Lecture Notes of the Institute for Computer Sciences, Social Informatics and Telecommunications Engineering 205

More information about this series at http://www.springer.com/series/8197

Michele Magno · Fabien Ferrero
Vedran Bilas (Eds.)

Sensor Systems and Software

7th International Conference, S-Cube 2016
Sophia Antipolis, Nice, France, December 1–2, 2016
Revised Selected Papers

 Springer

Editors
Michele Magno
ITET
ETH Zurich
Zurich
Switzerland

Vedran Bilas
Faculty of Electrical Engineering
University of Zagreb
Zagreb
Croatia

Fabien Ferrero
Laboratoire d'Electronique
Nice Sophia Antipolis University
Sophia Antipolis
France

ISSN 1867-8211 ISSN 1867-822X (electronic)
Lecture Notes of the Institute for Computer Sciences, Social Informatics
and Telecommunications Engineering
ISBN 978-3-319-61562-2 ISBN 978-3-319-61563-9 (eBook)
DOI 10.1007/978-3-319-61563-9

Library of Congress Control Number: 2017945727

Printed on acid-free paper

This Springer imprint is published by Springer Nature
The registered company is Springer International Publishing AG
The registered company address is: Gewerbestrasse 11, 6330 Cham, Switzerland

Preface

The 7th EAI International Conference on Sensor Systems and Software—S-CUBE 2016—an international conference in the field of sensors systems, hardware, software, and applications, was held during December 1–2, 2016, in Sophia Antipolis, Nice. The conference broadly focuses on the design, development, and optimization of sensor systems, and this international event provides the opportunity for researchers, technologists, and industry specialists in sensor systems and software to meet and to exchange ideas and information. The conference gave researchers an opportunity to discuss new technologies, interesting approaches, and hardware and software methods for sensing systems and their applications. The proceedings of S-CUBE 2016 are published by Springer in the series *Lecture Notes of the Institute for Computer Sciences, Social Informatics and Telecommunications Engineering* (LNICST).

This seventh edition of the conference was very rich and varied. The Technical Program Committee accepted 15 high-quality technical papers, which were presented at the conference. Each paper had at least two reviews. This year we chose four invited speakers: Daniela De Venuto, associate professor at Politecnico di Bari, Italy; Matthieu Gautier, associate professor at IRISA, University of Rennes; Mojtaba Masoudinejad, research associate at University of Dortmund; and Stephan Mach, PhD student at ETH Zurich. Their excellent talks focus on hot topics of sensor systems and a related paper is published in this volume.

S-CUBE 2016 was organized by the European Alliance for Innovation (EAI), ETH Zurich, and University Nice Sophia-Antipolis. The conference would not be successful without the hard work of many persons. First, our thanks go to the members of the conference committees and the reviewers for their dedicated and passionate work. In particular, the local and program chairs, Prof. Fabien Ferrero and Prof. Leonardo Lizzi, and the general chair, Dr. Michele Magno, for their important support to make the conference a successful event. It is also important to mention the Technical Program Committee Co-chairs, Dr. Emanuel Popovici and Prof. Vedran Bilas, for their support and effort in attracting a large number of submissions from around the world. We also thank Ms. Anna Horvathova and Ms. Sinziana Vieriu of EAI for their hard work and dedication in taking great care of the conference organization. Last, but not the least, our sincere thanks to the Steering Committee member, Andrey Somov, for his steady guidance and help. We are grateful to all the authors who have submitted papers to the conference, for none of this would happen without their valuable contributions. We would also like to thank our sponsors for their support and University Nice Sophia Antipolis for hosting us in this wonderful location.

February 2017

Michele Magno
Fabien Ferrero
Vedran Bilas

Organization

Steering Committee

Steering Committee Chair

Imrich Chlamtac   Create-Net, Italy

Steering Committee Member

Andrey Somov   University of Exeter, UK

Organizing Committee

General Chair

Michele Magno   ETH Zurich, Switzerland

Program Chairs

Fabien Ferrero   University of Nice Sophia Antipolis, France
Emanuel Popovici   University of College Cork, Ireland
Verdan Bilas   University of Zagreb, Croatia

Publicity and Social Media Chair

Lukas Cavigelli   ETH Zurich, Switzerland

Posters Chair

Leonardo Lizzi   University of Nice, France

Web Chair

Andres Gomez   ETH Zurich, Switzerland

Local Chair

Fabien Ferrero   University of Nice Sophia Antipolis, France

Conference Manager

Anna Horvathova   EAI - European Alliance for Innovation

Technical Program Committee

David Boyle   Imperial College London, UK
Matteo Ceriotti   University of Duisburg-Essen, Germany
Amir-Mohammad Rahmani   University of Turku, Finland

Contents

Invited Papers

SNW-MAC: An Asynchronous Protocol Leveraging Wake-Up Receivers for Data Gathering in Star Networks

Fayçal Ait Aoudia[1], Matthieu Gautier[1(✉)], Michele Magno[2], Olivier Berder[1], and Luca Benini[2]

[1] University of Rennes 1, IRISA, Rennes, France
matthieu.gautier@irisa.fr
[2] ETH Zürich, Zürich, Switzerland

Abstract. A widespread approach to extend lifetime of battery-powered wireless sensor nodes is duty-cycling, which consists in periodically switching on and off node transceiver. However, energy waste in idle listening periods is still a bottleneck. These periods can be completely removed using emerging ultra-low power wake-up receivers, which continuously listen to the channel with negligible power consumption. In this paper, an asynchronous medium access control protocol is proposed for data gathering in a star network topology. The protocol exploits state-of-the-art wake-up receivers to minimize the energy required to transmit a packet and to make collisions impossible. The proposed approach has been implemented on a real hardware platform and tested in-field. Experimental results demonstrate the benefits of the proposed approach in terms of energy efficiency, power consumption and throughput, which can be up to more than two times higher compared to traditional schemes.

1 Introduction

Wireless Sensor Networks (WSN) constitute a key technology to fulfill the increasing need of interaction between virtual and physical worlds for applications in environmental, healthcare, security, and industrial domains. WSN nodes are made of several subsystems such as processing unit, sensors, wireless communication and energy management to achieve the goal of collecting and processing data from sensors, and wirelessly send information to a remote host [5]. Typical WSNs usually have limited energy resources. As communication is the most power hungry task, great efforts are made to design network protocols at the Medium Access Control (MAC) layer [5] and techniques that rely on duty-cycling [16] turn out to be good candidates that fulfil the energy requirements of WSNs.

In duty-cycling, nodes are periodically powered on and off according to their own specific schedule while establishing on demand *rendez-vous* that can be initiated by the transmitter or the receiver [10]. Because idle listening periods are needed to perform the *rendez-vous* process, these approaches are referred to

© ICST Institute for Computer Sciences, Social Informatics and Telecommunications Engineering 2017
M. Magno et al. (Eds.): S-Cube 2016, LNICST 205, pp. 3–14, 2017.
DOI: 10.1007/978-3-319-61563-9_1

as *pseudo*-asynchronous in the literature [5]. Employing Ultra Low Power (ULP) Wake-up Receiver (WuRx) circuits allows significant simplification of the MAC protocols, as it enables asynchronous on-demand communication. The energy overhead incurred by the rendez-vous process is therefore eliminated [8].

The main feature of ULP WuRx is to consume power in the micro or nano Watt range, which is negligible when compared with the main radio that consumes milliwatts when active [3,11,13,17]. ULP WuRx can therefore continuously listen to the wireless medium while keeping the main transceiver in sleep state. When the node is in sleep state, the ULP WuRx is the only active component waiting for a specific signal, called Wake-up Beacon (WuB), sent by a neighboring node [3,11,13,14]. Moreover, many ULP WuRx embed address matching features, which allow nodes to wake up only a specific node and not all their neighbors [17,18].

Specific MAC protocols need to be designed to exploit the new potentiality offered by ULP WuRx. The first contribution of the paper is a novel asynchronous MAC protocol that focuses on star network topology, where all nodes are connected to a central sink that collects the data. SNW-MAC (Star Network WuRx - MAC) leverages ULP WuRx to minimize the energy required to transmit a packet and to make collisions impossible in the context of star networks. The second contribution of the paper is the experimental evaluation. SNW-MAC was implemented and tested in field conditions, using the Powwow platform [4] that embeds energy harvesting capabilities and a state-of-the-art ULP WuRx [11]. A comparison with state-of-the-art has been performed by implementing two traditional low-power MAC protocols on the same hardware.

The remainder of this paper is organized as follows. After giving a state-of-the art of MAC protocols that leverage WuRx, Sect. 2.1 introduces the star network topology and details the design of SNW-MAC. The experimental setup used to evaluate our approach is exposed in Sect. 3. Section 4 presents the experimental results with the in-field deployment of six Powwow nodes powered by indoor light. Finally, Sect. 5 concludes this paper.

2   Star Network WuRx - MAC Protocol

2.1   State-of-the-Art MAC Protocols Leveraging WuRx

As ULP WuRx is an emerging technology, only a few research studies were conducted on designing dedicated MAC protocols. WUR-MAC [12] was the first MAC protocol that takes advantage of ULP WuRx, using a multi-channel transmitter-initiated approach based on the request-to-send/clear-to-send handshake mechanism. Each node captures all incoming request-to-send and clear-to-send frames, and therefore has the information about which channel is used by its neighbours. When it wants to communicate, it randomly chooses a free channel and sends a request-to-send frame containing the chosen channel. *Sutton et al.* proposed Zippy [18], a flooding protocol based on ULP WuRx. To the best of our knowledge, this is the only solution that has been implemented on real sensor nodes. In a previous work, we introduced OPWUM [2], an opportunistic

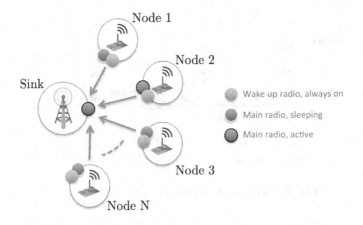

Fig. 1. Star network topology.

forwarding MAC using timer based contention for next hop relay selection and leveraging ULP WuRx. The protocol proposed in the present work is specially designed for star networks, and, unlike most of the previously cited protocols, was implemented on sensor nodes and compared to state-of-the-art MAC protocols.

In this section, the proposed SNW-MAC protocol exploiting ULP WuRx for data gathering star networks is presented. SNW-MAC enables asynchronous communication, minimizing the energy required to transmit a packet and making collisions impossible in the context of star networks. It is assumed that a physical layer (PHY) providing an error detection mechanism is used. For example, the widespread IEEE 802.15.4 PHY provides a Cyclic Redundancy Check (CRC) error detecting code.

2.2 Design of SNW-MAC

The target star network topology is illustrated in Fig. 1. The network is composed of two types of nodes. The sink initiates the communication and gathers the data from the nodes. It uses only one main transceiver (IEEE 802.15.4 PHY in our experiments), which is always on. On the other hand, the nodes are equipped with both a main transceiver and an ULP WuRx. The WuRx is always on, while the main transceiver is turned on only on demand from the sink.

SNW-MAC relies on receiver-initiated approach to minimize the energy consumption of WSN nodes. Packet transmission using SNW-MAC is illustrated by Fig. 2. The sink initializes a communication by sending a WuB containing the address of a specific sensor node, and then listens to the channel to receive the data packet. The targeted sensor node is awaken by its ULP WuRx, and starts sending the data packet. Compared to traditional receiver-initiated protocols, this approach reduces the energy consumption of the sink and the nodes as no rendez-vous process is required. The sink energy consumption is further reduced as useless periodic WuBs sending are avoided.

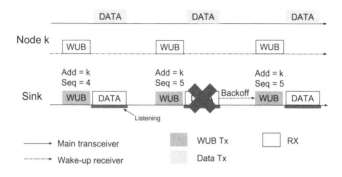

Fig. 2. Packet transmission using the SNW-MAC.

2.3 Error Control and Retransmission

By coordinating data packet transmission at the sink, SNW-MAC cancels the risk of collisions compared to traditional pseudo-asynchronous schemes as each node is specifically polled. However, wireless channel interferences may lead to corrupted frames, and energy-efficient error control and packet retransmission is therefore an important issue. As the sink is entirely in charge of coordinating the packet transmission, it is responsible for detecting transmission error and scheduling another attempt. To this aim, a 19 bit long WuB is used and its structure is described in Fig. 3. It is composed of 3 synchronization bits, the 8 bit address of the wireless sensor node to be polled and the 8 bit sequence number of the expected data packet.

The sink keeps an updated table that associates for each node the next packet sequence number to poll. When a sensor node ULP WuRx acquires a WuB, it reads both the address and the sequence number. Thanks to the capability of the ULP WuRx to directly recognize the address on the board, it wakes up the node MCU only if the address is valid, and then sends to it the sequence number using the serial port. All the packets, which have sequence number lower than the one received are considered as either successfully received or dropped because of a too high number of transmission attempts, and are thus erased from the transmission buffer. The packet which has the sequence number asked by the sink is then sent. Using this mechanism, when the sink detects a transmission failure, e.g. the received data packet is corrupted, it sets a random backoff and then, when the backoff expires, it initiates a new communication using the same sequence number, as illustrated by Fig. 2. Compared to traditional error-control schemes that use ACK frames, the energy overhead is significantly reduced for sensor nodes as they do not need to listen to ACK frames after each data packet transmission.

Sync bits	Sensor address	Sequence number
3 bits	8 bits	8 bits

Fig. 3. Structure of the Wake-up Beacon used in SNW-MAC.

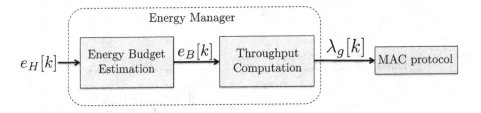

Fig. 4. Software architecture.

On the sink side, as no ACK frame is sent, energy is also saved. Nonetheless, this energy saving is counterbalanced by longer WuBs sent by the sink due to the sequence number. Using SNW-MAC, only the data frame is sent by the nodes, thus minimizing the per-packet energy consumption.

3 Experimental Setup

SNW-MAC was implemented in a complete WSN platform that embeds energy harvesting mechanisms. This section introduces the software and hardware setups used for the experimentations.

3.1 Software Architecture

The software architecture of the node is shown in Fig. 4 and is composed of two components: the Energy Manager (EM) and the MAC protocol.

Energy Management for Energy Harvesting Sensor Node. The EM goal is to dynamically adjust the performance of the node according to the time-varying energy that the node can harvest in its environment. Assuming that the time is divided into time slots of equal duration T, the throughput $\lambda_g[k]$ (in packets per second) of the node for the current slot k is set by the EM at the beginning of each slot according to the variation of the harvested energy $e_H[k]$.

Two submodules compose the proposed EM as shown by Fig. 4. The Energy Budget Estimation (EBE) module evaluates the energy budget $e_B[k]$ that the node can consume during the slot to remain sustainable. The EBE used in our work relies on a simplified version of Fuzzyman [1] and its operating is out of the scope of this paper.

The second module is the Throughput Computation (TC) module, which calculates $\lambda_g[k]$ according to the energy budget. As wireless communications are usually the most consuming task over all the other tasks such as sensing and computing [15], the throughput of the node given an energy budget is strongly tied to the MAC protocol. By denoting e_T and τ_T respectively the energy cost and the total time to transmit a single packet, the energy consumed by the node over one time slot k is:

$$e_C[k] = \lambda_g[k]Te_T + (T - \tau_T\lambda_g[k]T)P_S, \qquad (1)$$

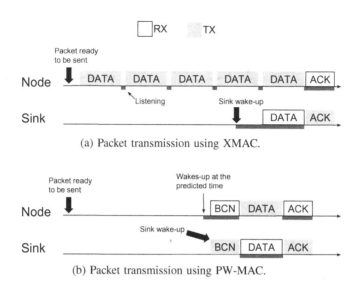

(a) Packet transmission using XMAC.

(b) Packet transmission using PW-MAC.

Fig. 5. X-MAC and PW-MAC protocols.

where P_S is the power consumption of the node when both the MCU and the radio chip are sleeping. Therefore, in order for the consumed energy $e_C[k]$ to be equal to the energy budget $e_B[k]$, the throughput is set to the following value:

$$\lambda_g[k] = \frac{\frac{e_B[k]}{T} - P_S}{e_T - \tau_T P_S}. \qquad (2)$$

This equation is obtained by replacing $e_C[k]$ by $e_B[k]$ in (1).

For SNW-MAC, each sensor node piggybacks its throughput in data packets. The sink keeps an updated table that associates for each node its throughput, and polls each node at the right time. Because the throughput is typically a 16 bit integer, minimal overhead is incurred by the piggybacking of this information. Moreover, the sink can use it to monitor the sensor node activity.

State-of-the-Art MAC Protocols Used for Comparison. The SNW-MAC protocol is compared to PW-MAC [19] and X-MAC [7], two well-known state-of-the-art pseudo-asynchronous MAC protocols. Figure 5a illustrates a packet transmission using the transmitter-initiated X-MAC. When a data packet must be sent, the node continuously transmits it, each transmission being followed by a listening period. This process continues until an ACK frame from the sink is acquired. The sink periodically wakes up and listens to the channel. If it detects an activity, it stays awake until it receives a complete data packet, and then acknowledges the received packet.

PW-MAC is a receiver-initiated protocol that focuses on energy efficiency on both the receiver side and sender side. Using PW-MAC, nodes accurately predict the time at which the sink will wake-up by using an on-demand prediction error

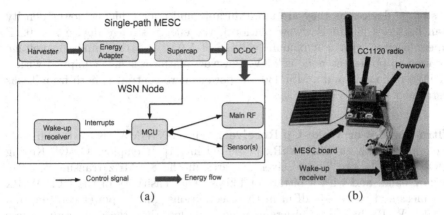

Fig. 6. Hardware architecture of a WSN node using energy harvesting and a WuRx: (a) functional description (b) Powwow node used for experiments.

correction mechanism and by considering clock drift and software and hardware latency. Moreover, to avoid repeated wake-up schedule collisions while allowing wake-up time prediction, independently generated pseudo-random sequences are used to control each node wake-up time. In this work, we focus on star networks with downlink data gathering. Therefore, using pseudo-random sequences to generate the wake-up schedule is unnecessary as the sink is the only receiver. Instead, the sink uses a periodic wake-up schedule. Figure 5b illustrates a packet transmission using PW-MAC. When a node needs to send a packet, it computes a prediction of the next wake-up time of the sink and wakes up at this predicted time. It then waits for a beacon from the sink (represented by the BCN frame in Fig. 5b). Once the beacon is acquired, it sends the data packets and then waits for the ACK frame. At each packet transmission, the prediction error is computed, and if it is found to be larger than a fixed threshold, the node requests an update of the prediction state.

3.2 Hardware Architecture

The hardware architecture of the node is given in Fig. 6 as well as a picture of the Powwow platform that has been used for experiments [4].

Architecture of Energy Harvesting Powwow Platform. Multiple energy harvesting platforms have been proposed by academia and industry over the last decade. Powwow platform relies on a single-path architecture version of the Multiple Energy Source Converter (MESC) architecture proposed in [9]. In single-path architecture, there is only one energy storage device and all the harvested energy is used to charge the storage device which directly powers the node through a DC-DC converter. Figure 6 shows the block architecture of MESC that can be used with a variety of energy harvesters (e.g. photovoltaic cells, thermoelectric generators and wind turbines). Supercapacitors were chosen as storage devices as they are more durable and offer a higher power density than batteries [6]. In Powwow platform, the energy storage device is a 0.9 F supercapacitor with a maximum voltage of 5.0 V, and the minimum voltage required to power the node is 2.8 V. Powwow platform is also equipped with a CC1120 radio chip and a MSP430 low power micro-controller, both from Texas Instruments.

Ultra-low Power Wake-Up Receiver. When SNW-MAC is used, each node is equipped with an ULP WuRx presented in [11]. It employs On-Off Keying (OOK) modulation. The receiver operates in the 868 MHz transmission frequency band, and with a bitrate of 1 kbps. The sensitivity of the ULP WuRx was measured to be −55 dBm in these conditions. As the power consumption of ULP WuRx has to be orders of magnitude less than the main radio, these devices are usually characterized by low sensitivity and low data rate [11]. For this reason, sending WuBs to an ULP WuRx can be energy-wise costly as it is done at low bitrate and high transmission power to achieve the same range as the main radio.

Moreover, the ULP WuRx embeds an ULP 8-bit microcontroller from Microchip (PIC12LF1552), which was selected for its low current consumption (20 nA in sleep mode) and its fast wake-up time (approximately 130 μs at 8 MHz). The PIC microcontroller is awaken by the analog front-end of the ULP WuRx when a carrier is detected. It then reads the address embedded in the WuB, and performs address matching. If the received address is valid, it wakes up the node MCU using an interrupt. Otherwise, it goes into sleep state, hence minimizing the power consumption of the ULP WuRx.

One of the requirements of an ULP WuRx is the very low power consumption as it is always active, even when all the other components are in sleep state. The power consumption of the ULP WuRx was measured to be 1.83 μW when the radio front-end is active and the PIC is in sleep state and 284 μW when the PIC is active at 3.3 V and is parsing the received data at 2 MHz.

SNW-MAC, X-MAC and PW-MAC protocols were implemented on the Powwow platform, as well as the energy management scheme. The parameters used for experimentations are shown by Table 1.

Table 1. Parameters used for the experimentations.

Parameters		Values
MAC	Sink wake-up interval (X-MAC and PW-MAC)	250 ms
	Maximum number of retransmissions	2
PHY	WuB bitrate	1 kbps
	Data/ACK/beacon bitrate	20 kbps
	WuB transmission power	12.5 dBm
	Data/ACK/beacon transmission power	−6 dBm

4 Experimental Results

The evaluated MAC protocols were implemented on a testbed made of 6 Powwow nodes including one sink, in a star topology. The nodes were exclusively powered by indoor fluorescent light, allowing reproducibility of the experiments. Moreover, the nodes were deployed under different lightning conditions, as shown by Fig. 7. Nodes 1, 2 and 5 were located on desks, directly under the ceiling lights while node 3 was deployed in a more shadowed area and node 4 was located on a book-case, close to the ceiling, thus receiving less light than the others. Each experiment lasted for 3 h, and the Powwow nodes have been equipped with an ULP WuRx only when the SNW-MAC protocol was evaluated. The metrics used for comparison are the average throughput, in packets per minute, and the Packet Delivery Ratio (PDR). Figure 8 shows the obtained results. First, Fig. 8a shows the average energy budget allocated by the EBE. As the amount of harvested energy varies for different nodes, the average allocated energy budget also differs. The results obtained for each node are obviously linked to this energy budget.

Figure 8b presents the throughput achieved with the different MAC protocols. SNW-MAC significantly outperforms the two other protocols, allowing up to two times higher throughput than PW-MAC for the node 2 due to the lower energy cost of packet transmissions. Finally, Fig. 8c shows the PDR achieved by the three protocols. SNW-MAC is the only protocol to achieve a 100% PDR on all the nodes. These results demonstrate the high reliability that ULP WuRx-based protocols enable.

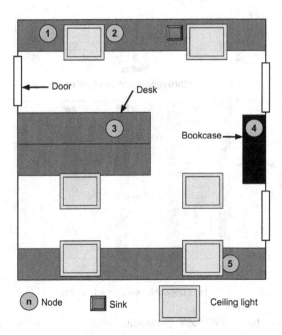

Fig. 7. Setup of the star network.

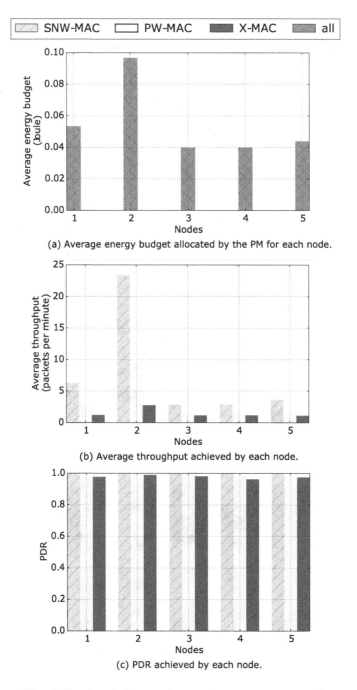

(a) Average energy budget allocated by the PM for each node.

(b) Average throughput achieved by each node.

(c) PDR achieved by each node.

Fig. 8. Results of the experimentations on a star network.

5   Conclusion

This paper proposes an asynchronous MAC protocol in the context of data gathering sensor networks with a star topology. The proposed solution leverages ultra-low power wake-up receivers to increase the energy efficiency of wireless sensor networks. This new scheme is designed to be implemented on real hardware. Experimental results have shown that the proposed approach concretely permits up to 2 times higher throughput compared with state-of-the-art MAC protocols such as PW-MAC and X-MAC. Future work is to evaluate the scalability of the proposed approach compared to traditional pseudo-asynchronous MAC by analytically computing the packet arrival rate.

Acknowledgment. This work was supported by "Transient Computing Systems", a SNF project (200021_157048), by SCOPES SNF project (IZ74Z0_160481) and by "POMADE" project, funded by CD22 and the Brittany region.

References

1. Ait Aoudia, F., Gautier, M., Berder, O.: Fuzzy power management for energy harvesting wireless sensor nodes. In: IEEE International Conference on Communications (ICC), May 2016
2. Ait Aoudia, F., Gautier, M., Olivier Berder, O.: OPWUM: Opportunistic MAC protocol leveraging wake-up receivers in WSNs. J. Sens. **2016**, 9 (2016). Article ID 6263719
3. Ammar, Y., Bdiri, S., Derbel, F.: An ultra-low power wake up receiver with flip flops based address decoder. In: International Multi-Conference on Systems, Signals and Devices (SSD), pp. 1–5, March 2015
4. Berder, O., Sentieys, O.: PowWow: power optimized hardware/software framework for wireless motes. In: International Conference on Architecture of Computing Systems (ARCS), pp. 1–5, February 2010
5. Huang, P., Xiao, L., Soltani, S., Mutka, M.W., Xi, N.: The evolution of MAC protocols in wireless sensor networks: a survey. IEEE Commun. Surv. Tutorials **15**(1), 101–120 (2013)
6. Kailas, A., Brunelli, D., Weitnauer, M.A.: Comparison of energy update models for wireless sensor nodes with supercapacitors. In: Proceedings of the 1st International Workshop on Energy Neutral Sensing Systems, ENSSys (2013)
7. Klues, K., Hackmann, G., Chipara, O., Lu, C.: A component-based architecture for power-efficient media access control in wireless sensor networks. In: Proceedings of the 5th International Conference on Embedded Networked Sensor Systems SenSys, November 2007
8. Le, T.N., Magno, M., Pegatoquet, L., Berder, O., Sentieys, O., Popovici, E.: Ultra low power asynchronous MAC protocol using wake-up radio for energy neutral WSN. In: Proceedings of the 1st ACM International Workshop on Energy Neutral Sensing Systems ENSSys, November 2013
9. Le, T.N., Pegatoquet, A., Berder, O., Sentieys, O., Carer, A.: Energy-neutral design framework for supercapacitor-based autonomous wireless sensor networks. ACM J. Emerg. Technol. Comput. Syst. (JETC) **12**(2), 19:1–19:21 (2015)

10. Lin, E.-Y.A., Rabaey J.M., Wolisz, A.: Power-efficient rendez-vous schemes for dense wireless sensor networks. In: IEEE International Conference on Communications, ICC, June 2004
11. Magno, M., Jelicic, V., Srbinovski, B., Bilas, V., Popovici, E., Benini, L.: Design, implementation, and performance evaluation of a flexible low-latency nanowatt wake-up radio receiver. IEEE Trans. Industr. Inf. **12**(2), 633–644 (2016)
12. Mahlknecht, M.S., Durante, W.-M.S.: Energy efficient wakeup receiver based MAC protocol. In: 8th IFAC International Conference on Fieldbuses and Networks in Industrial and Embedded Systems (2009)
13. Mazloum, N.S., Edfors, O.: Performance analysis and energy optimization of wake-up receiver schemes for wireless low-power applications. IEEE Trans. Wireless Commun. **13**(12), 7050–7061 (2014)
14. Oller, J., Demirkol, I., Casademont, J., Paradells, J.: Design, development, and performance evaluation of a low-cost, low-power wake-up radio system for wireless sensor networks. ACM Trans. Sens. Netw. **10**(1), 24 (2013)
15. Rault, T., Bouabdallah, A., Challal, Y.: Energy efficiency in wireless sensor networks: a top-down survey. Comput. Netw. **67**, 104–122 (2014)
16. Schurge, C., Tsiats, V., Ganeriw, S., Srivasta, M.: Optimizing sensor networks in the energy-latency-density design space. IEEE Trans. Mob. Comput. **1**(1), 70–80 (2002)
17. Spenza, D., Magno, M., Basagni, S., Benini, L., Paoli, M., Petrioli, C., Cycling, B.D.: Wake-up radio with selective awakenings for long-lived wireless sensing systems. In: IEEE INFOCOM, pp. 522–530, April 2015
18. Sutton, F., Buchli, B., Beutel, J., Thiele, L.: Zippy: on-demand network flooding. In: ACM Conference on Embedded Networked Sensor Systems, SenSys, pp. 45–58, November 2015
19. Tang, L., Sun, Y., Gurewitz, O., Johnson, D.V.: PW-MAC: an energy-efficient predictive-wakeup MAC protocol for wireless sensor networks. In: IEEE INFOCOM, pp. 1305–1313, April 2011

Towards P300-Based Mind-Control: A Non-invasive Quickly Trained BCI for Remote Car Driving

Daniela De Venuto[✉], Valerio F. Annese, and Giovanni Mezzina

Department of Electrical and Information Engineering, Politecnico di Bari,
Via Orabona 4, 70125 Bari, Italy
{daniela.devenuto,valeriofrancesco.annese}@poliba.it

Abstract. This paper presents a P300-based Brain Computer Interface (BCI) for the control of a mechatronic actuator (i.e. wheelchairs, robots or even cars), driven by EEG signals for assistive technology. The overall architecture is made up by two subsystems: the Brain-to-Computer System (BCS) and the mechanical actuator (a proof of concept of the proposed BCI is shown using a prototype car). The BCS is devoted to signal acquisition (6 EEG channels from wireless headset), visual stimuli delivery for P300 evocation and signal processing. Due to the P300 inter-subject variability, a first stage of Machine Learning (ML) is required. The ML stage is based on a custom algorithm (t-RIDE) which allows a fast calibration phase (only ~190 s for the first learning). The BCI presents a functional approach for time-domain features extraction, which reduces the amount of data to be analyzed. The real-time function is based on a trained linear hyper-dimensional classifier, which combines high P300 detection accuracy with low computation times. The experimental results, achieved on a dataset of 5 subjects (age: 26 ± 3), show that: (i) the ML algorithm allows the P300 spatio-temporal characterization in 1.95 s using 38 target brain visual stimuli (for each direction of the car path); (ii) the classification reached an accuracy of $80.5 \pm 4.1\%$ on single-trial P300 detection in only 22 ms (worst case), allowing real-time driving. For its versatility, the BCI system here described can be also used on different mechatronic actuators.

Keywords: BCI · Machine Learning · Classification · EEG · ERP · P300

1 Introduction

Only a few years ago the idea of mind controlling a robot or a prosthesis seemed to belong only to science fiction films. Nowadays, the possibility of using brain signals to control external actuators is reality. A Brain-Computer Interface (BCI) is a system providing a direct communication channel between human brain and an external mechanical device, via computer, µPC or FPGA. The functioning principle is based on the detection of specific Brain Activity Pattern (BAP) concurrently to a particular stimuli-based task: the BAP detection related to a particular stimulus expresses the user's intention to perform the command/actuation to whom that stimulus is linked. At the current state of the art, there are four different BAPs widely used for BCI applications:

© ICST Institute for Computer Sciences, Social Informatics and Telecommunications Engineering 2017
M. Magno et al. (Eds.): S-Cube 2016, LNICST 205, pp. 15–28, 2017.
DOI: 10.1007/978-3-319-61563-9_2

sensorimotor rhythms (SMR), amplitude modulation of slow cortical potentials (SCP), visual cortex potentials (VEPs) and Event-Related Potentials (ERPs) [1]. The ERP-based BCI systems are mainly based on the P300. Differently from SMR or SCP, a P300-based BCI does not require intensive user training, because the P300 component results from endogenous attention-based brain function. Despite the P300 inter-subject variability in terms of latency and amplitude [2], which makes necessary a phase of Machine Learning (ML), the component is detectable on every cognitively healthy human being. Although W. Grey et al. [3], which developed a mind-controlled cursor, implemented the first BCI system in 1964, the scientific research in this field is experiencing an exponential growth due to the possibility to improve the life quality of paralytic, tetraplegic and motor impaired people. Nowadays, P300-based BCI systems cover a wide range of applications such as locomotion (i.e. wheelchairs [4], robot or neuro-prosthesis [5, 6]), rehabilitation (i.e. the "Bionic Eye" [7]), communication (i.e. the P300 speller [5]), environmental control (i.e. the "Brain Gate" [8]) and entertaining (i.e. neuro-games [8]). In the field of mind-controlled car, Luzheng Bi et al. [9] developed a P300-based BCI for destination selection in vehicles. However, despite the high accuracy ($93.6\% \pm 1.6\%$), the system does not allow real-time navigation since the selection time is about 12 s. Differently, D. Gohring et al. [10] reported the development of a semi-autonomous mind-controlled car. Although the prototype allows the free-drive mode, the proposed BCI is SMR-based, requiring a very intensive training stage.

In this paper a P300-based BCI for the control of a mechatronic actuator driven by electroencephalographic (EEG) signals for assistive technology is presented. A proof of concept of the proposed BCI is shown using an "ad-hoc" implemented Raspberry-based prototype car. The system has been tested on 5 subjects (age: 26 ± 3). The main innovations of the implemented BCI are: (i) the development of the first P300-based mind-controlled vehicle to be used in free-drive mode; (ii) the adoption of a custom algorithm, t-RIDE [2], for the ML allowing a complete P300 spatio-temporal characterization in only 1.95 s using 38 target brain visual stimuli (for each addressable command) resulting in a very fast training phase; (iii) a functional approach for the real-time classification based on features extraction (FE), combining fast interpretation of the user's intention (worst case: 19.65 ms ± 10.1 ms) and high accuracy in the P300 single-trial detection ($80.51 \pm 4.1\%$ on 5 subjects). The structure of the paper is described in the following. Section 2 outlines basic knowledge on the P300 component. Section 3 presents the architecture of the implemented BCI, focusing on the (ML and classification algorithms). Section 3.4 describes the development of the prototype car system. Section 4 reports the experimental results performed on 5 subjects. Section 5 concludes the paper with final observations.

2   Evoked Related Potentials: The P300 Component

The P300 is a positive deflection in the human brain event related potentials (ERPs) evoked when a subject is actively and cognitively engaged in the discrimination of one target stimulus by not-target ones, generally denoted as "oddball paradigm" (Fig. 1) [2, 11]. The 'Stimulus' is a single external event (audio, visual, tactile, etc.) delivered to the subject under test. The target stimulus is the event to be recognized among different ones (not-target). When a target is delivered, the subject under test performs a cognitive task i.e. to count in mind the number of target stimuli occurrences ("no-go task" i.e. response without any muscular movement).

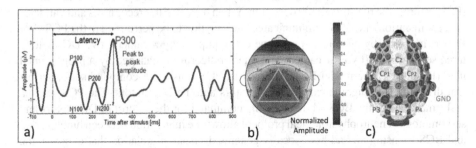

Fig. 1. (a) Time-domain P300 waveform; (b) cortical-area involved by the P300; (c) monitored electrodes. (Color figure online)

A trial is 1 s EEG signal starting from 100 ms before the stimulus delivery. A test is an assemble of stimuli (target and not-target ones) randomly delivered to the subject. In a single test, the probability of target occurrence has to be lower than the not-target one. The P300 characterization is based on its latency, amplitude and cortical-area involved (see Fig. 1). The P300 latency is heavily affected by trial-to-trial variability (P300 jitter) within a given experimental condition and ranges from 290 ms to 447.5 ms [12]. The P300 amplitude is the peak-to-peak amplitude between the previous deflection (N200) and the P300 maximum value (Fig. 1). The P300 amplitude can reach even 37.7 μV depending on the age and on the rarity of the target [12]. The cortical area involved by the P300 is not "a priori" known but, generally, it is the central parietal cortex [12]. The brain mapping of P300 is computed by a topography [2]. Differently form the classic oddball paradigm [2, 13, 14], for BCI applications more than two stimuli are delivered with uniform probability distribution. Each stimulus is linked to a particular actuation command. The subject select a single stimulus to be considered as the target and performs the cognitive task only on that particular stimulus according to his intentionality and to the command he wants to address. Only that particular stimulus will evocate the P300. The P300 detection on a particular stimulus allows understanding that the subject was focusing on that particular stimulus and that he wants to address the linked actuation command.

3   Overall Architecture

The overall architecture (Fig. 2) can be divided into two subsystems: the Brain Computer System (BCS) and the Prototype Car System (PCS) connected together through a Client-Server TCP/IP communication protocol. The BCS composed by the hardware acquisition system (wireless EEG headset station) and by the data processing algorithms aiming to interpret the user intentions. Due to the inter-subject variability, the system needs to be tuned on the particular user through a first stage of Machine Learning (ML). A custom algorithm, the tuned-Residue Iteration Decomposition (t-RIDE) [2, 13, 14], which characterizes the P300 waveform and extracts all the parameters to be used for the real time classification stage, performs the ML. A linear hyper-dimensional classifier combining low computational efforts and high accuracy basing on a stage of Feature Extraction (FE) performs the real-time P300 detection. When the classifier recognizes and validates the user intention, the BCS communicates the actuation to be performed to the PCS. The PCS is made up by an acrylic prototype car, equipped by a camera, two DC motors, three servomotors (two for camera and one for steering), managed by a programmed μPC (Raspberry Pi 2 model B+). Afterwards, PCS runs a pre-compiled set of scripts that drive the steering, the camera servomotors and the DC motors. The PCS sends a real-time video to the BCS while receiving command for the control of DC motors and servomotors. A neurophysiological protocol allows the interaction between human brain and BCS by using an "ad-hoc" locally generated visual stimulation that evocates the P300 potential.

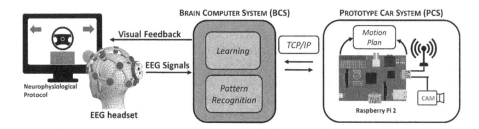

Fig. 2. Schematic overview of the developed BCI architecture.

3.1   Neurophysiological Protocol and Hardware Instrumentation

The adopted data acquisition hardware is a 32-channels wireless EEG headset with active electrodes (conditioning integrated circuit are embedded in the electrode performing amplification, filtering and digitalization) as the one used in [15–21]. According to the international 10–20 standard, the EEG recordings have been performed using six electrodes (C_z, CP_1, CP_2, P_3, P_z, P_4 – in red in Fig. 1c) referenced to AF_z electrode (in orange in Fig. 1c) and right ear lobe (A_2 – in green in Fig. 1c) is used as ground. The locations of the electrodes have been selected according to previous P300 studies [2, 13, 14]. EEG signals are recorded with sampling frequency of 500 Hz, 24-bit resolution, ±187.5 mV input range and filtered using a bandpass (Butterworth, 8th order 0.5–30 Hz) and power line notch filtered (Butterworth, 4th order 48–52 Hz - embedded into the front-end) [22–27]. The recording scheme is monopolar. The EEG signals are recorded while the user performs the neurophysiological protocol. The neurophysiological protocol is made up by 4 visual stimuli, individually and randomly flash on a display (25% occurrence probability) with an inter-stimuli time of 1 s. In the developed neurophysiological protocol there is no pre-defined target stimulus: the stimulus on which the user freely focuses his attention became the target (selective attention).

Each stimulus persists on the screen for 200 ms. Stimuli generation/delivered are driven by a Simulink model using a random numeric signal.

Each stimulus is related to a P300 latency and amplitude are related to the saliency of stimulus (in term of color, contrast, brightness, duration, etc.): the BCS associates to each direction different shapes and colors, in sharp contrast to each other. Figure 3 shows a sequence of driving environment snapshots provided by the BCS to the user. For instance, if the user wants to turn right, the target items is the one in Fig. 3c, while the other blinking stimuli are the not-target. EEG data collection, stimuli generation/delivery and signal processing are performed by the BCS. In this implementation, the BCS has been assumed as a PC (Intel i5, RAM 8 GB, 64 bit).

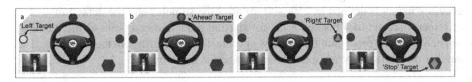

Fig. 3. The neurophysiological protocol is made up by 4 stimuli individually and randomly flashing on a display. Each stimulus is related to a particular command i.e. turn left (a), turn right (c), go ahead (b) and stop (d).

3.2 Machine Learning

The first step of the adopted pattern recognition strategy is to train the system via offline experiment with a learning stage. There are a number of methods reported in literature for P300 detection in single-trial and averaged-trials environments. The main challenge in this field is that the P300 is generally submerged by artifacts and background EEG, resulting in an extremely low Signal to Noise Ratio (SNR). The implemented ML is based on a novel algorithm based on the RIDE approach: the Tuned-Residue Iterative Decomposition (t-RIDE). A detailed description and a deep comparison between t-RIDE and other method at the state of the art (RIDE, ICA, PCA, Grand Average) are reported in [2]. The ML can be divided into four stages: pre-processing, P300 characterization, features extraction (FE) and weights/thresholds definition.

Pre-processing. This stage is intended to reduce the sources of noise, artifacts such as eye movements and head movements preserving the P300 and eliminating the critical issue affecting RIDE. Pre-processing is performed for each monitored channel. The acquired EEG signal is further low-pass filtered (Butterworth, 6th order, fstop = 15 Hz) and aligned to the stimulus signal. Subsequently, the EEG signal is decomposed in trial of 1 s, each epoch starts 100 ms before the rising edge of the stimulus (target and non-target). Trials are fitted in a 6th order polynomial. The resulting fitted curve is subtracted from the EEG signal, which is then centered (offset cancellation) and normalized. Finally all the trials are organized into a 3D matrix **DATA** $\in R^{S \cdot N \cdot M}$ where S is the number of samples into 1 trial (500 in our implementation), N is the number of monitored channels (6 in our work) and M is the number of delivered stimuli (target and not-target).

P300 Characterization. This stage is based on the custom algorithm t-RIDE [2, 13, 14]. The RIDE approach [2] is a multi-purpose method for ERP extraction and, for its generality, does not take advantages from the "a priori" information about P300. This leads to the necessity of a specialized staff setting static calculation parameters for RIDE (i.e. the computation window) as well as the impossibility to follow the latency modulation of the P300 component. Furthermore, RIDE includes neither pre-processing (which is application-dependent) nor spatial considerations. t-RIDE is a custom tuned version of RIDE for P300 extraction which includes three additional steps to RIDE: pre-processing, window optimization and spatial characterization [2, 13, 14]. Starting from a default window, t-RIDE automatically calculates the optimized one. Only one signal derived from the average of P_Z and C_Z is considered for window optimization. A first default window is defined as 250–400 ms after the stimulus and the default time-step increments are set to 4 ms and 8 ms for starting point and end point of the window, respectively. The procedure for window optimization is described in the following. The number of iterations for an optimal tuning phase is given by:

$$n_{IT} = \left\lceil \frac{t_{lim} - t_{e,win}}{t_{sh,r}} \right\rceil \tag{1}$$

where t_{lim} is the upper limit, $t_{e,win}$ is the selected window end time, $t_{sh,r}$ is the right-shift parameter. Therefore, n_{IT} different windows are considered, sweeping the entire time slot where the P300 is expected. By default configuration, the iteration cycle starts from a fixed window, then its start/end points are progressively right shifted by 4 ms and 8 ms respectively. Thus, the last window considered in the computation is 278 ms–456 ms. For each considered window, the RIDE approach extracts the P300 time-domain waveform. After n_{IT} iterations, the algorithm selects the optimized window i.e., the one with the highest P300 amplitude. As soon as the optimized window is defined, the **DATA** matrix is processed by t-RIDE. Time-domain results from each channel are subsequently interpolated in order to extract the spatial characterization (P300 topography). In this stage, the system stores the vectors $\mathbf{L} = (l_1,..., l_N) \in R^N$ and $\mathbf{A} = (a_1,..., a_N) \in R^N$ containing respectively the expected P300 latencies and amplitude for each channel ($N = 6$).

Feature Extraction (FE). The t-RIDE extracted P300 pulse undergoes a phase of FE to be used as 'golden reference' by the classifier. According to specialized medical staff P300 visual inspection guidelines, five features have been selected. They take into account the time-domain P300 shape information, exalting the differences between target and not-target typical trends. For the FE on the jth channel, the trial x(i) is windowed by a rectangular 200 ms window (number of samples ns = 100) centered on the expected latency l_j The extracted features are (see Fig. 4):

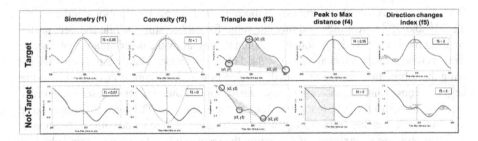

Fig. 4. Calculation example of the features set for target and not-target stimuli.

1. The **Simmetry** quantifies the symmetry degree of the signal with respect to the expected latency:

$$f_1 = 1 - \left| \frac{2}{ns - 1} \sum_{i=1}^{ns} [x(i) - x(ns - i)] \right| \tag{2}$$

2. The **Convexity** identifies the convexity degree of the considered data points with respect to the expected latency:

$$f_2 = 1 \leftrightarrow \sum_{i=1}^{\left(\frac{ns}{2}\right)-1} \frac{\partial x(i)}{\partial i} \geq \sum_{i=\left(\frac{ns}{2}\right)+1}^{ns} \frac{\partial x(i)}{\partial i} ; otherwise \quad f_2 = 0 \tag{3}$$

3. The **Triangle area (TA)** delivers the area of the triangle inscribed into the potentially P300 component deflection:

$$f_2 = 0.5 \cdot \begin{vmatrix} x1 & y1 & 1 \\ x2 & y2 & 1 \\ x3 & y3 & 1 \end{vmatrix} \tag{4}$$

where (x1, y1) is the minimum value in the 100 ms before the P300 learned latency as well as (x2, y2) is the minimum value of the 100 ms on its right side. (x3, y3) are the coordinates of maximum value of the extracted data points.

4. The **Peak to Max distance (PMD)** quantifies how close is the maximum point of the single trial with respect to the expected one:

$$f_4 = \left\{ \frac{(ns + 1)}{2} - \left| \frac{(ns + 1)}{2} - index(\max(x)) \right| \right\} \frac{2}{(ns + 1)} \tag{5}$$

5. The **Direction changes index (DCI)** quantifies the number of considered waveform direction changes. It can be obtained by counting the slope sign changes, referring to signal derivative.

Weights/Thresholds Definition. The FE is performed offline, on the same acquired raw data and performed on single-trials (for both targets and not-targets) i.e. on the

DATA matrix. A statistical analysis elaborates the features distributions and extracts the 25th and 75th percentiles and median value for each feature. While the percentiles are used for thresholds definition, the median values allow the determination of a set of weights (one set for each channel) to be used by the classifier. They are assigned considering the subtraction between the median value of the j-th feature vector referred to the target responses and the not-target ones. The ML orders their values in descending order and assigns 0.3 to the best feature and 0.1 to the worst one. The other 3 features have weight that decreasing from 0.3 to 0.1 with 0.05 steps. These values allow obtaining a sum that provides a maximum of 1. Finally, the responsivity of each monitored channel is evaluated in order to define a further set of spatial weights.

Summarizing, at the end of the ML, the following subject-depending parameters have been learned by the BCS:

1. **UP** $\in R^{5\times6}$: its generic element $up_{i,j}$ contains the upper thresholds for i-th feature (the 75th percentile) referred to the j-channel.
2. **DN** $\in R^{5\times6}$: its generic element $dn_{i,j}$ contains the lower thresholds for i-th feature (the 25th percentile) referred to the j-channel.
3. **W** $\in R^{5\times6}$: its generic element $w_{i,j}$ is the i-th weight referred to the j-channel.
4. **S** $\in R^6$ contains the indications about the responsivity of the channels.
5. **L** $\in R^6$ contains the expected P300 latencies for each channel.
6. **A** $\in R^6$ contains the expected P300 amplitude for each channel.

3.3   Real-Time Hyper-Dimensional Classification

For each subject, the "golden" learned P300 can be represented by a single point in a n-dimensional space where the features are the bases (n = number of features). The real-time classifier performs a FE on incoming streaming EEG data and compares the results with the "golden" reference: the decision about the absence/presence of P300 is based on the n-dimensional distance between reference and incoming trial exploiting thresholds. In order to reduce the computational times, the classification is performed on a down-sampled (from 500 sps to 100 sps) and windowed (M samples centered on the expected latency, M = 20–200 ms) version of EEG trials. The first step is data validation (*1st classifier rule*): in order to avoid that artifacts affect the results, data are validated only if they are similar in amplitude to the values in **A**. As soon as a new stimulus occurs, the BCS performs the FE on the single-trial for each channel basing on **L**. This leads to the computation of $\mathbf{f} \in R^{5\times6}$ where its generic element $f_{i,j}$ expresses the value of the i-th feature on the j-th channel. The classifier adopts the following decisional rule (*2nd classifier rule*):

$$F_{i,j} = \begin{cases} 0 & \leftrightarrow f_{i,j} < dn_{i,j} \\ 0.5 & \leftrightarrow dn_{i,j} \leq f_{i,j} \leq up_{i,j} \\ 1 & \leftrightarrow f_{i,j} > up_{i,j} \end{cases} \tag{6}$$

This procedure leads to the creation of the matrix $\mathbf{F} \in R^{5 \times 6}$. A weighted sum of $\mathbf{F}$ defines the presence of the P300 on the j-th channel, through the calculation of the vector $R \in R^6$, where the generic element is (3rd classifier rule):

$$r_j = w_{1,j} \cdot F_{1,j} + \ldots + w_{5,j} \cdot F_{5,j} \text{ for } j = 1, 2, \ldots, 6 \tag{7}$$

Afterwards, the classifier adopts the 4th decisional rule to evaluate the presence/absence of P300 on the j-th channel:

$$y_j = \begin{cases} 0 \leftrightarrow r_j \leq y_t \\ 1 \leftrightarrow r_j > y_t \end{cases} \tag{8}$$

Where y_j is the generic element of $\mathbf{Y} \in R^6$ and y_t is a decision threshold set to 0.5. The decision rule with $y_t = 0.5$ means that on the j-th channel, at least 3 features have been detected. The classification ends with the spatial validation (5th classifier rule): the classifier validate the P300 presence only if the P300 is simultaneously detected on 5 out of 6 channels detect w.r.t. channels, which deliver a high detection rate (vector $\mathbf{S}$). When the classification is over, the BCS sends to the PCS a 2 bits code informing Raspberry about the actuation through TCP/IP wireless communication.

3.4   The Prototype Car System (PCS)

Two 3.7 V batteries (Panasonic 18650) deliver a nominal supply voltage of 7.4 V. Through the DC-DC converter (XL-1509), this voltage is converted into a 5 V stable power supply for the entire prototype car. Raspberry Pi 2 (Model B+), equipped by a Wi-Fi antenna, a USB camera and a SD card, is the control unit of the prototype car. Raspberry controls three main aspects of the navigation i.e. obstacle detection and avoidance, servomotor orientation (both for car driving both for camera positioning) and DC motor power control. The obstacle detection and avoidance is based on three ultrasonic proximity sensors (HC-SR04) which point in three different directions (straight and sideways). The 'Trig' pins of the ultrasonic sensors are driven by a single output Raspberry pin and triggered at 10 Hz with a pulse wave of 10 μs. The sensors response delivered on their 'Echo' pin are connected to three different Raspberry input pins. An in-loco running python script continuously monitors the presence/absence of obstacles: when an obstacle is detected ahead with a distance lower than 50 cm, the prototype car stops. Differently, when the prototype car detect a side obstacle that is not in its trajectory, Raspberry alert the BCS, which adapt the neurophysiological protocol, which does not propose to curve on that direction. The DC motor power control is managed by Raspberry Pi using an h-bridge (L298N): GPIO pins controls the enable pins of the L298N ('ena', 'enb') using pulse with modulation (PWM). The motor power control depends on the directives sent by the BCS. Servomotor orientation is controlled by PWM using the PWM module (PCA 9685). There are three servomotors: while the first one manages the prototype car direction (and is controlled by the BCS), the other ones control the orientation of the USB camera, which streams a real-time video to the BCS.

4   Experimental Results

The entire architecture has been tested on a dataset from 5 different subjects (age: 26 ± 3). The subjects performed at first the learning protocol and, subsequently, the real-time prototype car control. The P300 amplitude range was 3–8 µV with a mean value of 4.7 µV $\pm$ 0.61 µV; the P300 latency was included in the range 300–403 ms, with a mean value of 349.25 ms $\pm$ 35.52 ms. Table 1A shows the subject-by-subject topographies of the amplitudes (for both target and not-target stimuli), latencies and time-domain waveform achieved by the t-RIDE algorithm. From the latency topography it is shown that the P300 is detected from the lateral mid-line electrodes (200–250 ms on P3 and P4) and the central electrodes (Fz, Cz, Pz) 300–400 ms after stimulus. Additionally, from the amplitude topographies it is clear that despite the subject-by-subject P300 variability, this component his deeply suitable for binary discrimination. The complete results of the ML stage are presented in Table 1B where, for each subject and feature are express as medium value $\pm$ std. deviation computed on all the monitored channels. The online validation approach included two different tests: (i) single direction repetitive selections and (ii) pattern recognition. In the first approach, the user is asked to select repeatedly a single target. The reached classification accuracies computed in these conditions are (see Table 2A): sub1: 73.68 $\pm$ 5.3%; sub2: 83.71 $\pm$ 4.6%; sub3: 80 $\pm$ 3.1%; sub4: 81.30 $\pm$ 4.8%; sub5: 83.84 $\pm$ 5.8%. The best classification accuracy is 89% while the worst one is 68.38%.

Table 1. (A) P300 subject-by-subject P300 spatio-temporal characterization; (B) detailed subject-by-subject trained parameters.

Table A

S	Latency (ms)	Amplitude (µV) Target Not Target	Time-Domain Response
1	[Pz] 300ms		[Pz] 5.1
2	[Pz] 344ms		[Pz] 5.2
3	[Pz] 338ms		[Pz] 5.3
4	[Pz] 308ms		[Pz] 5.4
5	[Pz] 344ms		[Pz] 5.5

Table B			S.1	S.2	S.3	S.4	S.5
A (µV)			7.2±0.7	5.2±0.4	4.3±0.57	4,1±0.93	4±1.06
L (ms)			360±107	340±10	330±47	330±7	300±45
f1	UP		0.68±0.01	0.68±0.03	0.68±0.03	0.67±0.03	0.65±0.02
	DN		0.43±0.09	0.23±0.07	0.19±0.10	0.43±0.14	0.30±0.08
	W		0.15	0.15	0.15	0.15	0.15
f2	UP		0.5±0	0.5±0	0.5±0	0.5±0	0.5±0
	DN		0.5±0	0.5±0	0.5±0	0.5±0	0.5±0
	W		0.3	0.3	0.3	0.3	0.3
F3 (µV·ms)	UP		125.5±24.8	84.9±18.1	65.6±12.9	44.5±11.9	38.7±8.8
	DN		39.6±12.3	44.8±2.2	19.7±1.9	18.8±1.9	26.6±6.86
	W		0.25	0.2	0.25	0.25	0.2
f4 (ms)	UP		0.31±0.08	0.31±0.14	0.35±0.23	0.33±0.07	0.33±0.12
	DN		0.11±0.04	0.07±0.05	0.15±0.07	0.25±0.03	0.24±0.03
	W		0.10	0.10	0.10	0.10	0.10
f5	UP		7.8±0.41	7.7±0.82	8±0.63	7.17±0.41	6.17±0.75
	DN		1.67±0.81	2.2±0.41	2.33±0.81	4.00±1.26	4.50±1.38
	W		0.2	0.252	0.2	0.2	0.15

The analysis demonstrated a channel-to-channel accuracy modulation: Table 2A highlights the subject-by-subject highest accuracy.

Differently, the pattern recognition test consists in the selection of a known stream of directions. The reference pattern to be perform by the user was made up by 10 commands covering all the addressable directions. The users performed this test more than once. The performed accuracies computed in this test are: sub1: 67.9 $\pm$ 6.7%; sub2: 72.5 $\pm$ 7.1%; sub3: 67.5 $\pm$ 4.4%; sub4: 69.2 $\pm$ 8.5%; sub5: 70.6 $\pm$ 3.7%. The best pattern recognition is 8/10 of the pattern (80%). The worst response is detecting 5/10 of the

Table 2. (A) P300 subject-by-subject P300 spatio-temporal characterization; (B) detailed subject-by-subject trained parameters.

TABLE A	CLASSIFICATION ACCURACY			
	SINGLE SELECTION		PATTERN RECOGNITION	
SUB	Accuracy(%)	Best Electrode	Accuracy (%)	Best Electrode
1	73.7±5.3	Pz(87%)	67.9±6.7	Pz(74%)
2	83.7±4.6	P4(91%)	72.5±7.1	P4(79%)
3	80±3.1	Cz(86%)	67.5±4.4	Cz(71%)
4	81.3±4.8	C3(95%)	69.2±8.5	C3(77%)
5	83.84±5.8	Cz(89%)	70.6±3.7	Cz(74%)

TABLE B	LEARNING COMPUTED ON SUB.				
CLASSIFICATION COMPUTER ON SUB.	1	2	3	4	5
1	75.4	36.84	21.35	34.40	30.17
2	47.50	85.1	34.57	9.85	11.25
3	12.41	32.71	79.3	17.23	27.87
4	40.20	10.75	18.21	82.3	21.61
5	13.13	31.9	26.50	24.47	84.8

pattern (50%). The most accurate channel for each subject is the same as the one resulted from the previous test, although with lower accuracy.

In order to highlight the necessity of the ML, in table B the classification accuracy of each subject basing on the learned parameters of the other subjects is presented. It is worth to notice that the procedure of classification basing on non-optimized thresholds for that specific subject does not maximize the accuracy of the P300 detection: the preponderance of the diagonal elements with respect to the off-diagonal ones highlights the high degree of subjectivity of the classification. In fact, the classification performed using sets of erroneous learning (such as those of others) exhibit low accuracies. Thus, table B highlights the need for a phase of learning on the specific subject.

Since the application is in real-time, special attention should be devoted to timing in order to guarantee the correct functioning. The advantages of t-RIDE respect the state of the art in terms of computational speed have been already discussed in [2]: t-RIDE allows to drastically reduce the duration of the training since it needs only 38 target stimuli for a complete characterization of P300 (190 s). The shortening of the training phase allows reducing the effect of the "habituation" which spoils the P300. t-RIDE computational time was only 1.95 s (against ICA: 3.1 s on the same dataset) [2] and it does not require a minimum number of channels. The fixed communication latency from EEG headset and gateway is 14 ms. The classifier needs to buffer 1 s data after the stimulus in order to perform the computation. The worst-case computational time for each feature extraction on single channel and single trial was 0.653 ± 0.32 ms. The worst-case total time for the FE stage on 6 channels was 19.58 ± 9.7 ms. The successive definition of the matrix F was performed in 0.026 ± 0.011 ms on all the channels. The computational time (for 6 channels) for the spatial validation was 0.041±0.008 ms. Given this computational details, the worst-case total time needed by the classifier to complete the classification for all the channels was 19.65 ± 10.1 ms. The FE stage is the most time consuming part of the process. The communication time between BCS and PCS takes about 3.35 ns (only 2 bits to be sent by Wi-Fi). As soon as Raspberry Pi receives the command, the actuation is performed in 3 ms (worst-case). The overall architecture completes a single actuation (from EEG raw data acquisition triggered by stimulus delivery to PCS actuation) in 1.03 s (worst-case).

5 Conclusion

The aim of the present work has been the study, the design, implementation and test of a brain-computer interface based on P300. The implemented neural interface allows remote control of a generic mechanical device such as a limb, a wheelchair or a robot. In order to validate the above BCI, in the present work the BCI has been applied to the remote control of a prototype vehicle, properly realized. The complete system architecture can be divided into two subsystems: the "Brain-to-Computer System" (BCS) and the "Prototype Car System" (PCS), communicating via TCP/ IP connection.

In order to adapt the system on the user, a first stage of Machine Learning (ML) is needed. The ML stage is based on the custom algorithm t-RIDE, which trains the following hyper-dimensional real-time classifier.

In order to satisfy real-time constraints, a linear thresholds classifier performs in real time the FE on raw data and detects the presence/absence of P300 basing on the learned references. The system has been validated on a dataset of 5 subjects driving the prototype car by their mind. The average classification accuracy on a single direction was $80.51 \pm 4.1\%$. The average classification accuracy in the detection of a 10-direction pattern was $69.6 \pm 1.9\%$. The classifier completes its process on all the channels in 19.65 ± 10.1 ms (worst-case).

References

1. Fernando, L., Alonso, N., Gomez-Gil, J.: Brain computer interfaces, a review. Sensors **12**(2), 1211–1264 (2012)
2. De Venuto, D., Annese, V.F., Mezzina, G.: Remote neuro-cognitive impairment sensing based on P300 spatio-temporal monitoring. IEEE Sensors J. **PP**(99) (2016). doi:10.1109/JSEN. 2016.2606553. Article no. 7562544
3. Graimann, B., Allison, B., Pfurtscheller, G.: Brain–Computer Interfaces: A Gentle Introduction. Brain-Computer Interfaces, pp. 1–27. Springer, Heidelberg (2009)
4. Grychtol, B., et al.: Human behavior integration improves classification rates in real-time BCI. Neural Syst. Rehabil. Eng. **8**(4), 362–368 (2010)
5. Ortner, R., et al.: An SSVEP BCI to control a hand orthosis for persons with tetraplegia. IEEE Trans. Neural Syst. Rehabil. Eng. **19**(1), 1–5 (2011)
6. Hochberg, L.R., et al.: Neuronal ensemble control of prosthetic devices by a human with tetraplegia. Nat. J. **442**, 164–171 (2006)
7. Stacey, A., Li, Y. Barnes, N.: A salient information processing system for bionic eye with application to obstacle avoidance. In: 2011 Annual International Conference of the IEEE Engineering in Medicine and Biology Society, Boston, MA, pp. 5116–5119 (2011).doi: 10.1109/IEMBS.2011.6091267
8. Nijholt, A.: BCI for games: a 'state of the art' survey. In: International Conference on Entertainment Computing. Springer, Heidelberg (2008)
9. Bi, L., et al.: A head-up display-based P300 brain–computer interface for destination selection. IEEE Trans. Intell. Transp. Syst. **14**(4), 1996–2001 (2013)
10. Göhring, D., Latotzky, D., Wang, M., Rojas, R.: Semi-autonomous car control using brain computer interfaces. In: Lee, S., Cho, H., Yoon, K.J., Lee, J. (eds.) Intelligent Autonomous Systems 12. Advances in Intelligent Systems and Computing, vol. 194, pp. 393–408. Springer, Heidelberg (2013)

11. De Tommaso, M., Vecchio, E., Ricci, K., Montemurno, A., De Venuto, D., Annese, V.F.: Combined EEG/EMG evaluation during a novel dual task paradigm for gait analysis. In: Proceedings of 2015 6th IEEE International Workshop on Advances in Sensors and Interfaces, IWASI, pp. 181–186 (2015). doi:10.1109/IWASI.2015.7184949. Article no. 7184949

12. Dinteren, V., et al.: P300 development across the lifespan: a systematic review and meta-analysis. PLoS One **9**(2), e87347 (2014)

13. De Venuto, D., Annese, V.F., Mezzina, G., Ruta, M., Di Sciascio, E.: Brain-computer interface using P300: a gaming approach for neurocognitive impairment diagnosis. In: Proceedings of 2016 IEEE HLDVT, Santa Cruza, USA (2016). doi:10.1109/HLDVT.2016.7748261. ISBN 978-1-5090-4270-8

14. Annese, V.F., Mezzina, G., De Venuto, D.: Towards mobile health care: neurocognitive impairment monitoring by BCI-based game. In: Proceedings of IEEE SENSORS 2016, Orlando, USA (2016). doi:10.1109/ICSENS.2016.7808745. ISBN 978-1-4799-8287-5

15. Annese, V.F., De Venuto, D.: Gait analysis for fall prediction using EMG triggered movement related potentials. In: Proceedings of 2015 10th IEEE International Conference on Design and Technology of Integrated Systems in Nanoscale Era, DTIS (2015). doi:10.1109/DTIS. 2015.7127386. Article no. 7127386

16. De Venuto, D., Annese, V.F., Ruta, M., Di Sciascio, E., Sangiovanni Vincentelli, A.L.: Designing a cyber-physical system for fall prevention by cortico-muscular coupling detection. IEEE Des. Test **33**(3), 66–76 (2016). doi:10.1109/MDAT.2015.2480707. Article no. 7273831

17. Annese, V.F., De Venuto, D.: FPGA based architecture for fall-risk assessment during gait monitoring by synchronous EEG/EMG. In: Proceedings of 2015 6th IEEE International Workshop on Advances in Sensors and Interfaces, IWASI 2015, pp. 116–121 (2015). doi: 10.1109/IWASI.2015.7184953. Article no. 7184953

18. Annese, V.F., De Venuto, D.: Fall-risk assessment by combined movement related potentials and co-contraction index monitoring. In: Proceedings of IEEE Biomedical Circuits and Systems Conference: Engineering for Healthy Minds and Able Bodies, BioCAS (2015). doi: 10.1109/BioCAS.2015.7348366. Article no. 7348366

19. Annese, V.F., Crepaldi, M., Demarchi, D., De Venuto, D.: A digital processor architecture for combined EEG/EMG falling risk prediction. In: Proceedings of the 2016 Design, Automation and Test in Europe Conference and Exhibition, DATE 2016, pp. 714–719 (2016). Article no. 7459401

20. Annese, V.F., De Venuto, D.: The truth machine of involuntary movement: FPGA based cortico-muscular analysis for fall prevention. In: 2015 IEEE International Symposium on Signal Processing and Information Technology, ISSPIT 2015, pp. 553–558 (2015). doi: 10.1109/ISSPIT.2015.7394398. Article no. 7394398

21. De Venuto, D., Annese, V.F., Sangiovanni-Vincentelli, A.L.: The ultimate IoT application: a cyber-physical system for ambient assisted living. In: Proceedings of IEEE International Symposium on Circuits and Systems, July 2016, pp. 2042–2045 (2016). doi:10.1109/ISCAS. 2016.7538979. Article no. 7538979

22. De Venuto, D., Carrara, S., Riccò, B.: Design of an integrated low-noise read-out system for DNA capacitive sensors. Microelectron. J. **40**(9), 1358–1365 (2009). doi:10.1016/j.mejo. 2008.07.071

23. De Venuto, D., Castro, D.T., Ponomarev, Y., Stikvoort, E.: Low power 12-bit SAR ADC for autonomous wireless sensors network interface. In: 3rd International Workshop on Advances in Sensors and Interfaces, IWASI 2009, pp. 115–120 (2009). doi:10.1109/IWASI. 2009.5184780. Article no. 5184780

24. De Venuto, D., Ohletz, M.J., Ricco, B.: Automatic repositioning technique for digital cell based window comparators and implementation within mixed-signal DfT schemes. In: Proceedings of International Symposium on Quality Electronic Design, ISQED, January 2003, pp. 431–437 (2003). doi:10.1109/ISQED.2003.1194771. Article no. 1194771
25. De Venuto, D., Ohletz, M.J., Riccò, B.: Digital window comparator DfT scheme for mixed-signal ICs. J. Electron. Test. Theory Appl. (JETTA) **18**(2), 121–128 (2005). doi:10.1023/A: 1014937424827
26. De Venuto, D., Ohletz, M.J., Riccò, B.: Testing of analogue circuits via (standard) digital gates. In: Proceedings of International Symposium on Quality Electronic Design, ISQED, January 2002, pp. 112–119 (2002). doi:10.1109/ISQED.2002.996709. Article no. 996709
27. De Venuto, D., Vincentelli, A.S.: Dr. Frankenstein's dream made possible: implanted electronic devices. In: Proceedings of Design, Automation and Test in Europe, DATE, pp. 1531–1536 (2013). doi:10.7873/DATE.2013.311. Article no. 6513757

A Dual Processor Energy-Efficient Platform with Multi-core Accelerator for Smart Sensing

Antonio Pullini[✉], Stefan Mach, Michele Magno, and Luca Benini

Integrated Systems Laboratory, ETH Zurich, Gloriastrsse, 35, 8092 Zurich, Switzerland
{antonio.pullini,stefan.mach,michele.magno,
luca.benini}@iis.ee.ethz.ch

Abstract. Energy-efficient computing has increasingly come into focus of research and industry over the last decade. Ultra-low-power architectures are a requirement for distributed sensing, wearable electronics, Internet of Things and consumer electronics. In this paper, we present a dual-mode platform that includes an ultra-low power Cortex Arm M4 microcontroller coupled with a highly energy efficient multi-core parallel processor. The platform is designed to maximize the energy efficiency in sensors applications by exploiting the Cortex Arm M4 to achieve ultra-low power processing and power management, and enables the multi-core processor to provide additional computational power for near-sensor data centric processing (i.e. accelerating Convolutional Neural Networks for image classification) increasing energy efficiency. The proposed platform enhances the application scenarios where on-board processing (i.e. without streaming out the sensor data) enables intensive computation to extract complex features. The platform is geared towards applications with limited energy budget, as for example in mobile or wearable scenarios where the devices are supplied by a battery. Experimental results confirm the energy efficiency of the platform, demonstrate the low power consumption, and the benefits of combining the two processing engines. Compared to a pure microcontroller platform we provide a boost of 80× in terms of computational power when running general purpose code and a boost of 560× when performing convolutions. Within a reasonable power budged of 20 mW compatible to battery-operated scenarios the system can perform 345 MOPS of general purpose code or 1.5 GOPS of convolutions.

Keywords: Low power design · Sensors platform · Energy efficiency · Power management · Multi-core processor

1 Introduction

Due to the vast improvements in sensors technology, digital processors, device minia-turization and thanks to the availability of ubiquitous wireless connectivity, intelligent sensor devices are becoming increasingly smart and this leads to always-on connected products. The Internet of Things (IoT) paradigm, promises to have trillions of those sensors devices in nearly future deployed around the world [1]. Partially this revolution has already started, and today sensors devices are gaining immense popularity, with

© ICST Institute for Computer Sciences, Social Informatics and Telecommunications Engineering 2017
M. Magno et al. (Eds.): S-Cube 2016, LNICST 205, pp. 29–40, 2017.
DOI: 10.1007/978-3-319-61563-9_3

people increasingly surrounded by "smart" objects, from phones to clothing, from glasses to watches, finding applications from home automation to healthcare [2].

The IoT is also creating formidable research challenges. In particular, trillions of sensors will produce huge amounts of data that need to be sent and stored somewhere. Moreover, the data by themselves do not provide value unless we can turn them into actionable, contextualized information. In fact, to produce useful information the data needs to be processed by some intelligent system somewhere along the line. Big-data mining techniques allow us to gain new insights by batch-processing and off-line analysis. Machine learning technologies are used with great success in many application areas, solving real-world problems in entertainment systems, robotics, health care, and surveillance [1]. More and more researchers are tackling classification and decision-making problems with the help of brain-inspired algorithms, featuring *many stages* of feature extractors and classifiers with lots of parameters that are optimized using the unprecedented wealth of training data that is currently available. However, machine learning requires complex software and significant computational power to be really effective [4, 5].

Today there are many IoT applications that use a centralized approach where data processing is done far from the sensor. In these applications, data is sent directly to a remote host capable of running complex and power hungry algorithms. This is, for example, the approach used by the cloud computing adopted by the biggest service companies as Google and Facebook and millions of users [6]. It is clear that, as the number of data generating remote sensors increase steadily, the communication infrastructure will be not sufficient to deal with the enormous amounts of data being generated all over the planet. For a truly scalable and robust IoT infrastructure to succeed, in-situ, close to the sensor and distributed real-time feature extraction, analysis, classification, and local decision-making are essential [7].

In recent years, there have been many research efforts to design new processors to match the requirements of computational resources required by in-situ signal processing with low power consumption needed for operating long-lasting sensors devices [7–10]. There are two approaches to improve the performance of ultra-low-power processors that have shown promise. The first one is to exploit parallelism as much as possible. Parallel architectures for near-threshold operation, based on multi-core clusters, have been explored in recent years with different application workloads for an implementation in a 90 nm technology [17]. A second very prolific research area is exploiting low-power fixed-function hardware accelerators coupled with programmable parallel processors to retain flexibility while improving energy efficiency for specific workloads [11, 12]. Such near-threshold parallel heterogeneous computing approaches hold great promise.

In this work, we present a complete hardware platform that includes an heterogeneous multi-core System on Chip (SoC), capable of operating on a wide voltage range, paired with an ultra-low power ARM Cortex M4 micro controller that are able to interface to a wide set of sensors. The platform is designed to achieve the best energy efficiency for a wide range of applications by combining the ultra-low power of the highly integrated ARM microcontroller and the powerful multicore SoC. The ARM M4, which is designed for battery powered applications such as wearable electronics, is used to configure the SoC processor, provides the power management of the board and can also process preliminary sensor data. In this way, the SoC processor is activated by the ARM M4 only when it has not enough computational resources (i.e. processing convolutional neural network for video processing) or in cases when it is more energy efficient to process the data on the SoC (i.e. if the SoC can accelerate the algorithm by a factor of 10× or more). The platform has been designed as a generic testbed and supports several peripherals where sensors can be attached.

The rest of the paper is organized as follows: Sect. 2 presents related work, Sect. 3 describes the SoC ultra low-power multi-core parallel platform (PULP), Sect. 4 illustrates the multi-processor platform that has been designed and developed, Sect. 5 shows the experimental results and Sect. 6 concludes the paper.

2   Related Works

Research on intelligent sensors systems has been very prolific in recent years with a variety of solutions in a wide range of application scenarios [1, 3]. There are many examples of implemented and deployed wearable devices that attempt to exploit intelligent sensing and wireless communication to monitor human activities [13–15]. The main challenges of IoT devices design are to prolong the operating lifetime and to enhance usability, maintenance, and mobility, while keeping a small and unobtrusive form factor [2]. Many IoT devices such as for example mobile and wearable sensing systems have to provide continuous data monitoring, acquisition, processing, and classification. Supporting such continuous operation using only ultra-small batteries poses unique challenges in energy efficiency [16].

As sensor data processing based on machine learning needs computational performance, most IoT applications today on the market have focused on using smartphones as a centralized hub that provides a powerful computing platform and allows a network of smaller sensors to be connected. Pushing on energy efficiency, state-of-the-art commercial ultra-low power processors are trying to exploit novel solutions to extract as much as possible out of silicon. A novel approach to further improve the energy efficiency is near-threshold computing, which exploits the fact that CMOS technology is most efficient when operated near the device voltage threshold [19]. In particular in [20–22] the authors show examples of near-threshold ultra-low power microcontrollers, with the latter also exploiting SIMD parallelism to improve performance. There are microcontrollers that can embed custom hardware accelerators [23] as well to improve the computational performance. However, such approaches limit the flexibility of the solution affecting the cost and scale economy. In this paper, we show the potential of combining an ARM Cortex M4 with a state-of-the-art multi-core accelerator in a single platform to maximize the energy efficiency of a wide range of sensor applications providing extraordinary computational power.

3   Pulp Overview

The main aim of this work is to build a multi-modal and multi-processor sensing platform that embeds an ultra-low-power parallel-processor called PULP (Parallel Ultra Low

Power Platform) [17]. The PULP processor has been designed specifically to take advantage of the energy-efficient near-threshold regime. The degradation of performance, caused by the aggressive voltage scaling, is recovered by increasing the parallelism. The PULP platform is built upon a cluster of tightly coupled cores. To avoid the huge overhead of a cache coherent system, the cores do not have private data caches but share data through a Tightly Coupled Data Memory (TCDM). The TCDM is composed of several single ported memory cuts connected to the processors with a non-blocking logarithmic interconnect. The interconnect grants single cycle access when there is no contention and, by using appropriate banking factors and interleaving, on average the access contention remains below 10% even for load/store intensive applications. The Instruction-Cache (I-Cache) is shared among all cores and is implemented with Standard Cell Memory (SCM) cuts to optimize the energy of instruction fetching. Data transfer between L1 TCDM and the main SoC memory is done by a system DMA capable of queuing multiple transfers with ultra-low latency programming interface dedicated to each core. The system is completely event based: the cores, when waiting for synchronization events or for I/O, are forced in an idle state by a dedicated hardware Event Unit. The event unit performs the gating of the cores and provides hardware support for fast core synchronization (Fig. 1).

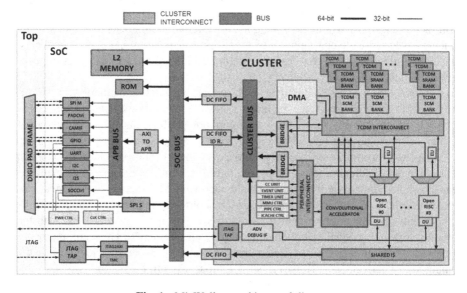

Fig. 1. MiaWallace architectural diagram

The SoC named MiaWallace in this work is an implementation of the PULP platform in UMC 65 nm with the addition of a convolutional hardware accelerator. It has four cores and features an L1 TCDM of 80 KB (64 KB SRAM and 16 KB SCM based), a 4 KB instruction cached based entirely on SCM, a 256 KB L2 memory and a full set of peripherals. The cores are compliant with the OpenRISC ISA, with instruction set extensions for DSP applications to improve performance [24].

The dedicated Hardware Convolution Engine (HWCE) is directly connected to the L1 TCDM memory through the logarithmic interconnect just like processor cores. It uses three dedicated ports toward the shared memory to sustain the full bandwidth required by its engine. Its core is made of two sum of products unit, each of which is capable of performing a 5×5 convolution on 16 bits input data. Although it is optimized for 5×5 convolutions it can, with a little loss of performance perform convolutions of different sizes allowing applications that use convolutions (such as convolutional neural networks) to be processed efficiently [12].

The PULP includes two SPI (Serial Peripheral Interface) interfaces (one master and one slave), I2C, I2S, GPIOs, a boot ROM and a JTAG interface suitable for testing purposes. Both SPI interfaces can be configured in *single* mode or *quad* mode depending on the required bandwidth, and they are suitable for interfacing the SoC with a large set of off-chip components (non-volatile memories, voltage regulators, cameras, etc.).

PULP is able to operate in two different modes: *slave* mode or *stand-alone* mode. When configured in slave mode, PULP behaves as a many-core accelerator of a standard *host* processor (e.g. an ARM Cortex M4 low-power microcontroller). In this configuration the host microcontroller is responsible for loading the application and the data on to the PULP L2 memory through the SPI master interface. After this the microcontroller initiates and synchronizes the computation through dedicated memory mapped signals (e.g. fetch enable) and GPIOs. When configured in stand-alone mode, the boot code in the on-chip ROM is able to detect a flash memory on its SPI master interface and, if present, will load the program to the L2 memory and starts the execution.

The SoC is divided in two voltage domains, one for the cluster and one for the peripherals and L2 memories. The cluster works on a wide range of voltages starting as low as 0.62 V while the minimum operating voltage of the peripheral domain is limited by the L2, whose performance degrades severely below 0.8 V. Figure 2 shows the chip micrograph and a table with the main features.

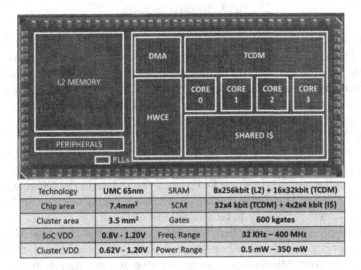

Technology	UMC 65nm	SRAM	8x256kbit (L2) + 16x32kbit (TCDM)
Chip area	7.4mm²	SCM	32x4 kbit (TCDM) + 4x2x4 kbit (I$)
Cluster area	3.5 mm²	Gates	600 kgates
SoC VDD	0.8V - 1.20V	Freq. Range	32 KHz – 400 MHz
Cluster VDD	0.62V - 1.20V	Power Range	0.5 mW – 350 mW

Fig. 2. Chip micrograph and main features

4   Platform Architecture

Figure 3 shows the architectural block diagram of the implemented platform. The designed multi-processor platform features an ARM Cortex M4 ultra low-power microcontroller as well as the Mia Wallace SoC as the main architectural blocks. The two devices are interconnected by various interfaces. In particular, PULP's slave SPI interface is driven by the microcontroller to have access to the entire memory space of the PULP system. With this interface, the microcontroller can assume the role of a host controller using PULP as an accelerator. Additionally, a shared I^2C Bus and GPIO connections between the two devices allow for user-programmable signaling or data exchange.

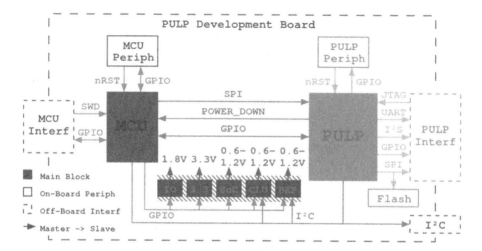

Fig. 3. Sytem architecture

Both PULP and the microcontroller are connected to a set of LEDs and push buttons to allow for basic user interaction. A flash memory for loading PULP programs in standalone mode is part of the platform. Although in the current version of the platform we didn't embed any sensors, all interfaces of both devices are accessible via pin headers and connectors so that a multitude of sensors or other peripheral devices can be attached to the system. Thus, serial interfaces such as I^2C, UART, SPI, QUAD-SPI, I^2S and GPIOs are all available for sensors board extension.

As the platform is mainly targeting mobile and wearable applications, to ensure simplicity and portability, the platform is powered from a single power source such as a laboratory power supply or a single Li-Po battery cell. A set of DC-DC converters are a part of the platform in order to provide the necessary supply voltages for PULP, the microcontroller and peripherals to be attached to the system.

All the supplies can be controlled by both the microcontroller and the MiaWallace SoC, however to achieve ultra-low power consumption the microcontroller can completely shut down MiaWallace and ensure correct wakeup after deep sleep modes.

To improve the energy efficiency of the platform and provide flexibility, different power supplies have been optimized for different current ranges and average on times.

Table 1 shows the main features of the power converters we have evaluated. High Efficiency Power Converter (HEPCO) has been designed to extend the voltage range of commercially available DC/DC components while keeping the maximum possible efficiency.

Table 1. Efficiency and Ripple for different DC/DC converters

Converter	1.2 V				0.6 V			
	0.1 mA		10 mA		0.1 mA		10 mA	
	Eff (%)	Rip (V)	Eff	Rip	Eff	Rip	Eff	Rip
TPS62080 PFM/PWM	40	0.4	80	0.2			73	0.2
TPS62080snooze mode	57	4.2	79	0.9	48	4.8	71	0.8
TPS62361B	30	0.9	84	0.5	23	2.4	78	0.8
HEPCO w/TPS62736	82	1.9	88	0.5	74	3.9	80	1.7
HEPCO w/TPS62737	76	3.2	79	2.9	63	9.2	68	8.0

For the cluster domain we choose the TPS62361B, which has an operating range compatible with our requirements and it has a very fine tuning range to find the optimal operating point for a given application. The minimum current of the cluster is above the point for which this converter starts to lose efficiency. For the peripheral domain of the MiaWallace we use the HEPCO implemented with the TPS62736 due to its high efficiency at lower currents.

The choice of the microcontroller was driven by the low power features available and the flexibility on the power modes. After comparing various microcontrollers available today on the market we choose the Ambiq Apollo MCU. The microcontroller combines ultra-low-power sensor conversion electronics with a 32-bit ARM Cortex-M4F processor. It also integrates 512 KB of flash memory, 64 KB of RAM and a Floating Point Unit which is a big advantage compared to the other MCUs in the ultra-low power world.

Other main components of the Apollo MCU include: 10 bit ADC with 8 channels, temperature sensor, I2C/SPI interface, 50 GPIO, and one UART. Furthermore, the Apollo MCU includes a set of timing peripherals based on Ambiq's AM08XX and AM18XX Real-Time Clock (RTC) families. The RTC, timers, and counters may be driven by three different clock sources: a low frequency RC oscillator, a high frequency RC oscillator, and a 32.768 kHz crystal (XTAL) oscillator. With its extremely low active mode power of <40 µA/MHz, it is possible to perform complex sensor processing algorithms on the Apollo MCU. The Apollo MCU also includes a Power Management Unit (PMU) that controls the transitions of the MCU between the following power modes:

Active mode: in this state, the processor M4F is switched on, all clocks are active and instructions are being executed. The MCU will return to active mode during reset, when an interrupt is received by the **Nested Vectored Interrupt Controller** or a Debug Event is received.

Sleep mode: during this mode, the M4F is powered up, the clocks (HCLK, FCLK) are not active. The difference between this state and the Deep Sleep Mode is that the M4F logic is still on and it can return to Active State rapidly on a wakeup event.

Deep Sleep mode: in this state, the M4F enters a State Retention Power Gating (SRPG) where the main power is removed, but the registers in the MCU retain their values. The clocks are not active, and the clock sources for HCLK and FCLK can be deactivated. Table 2 shows measurements performed on the MCU during different operating modes relevant for the project.

Table 2. Ambiq Apollo operating modes and current consumption

Scenario	Power consumption
Deep sleep, RTC disabled	100 nA @ 2 V
Deep sleep, 8/64 KB ram block retention, RTC on 1 s, incrementing one variable	125 nA @ 2 V
Deep sleep, 64/64 KB ram block retention, RTC on 1 s, incrementing one variable	435 nA @ 2 V
Normal sleep, RTC disabled, 8/64 KB ram block retention	50 μA @ 2 V
Active mode, 64/64 KB ram retention	1.3 mA @ 2 V

5   Experimental Results

5.1   Experimental Setup

The platform has been designed and implemented on a small-outline PCB just 8.7 cm × 5.7 cm in size and is shown in Fig. 4. The whole platform can then be supplied by a single battery.

Fig. 4. PCB photo

Before measurements take place, programs for PULP and the microcontroller are loaded into PULP's flash memory and the ARM's onboard flash via the JTAG and SWD debug ports, respectively. The platform is supplied by and measurements are then taken with the Keysight N6705B DC power analyzer. This approach allows for precise measurements of dissipated power in the individual components of the platform as well as for the calculation of converter efficiencies.

5.2 Computational Performance

MiaWallace with its wide operating range and the availability of the HWCE enables multiple working modes that could cover many applications typical of the IoT domain. Detailed measurements of performances and power consumption of the SoC in stand-alone mode have been performed using an Advantest SoCV93000 ASIC tester. Figure 5a shows the maximum operating frequency for different voltage points over the whole operating range, while Fig. 5b shows how the energy efficiency changes in the same range. When the HWCE is on, we consider the power in different conditions depending on the computation over communication ratio (CCR) which depends highly on the topology of the CNN. The number of operation per second is assuming that the cores can perform 1 instruction per cycle. This assumption is true for many DSP kernels especially where the operands are smaller than 32 bits and the system can benefit from the available vector support extensions.

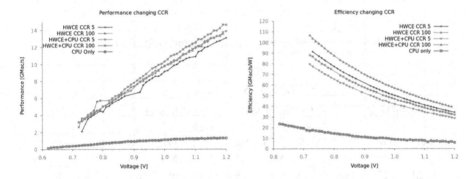

Fig. 5. Performance and efficiency of the SoC for different operating points

Both figures clearly show the boost in efficiency and performance given by the accelerator. A high accuracy CNN architecture as GoogleLeNet requires nearly 2.5 GOPs to process a frame of 320 × 240 pixels. The peak performance curve shows that even at modest voltages the system can sustain a full blown convolutional neural network when using the HWCE. From both graphs we can see that when using the CPU only the system can operate at very low voltages. This is possible thanks to the heterogeneity of the L1 TCDM and the use of the SCMs. This ULP mode is very useful for example in all the applications where the environment has to be monitored continuously (light, noise, temperature) and only upon an event the full processing is performed. The system can sustain a maximum of 14 GMAC/s at 1.2 V and reach an energy efficiency of 108 GMAC/s/W.

5.3 System Profiling

After measuring the SoC and the power supply in isolation we implemented a simple power management firmware in the Apollo MCU and we measured the whole system in different operation points and during a synthetic application in which we moved through the different power modes. Figure 6 shows the profile with the states and the measurements results of the whole sequence while Table 3 gives more details about the states.

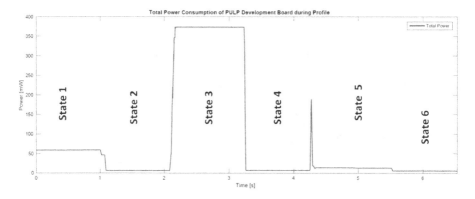

Fig. 6. Power profiling of the whole platform tested in our lab

Table 3. State Details

State	Ambiq Apollo state			MiaWallace SoC state			MiaWallace cluster state				
	Vdd V	Freq Mhz	Pwr mW	Vdd V	Freq Mhz	Pwr mW	Vdd V	Freq Mhz	Pwr mW	Conv Eff%	Perf GMAC/s
1	2.1	20	0.2	1.13	50	9.1	1.16	50	38	85.8	1.8
2	2.1	20	0.3	1.13	50	0.7	OFF	n/a	<1u	91.1	n/a
3	2.1	20	0.3	1.13	200	34.5	1.16	350	330	86	12.5
4	2.1	20	0.3	1.13	200	1.3	OFF	n/a	<1u	87.2	n/a
5	2.1	20	0.2	0.79	5	0.7	0.68	5	1.8	79.3	0.02
6	2.1	20	0.3	1.13	5	0.2	OFF	n/a	<1u	90	n/a

6   Conclusions

In this paper we presented a multi-modal multi-processor platform designed to maximize the energy efficiency of smart sensing applications. The platform can be supplied by a single battery and can host a wide range of sensors trough several peripherals. The platform exploits the combination of the two processors to achieve energy efficiency. In particular, with the ultra-low power commercial microcontroller, it is possible to achieve very low power states and manage the power supply of the rest of the platform.

On the other hand, the presence of the multi-core energy efficient accelerator brings extraordinary computational resources even when working in a very tight power envelope. The platform has been designed carefully also to achieve conversion efficiency on the power domains needed for the PULP processor. Experimental results on the developed platform shows the energy efficiency and the low power of the platform. The platform is ready to host sensors and applications that will be studied in future works.

References

1. Gubbi, J., Buyya, R., Marusic, S., Palaniswami, M.: Internet of Things (IoT): a vision, architectural elements, and future directions. Future Gener. Comput. Syst. **29**(7), 1645–1660 (2013)
2. Da Xu, L., He, W., Li, S.: Internet of Things in industries: a survey. IEEE Trans. Ind. Inform. **10**(4), 2233–2243 (2014)
3. Govindaraju, V., Rao, C.: Machine Learning: Theory and Applications. Elsevier, Amsterdam (2013)
4. Michalski, R.S., Carbonell, J.G., Mitchell, T.M. (eds.) Machine learning: an artificial convolutional networks. In: Proceedings of the 52nd Annual Design Automation Conference, p. 108. ACM (2013)
5. Hashem, I.A.T., Yaqoob, I., Anuar, N.B., Mokhtar, S., Gani, A., Khan, S.U.: The rise of "big data" on cloud computing: review and open research issues. Inf. Syst. **47**, 98–115 (2015)
6. Hwang, K., Dongarra, J., Fox, G.C.: Distributed and Cloud Computing: From Parallel Processing to the Internet of Things. Morgan Kaufmann, Boston (2013)
7. Kahng, A.B., Kang, S., Kumar, R., Sartori, J.: Enhancing the efficiency of energy-constrained DVFS designs. IEEE Trans. Very Large Scale Integr. (VLSI) Syst. **21**(10), 1769–1782 (2013)
8. Wang, Z., Liu, Y., Sun, Y., Li, Y., Zhang, D., Yang, H.: An energy-efficient heterogeneous dual-core processor for Internet of Things. In: 2015 IEEE International Symposium on Circuits and Systems (ISCAS), Lisbon (2015)
9. Dreslinski, et al.: Centip3De: a 64-core, 3D stacked, near-threshold system. IEEE Micro **33**(2), 8–16 (2013)
10. Jeon, D., Kim, Y., Lee, I., Zhang, Z., Blaauw, D., Sylvester, D.: A 470 mV 2.7 mW feature extraction-accelerator for micro-autonomous vehicle navigation in 28 nm CMOS. In: Proceedings of 2013 IEEE International Solid-State Circuits Conference Digest of Technical Papers (ISSCC), pp. 166–168 (2013)
11. Yoon, J.-S., Kim, J.-H., Kim, H.-E., Lee, W.-Y., Kim, S.-H., Chung, K., Park, J.-S., Kim, L.-S.: A unified graphics and vision processor with a 0.89 uW/fps pose estimation engine for augmented reality. IEEE Trans. Very Large Scale Integr. (VLSI) Syst. **21**(2), 206–216 (2013)
12. Ghasemzadeh, H., Jafari, R.: Ultra low-power signal processing in wearable monitoring systems: a tiered screening architecture with optimal bit resolution. ACM Trans. Embed. Comput. Syst. (TECS) **13**(1) (2013). Article No. 9
13. Magno, M., Brunelli, D., Sigrist, L., Andri, R., Cavigelli, L., Gomez, A., Benini, L.: InfiniTime: multi-sensor wearable bracelet with human body harvesting. Sustain. Comput. Inform. Syst. **11**, 38–49 (2016)
14. Cavigelli, L., Magno, M., Benini, L.: Accelerating real-time embedded scene labeling with convolutional networks. In: Proceedings of the 52nd Annual Design Automation Conference, p. 108. ACM, June 2015
15. Magno, M., Spagnol, C., Benini, L., Popovici, E.: A low power wireless node for contact and contactless heart monitoring. Microelectron. J. **45**(12), 1656–1664 (2014)

16. Magno, M., Salvatore, G.A., Mutter, S., Farrukh, W., Troester, G., Benini, L.: Autonomous smartwatch with flexible sensors for accurate and continuous mapping of skin temperature. In: 2016 IEEE International Symposium on Circuits and Systems (ISCAS), pp. 337–340. IEEE, May 2016

17. Rossi, D., et al.: A -1.8 V to 0.9 V body bias, 60 GOPS/W 4-core cluster in low-power 28 nm UTBB FD-SOI technology. In: SOI-3D-Subthreshold Microelectronics Technology Unified Conference (S3S). IEEE, Rohnert Park (2015)

18. Conti, F., Benini, L.: A ultra-low-energy convolution engine for fast brain-inspired vision in multicore clusters. In: 2015 Design, Automation and Test in Europe Conference and Exhibition (DATE), Grenoble, pp. 683–688 (2015)

19. Dreslinski, R., Wieckowski, M., Blaauw, D., Sylvester, D., Mudge, T.: Near-threshold computing: reclaiming Moore's law through energy efficient integrated circuits. In: Proceedings of the IEEE, vol. 98, pp. 253–266, February 2010

20. Ickes, N., Sinangil, Y., Pappalardo, F., Guidetti, E., Chandrakasan, A.P.: A 10 pJ/cycle ultra-low-voltage 32-bit microprocessor system-on-chip. In: 2011 Proceedings of the ESSCIRC (ESSCIRC), pp. 159–162. IEEE, September 2011

21. Bol, D., De Vos, J., Hocquet, C., Botman, F., Durvaux, F., Boyd, S., Flandre, D., Legat, J.-D.: SleepWalker: a 25-MHz 0.4-V Sub-mm2 7-uW/MHz microcontroller in 65-nm LP/GP CMOS for low-carbon wireless sensor nodes. IEEE J. Solid-State Circ. **48**, 20–32 (2013)

22. Botman, F., Vos, J.D., Bernard, S., Stas, F., Legat, J.-D., Bol, D.: Bellevue: a 50 MHz variable-width SIMD 32 bit microcontroller at 0.37 V for processing-intensive wireless sensor nodes. In: Proceedings of 2014 IEEE Symposium on Circuits and Systems, pp. 1207–1210 (2014)

23. Fujita, T., Tanaka, T., Sonoda, K., Kanda, K., Maenaka, K.: Ultra low power ASIC for R-R interval extraction on wearable health monitoring system. In: 2013 IEEE International Conference on Systems, Man, and Cybernetics (SMC), pp. 3780–3783, October 2013

24. Gautschi, M., et al.: Tailoring instruction-set extensions for an ultra-low power tightly-coupled cluster of OpenRISC cores. In: 2015 IFIP/IEEE International Conference on Very Large Scale Integration (VLSI-SoC), Daejeon, pp. 25–30 (2015)

Smart Sensing Devices for Logistics Application

Mojtaba Masoudinejad[✉], Aswin Karthik Ramachandran Venkatapathy,
Jan Emmerich, and Andreas Riesner

TU Dortmund University, Dortmund, Germany
Mojtaba.Masoudinejad@tu-dortmund.de
http://www.flw.mb.tu-dortmund.de/

Abstract. This paper provides an abstract view of the Industry 4.0 as
the next industrial revolution. Cyber Physical Systems (CPS) as smart
connected solutions are considered to be the key answer to the needs
of future industry. Effects of this revolution on the logistics sector is
analysed and integration of CPS in this field is presented.

To evaluate the quality of CPS solutions in the field of logistics,
PhyNetLab and its subcomponents are presented as a physical testbed
for testing CPS nodes, structural designs, communication platform and
protocols in addition to the energy challenges for materials handling and
warehousing application.

inBin and P-ink as two CPS solutions are reviewed in the context of
the order-picking. Also, iCon as an alternative outdoor asset tracking
solution is presented.

Keywords: Smart sensing · Logistics · Industry 4.0 · Wireless sensor
network · PhyNetLab · inBin · P-ink · iCon

1 Introduction

Industry as a major part of the economy, responsible for production and manufacturing have seen different paradigm shifts since the beginning of industri-
alization. Mechanization, electrification and automation (or digitalization) are
the three past revolutions. Future technologies are orienting into the direction of
making machines and services more "smart", resulting in a new shift in industry [1]. This transfer is pushed by the development of new technologies and
forced from application and costumer side for better solutions [1].

In a traditional system, several sensors provide data to a central decision
making unit. After deciding about the required action, it propagates them to
actuators. However, the current need of fast changing products and systems
pushes industries towards more flexible solutions. Therefore, future systems have
to be easily reconfigurable. Preference is in less central structure and more use of
multi-agent solutions which communicate with each other [2]. This helps to avoid
complex and tedious task of central reconfiguration after system modifications.
Hence, intelligent modularity and communication are the two critical aspects of
the next industrial revolution named Industry 4.0.

© ICST Institute for Computer Sciences, Social Informatics and Telecommunications Engineering 2017
M. Magno et al. (Eds.): S-Cube 2016, LNICST 205, pp. 41–52, 2017.
DOI: 10.1007/978-3-319-61563-9_4

1.1   Industry 4.0

In the Industry 4.0 vision, an efficient smart manufacturing system or production line is made of multiple modules. These modules communicate not only with each other and the environment, but also products communicate with them as well to influence the manufacturing configuration and control the production scenario [3]. This is mainly required to realize the individual production in the batch size of one single product while still maintaining the economic condition of the mass production [1]. It makes topologies to be more fluid to automatically reconfigure instead of having a production process with fixed rules [3].

Smart networking of multi entity system will make the future systems more mobile and flexible. It also makes the integrity of the costumers easier and opens new business model innovations [4]. This costumer integrity can be from a simple action such as automatic brewing of a coffee when the costumer enters the coffeehouse till halt of an assembly line by clicking on a button [5].

Recent developments made the future modules for the Industry 4.0 such as sensors, data acquisition systems and networks more available and affordable [6]. For instance, a smart sensor is not only responsible for the sensing, but also it processes the data and analyses it independently as a complete entity. This information can even lead into a decision directly made by the sensor unit. It transmits this data via network to a smart actuator to do the proper action [4].

Although there are different understanding and definition of *smart* in the context of the Industry 4.0, most of them are focusing on two main aspects: first, they are all embedded devices and second, they are able to communicate. This communication can be within different levels; from closed local Wireless Sensor Networks (WSN) to globally spread devices communicating over the internet. These two aspects lead into the definition of the Cyber Physical Systems (CPS). Unlike traditional embedded systems mostly designed for the stand-alone operation, CPS is focusing on the networking of multiple devices. Also, this data exchange possibility is the key differentiation of devices in this new era [4].

1.2   Cyber Physical Systems

Although CPS consists of two main aspects of the connectivity and intelligence (including computational power and data management), there is a 5C structure to explain the work-flow of CPS construction [6]:

- **Smart connection:** easy setup (plug&play) and reliable network connection
- **Data/information conversion:** converting available data into meaningful and useful information
- **Cyber machine:** collecting data from the network and understanding the status of the node among the whole fleet
- **Cognition:** presenting proper monitoring information for the higher levels (or experts) to define priorities, optimization points and maintenance needs
- **Configuration:** feedback from cyber level to the physical level

Exploitation and integration of CPS with such specifications in the industry would transform today's factories into Industry 4.0 factories with significant potentials. A report from Fraunhofer Institute and the industry association Bitkom predicts that introducing Industry 4.0 will boost the German gross value by a cumulative 267 billion Euro by 2025 [6].

Although transition into this direction will bring new potentials for the industry, it amplifies the already existing complexities in the supply chain. All compartments of the supply chain have to be extremely flexible with the shortest reaction time while still acting reliable to assure costumers' needs [3]. Logistics as a major section of the supply chain need to grow hand in hand with this revolution to avoid problems and bottlenecks in the supply chain.

In the remaining of this paper, first the effect of Industry 4.0 on the future logistics is seen. To analyse possible CPS with focus on the logistics, PhyNetLab as a testbed platform is presented. Then, two types of CPS nodes operating in this testbed are presented. Subsequently, two CPS solutions for the order-picking application are discussed. And finally an energy-neutral logistics asset-tracker called iCon is presented before a short conclusion.

2   Logistics

Logistics in its general substance can be considered as all set of services covering the planning, organization, management, control and execution of flowing goods and information. It includes multiple tasks, from purchasing, production, warehousing and freight transport to added value services, distribution and reverse logistics in the whole supply chain [7,8]. Based on this definition, logistics is a vital section for the industry and supply chain. The estimated potential market volume of the logistics sector of the 28 European Union member states in 2012 was about 878 billion Euro. However, transport and warehousing are representing the majority of the added values in this sector [8].

According to the latest investigations published in [8], the existing European logistics sector is dealing with three clear problem areas as:

- continuous rise in costs
- external (non-logistics) effects such as energy and emission
- the quality and quantity of the relevant staff

moreover, there are some not critical issues pushing this sector to improve. Some of them are [5]:

- transparency and integrity control along the whole supply chain
- real time detailed shipment tracking
- integrity control for sensitive goods
- assets control and monitoring for analysis and optimization

In addition to the available concerns pushing for new solutions, influence of reconfigurable manufacturing systems foreseen in the Industry 4.0 revolution demands special solutions as well. On the other hand, advances in the networking solutions and protocols, energy efficient and energy aware hardware in addition to the maturity and affordability of the smart sensors provides new opportunities to fulfil the Industry 4.0 in the logistics sector.

Flexibility of a system have always been an asset in the logistics [9, 10]. Modularization as a priority for flexibility requires to decompose the logistics system into its basic functions and introduce proper module for each of them able to communicate with each other. This will reduce the operating challenge in the highly dynamic Industry 4.0 environment [11]. Therefore, using these systems able to understand their condition and react based on that will tackle the flexibility issue [12].

Modularization of logistics tasks using CPS will also reduce the need for central systems and make them much more dynamic [9]. This will reduce the need for human interaction required for continuously reconfigure the system based on new needs. In addition, in those cases where operators have to be available, these solutions can improve the human working quality or reduce the injury risks at the work space. They also help them to decide more efficiently and reduce the chance of failure. A simple example would be a connected forklift which can alert all other entities in its surrounding about its driving path [5].

Among the logistics modules heavily intermeshed with cyber technologies are sensors, data acquisition and actuators. These modules are directly in the front line of application. Therefore, any improvement in them will bring added value and help to optimize the utilization of available resources [4]. Some of these modules are presented hereafter as examples.

3   PhyNetLab

In the logistics application, different physical analysis have to be done before deployment of a new system into the operational field. Though simulation and emulation tools provide understanding of system's subsections, they are not able to mimic all the complexities and dynamics of a working network. Some of these dynamics in addition to the logistics scenarios complexities are: radio interferences, resource limitations, energy harvesting potentials [13]. These dynamics has to be analysed before a large-scale deployment which can be in the size of some hundred thousand of CPS entities.

PhyNetLab, is a research testbed platform with more than $1,000\,m^2$ surface, with a section as an automated warehouse for the storage of materials. It replicates a real world industrial materials handling and warehousing facility [13]. In addition to its physical space, its hardware platform provides a variety of wireless communication possibilities with protocols on the sub 1 GHz band in addition to the 2.4 GHz band [14]. It is developed to deploy an ultra-low-power WSN to test different decentralized in-house materials handling scenarios in addition to the evaluation of different logistics CPS modules in operation [14].

In addition to the evaluation of the logistics CPS modules, PhyNetLab provides the opportunity to test different technical aspects of WSNs such as radio configuration and routing algorithms. Moreover, different debatable topics such as security, privacy, business structure and integration to other available IT infrastructure can be analysed in the PhyNetLab under real-world constraints [13].

Although this platform represents the real physical environment, introducing the same number of entities acting in a real application will conquer the limitations for experimentation. Therefore, PhyNetlab is deployed in three tiers [14] which an abstract view of them can be seen in Fig. 1.

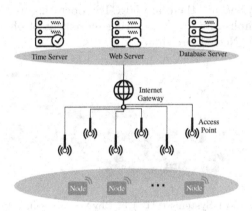

Fig. 1. An abstract overview of the three tiers structure of the PhyNetLab

By looking back into the 5C structure for the CPS development, it can be seen that the middle layer of the PhyNetLab provides the infrastructure for *simple connection* of any new node added to the system. Moreover, it is the back-end for the *cyber machine* in the nodes. It feeds them with the required data from the rest of the system. The two upper layers provide *cognition* from the field to users and experts. Moreover, the web server has options for a system designer to develop and roll-out new *configuration* for the system.

In the PhyNetLab different type of CPS nodes can be operating in the field level which two current types of them are introduced here.

3.1 Cellular Transport System

Traditionally, conveyors were responsible for the in-house materials handling. However, the best logistic area is in theory an empty room with flexible transport options. By the advancement in the field of robotics, mobile transport systems are able to replace the fixed conveyors. These devices are able to freely move in the whole area without blocking a part of the system as the conveyors do.

Cellular Transport System (CTS) is a mobile robot for materials handling in the PhyNetLab. It is designed in a way that can also enter the warehouse section and be lifted to any desired level. Therefore, it is able to pick a handling unit (a standard size bin in the PhyNetLab) from any source and deliver it to any destination in the system.

In addition to the normal operational sensors, logic and actuators, each CTS is equipped with a laser scanner that continuously scans its surrounding to avoid collision with other devices or human operators. By means of wireless triangulation, each CTS finds out its current location and plans its path internally with an acceptable accuracy using artificial intelligence. However, they send this information into the system's higher levels, but only for monitoring purpose and it is not propagated into the other nodes.

Within the PhyNetLab, there are 50 CTSs operating as CPS nodes in the field level to accomplish any task requiring movement of objects. Some CTSs operating in the PhyNetLab are shown in Fig. 2.

Fig. 2. Cellular Transport Systems (CTS) in PhyNetLab courtesy Fraunhofer IML, Dortmund

3.2 PhyNode

The main operational research goal of the PhyNetLab is evaluation of different logistics CPS nodes in diverse structures and scenarios. In one hand, a large number of them are needed to replicate a real scale system; on the other hand, thy have to be modifiable to represent different nodes and applications. Therefore, a design with two sections is considered. Each system is made of a main board (MNB) enabling the *configuration* aim of the 5C structure. An abstract view of the PhyNode's MNB can be seen in Fig. 3.

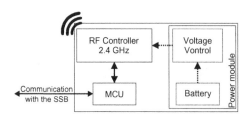

Fig. 3. Schematic structure of the PhyNode's MNB

In addition, a Swappable Slave Board (SSB) makes integration of different hardware designs to be implemented in the platform easily by changing the SSB. A general design of the SSB is shown in Fig. 4.

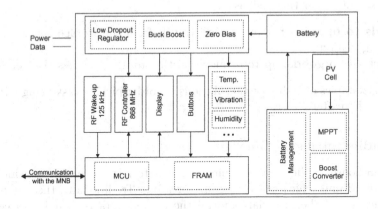

Fig. 4. Schematic structure of the PhyNode's SSB

Five different versions of this SSB with differences in the hardware (replicating dissimilar nodes) are designed and produced. A complete PhyNode including both MNB and the full version of SSB is shown in Fig. 5.

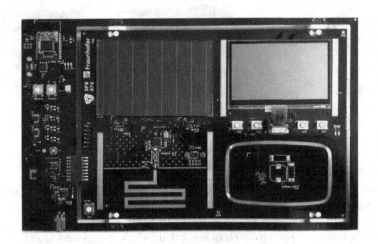

Fig. 5. Overview of a complete PhyNode

In the PhyNetLab, 350 PhyNodes are mounted on transport bins operating in the field level. Therefore, overall 400 nodes are operational as a combination of CTSs and PhyNodes.

4   Order-Picking Application

Order picking as a major section of in-house logistics is getting more and more momentum specially with the raise of online stores. Traditionally, there are two type of strategies for this task as:

- **goods to operator:** ordered good travels from the storage space into the picking station
- **operator to goods:** operator moves in the storage to access the item

Two examples of Industry 4.0 solutions for order picking task using CPS are presented hereafter.

4.1   inBin: Intelligent Bin

In the in-house application, the nun-bulky materials are mostly flowing in a standardized unit which can be a pallet or a bin. Traditionally, these units are only a carrier of the materials and all the related data is stored in a central system. With the advancements in the low-energy electronics and energy harvesting, an electronic board with the concept of PhyNode can be mounted on a normal bin. This intelligent module stores all the related data locally and makes them available all the time travelling with the bins. This will make an intelligent bin (inBin) which its evolution over the time can be seen in Fig. 6.

2009   2012   2014

Fig. 6. Three generations of inBin over time

By storing the content data in the inBin, there would be no need for a central warehouse management system. As soon as a new picking order is triggered by user through the web server, a request of picking propagates in the whole system. Those inBins able to fulfil the order, reply to the request and build up a subgroup. They communicate to each other within their group and select the best matching solution based on their own criteria. It can be the longest storage time, products expiry date, lowest distance to pickup or any other criteria. The selected inBin starts communicating about its selection.

In the *operator to goods* concept this signal would be received by the operator's interface which can be a hand-held device or a voice signal through its related gadget. Operator moves to the storage place and meanwhile a lighting signal on the inBin helps the operator to find the bin easier. After picking the item, operator acknowledges the number of picked items and inBin updates its internal database and logs the pick's data.

In the *goods to operator* concept, for instance in the case of using PhyNetLab, communicated signal from inBin reaches the CTSs. They do also an intelligent selection internally and the chosen CTS starts communicating with the inBin. CTS picks the inBin and brings it to the operator's station. After confirmation of operator, inBin communicates with the CTS for return into the storage.

4.2 P-ink: Pick by Ink

In the *operator to goods* order-picking strategy, operator can be informed in different ways where the desired item is stored. It can be by use of an order-picking list, using a voice commanding system or a light alerting mechanism. Generally, systems based on the visual sense are easier for the operator to work with. However, typical visual solutions require long cabling in the whole warehouse for communication. This cabling makes them expensive and system structure would be reluctant to any change.

P-ink is a CPS alternative pick by light order-picking solution. It uses a large flexible segmented e-ink display to show the meta-information such as the items details relevant for the order-picking operator. Flexibility of the display makes it easy to be integrated in the available standard systems (Fig. 7).

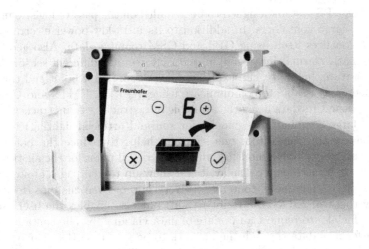

Fig. 7. A P-ink system easily mounted on a standard size bin   courtesy Fraunhofer IML, Dortmund

It is using ultra-low-power logic and communication hardware. The industrial grade hardware with compliant wireless communication standards using 868 MHz ISM band bidirectional communication removes the need for cabling and brings flexibility to easily restructure the storage area. Local storage of data reduces the communication overhead compared to the centralized systems. Also, a node density of up to 4,000 nodes with latency of up to 3 s (for requests from the top most layer) per industrial warehouse can be reached. The wireless connectivity makes over the air programming possible and it is easy to update the logistics softwares interacting with the system.

P-ink can be also used as a decentralized warehouse management system and increase the traceability of the items in a warehouse. It helps to create better allocation of storage spaces in real time with close integration to other controlling (normative) layers of industrial software.

MEMS sensors such as a vibration sensor embedded in the P-ink, provide data that can be integrated into the process. For example, critical state detection of an article from the container when a specific kind of vibration is detected.

5   iCon: Intelligent Container

In the not-enclosed logistics applications, asset state and tracking has a very high priority. According to a report [5] published by Cisco, it accounts for about 25% of the total value stack of the whole IoT. For most active components of the logistics sector such as vehicles, trucks, airplanes and ships, integration of tracking solutions is roughly easy. However, number of passive modules is much larger than the active ones and their tracking is much harder mainly because of the lack of energy supply.

iCon is a CPS system designed to be installed on the passive logistic modules such as air-cargo containers. In addition to its ultra-low-power electronic logic system, it localizes itself using GPS and GSM roaming data. Also geo-fencing with automatic alarm is integrated in it. iCon integrates different sensors including temperature, humidity, sun exposure, air pressure, dew point and three axis accelerometer. It is able to communicate using 4G LTE, UMTS and GSM network to transmit its data using the available infrastructure to its tracker (Fig. 8).

Using large combined PV panels (for sun and artificial lighting) it assures reduced harvesting time from one side and helps to reduce the battery size (already enough for 6 to 8 months) which is a critical point for the air transport. Moreover, by using e-paper display it can show up to 100 pages of stored documents such as container's contents, delivery info or even customs documents. Not only this will reduce the fright weight, but also enables the user (such as customs officials) to request an update of data via an app. The container owner can transfer new data through the network to be shown on the display.

iCon is able to do short range communication (up to 300 m) with other intelligent logistics modules. This can even reduce the energy requirements by collecting the data from multiple iCons and transmission through only one single data link.

Fig. 8. An iCon device showing customs documents courtesy Fraunhofer IML, Dortmund

6   Conclusion

It had been shown that the next big change in the manufacturing and production or in general, industry is going to be happening in the context of Industry 4.0. This advancement is mostly seen by breaking the available industry into its fundamental sections and provide intelligent modules responsible for each. These modules have to communicate among each other to enable self reconfiguration to adapt the industry to the current dynamics.

Cyber Physical Systems as intelligent devices with communication possibilities are considered as the key pile of this revolution. The 5C structure for development of CPS was reviewed.

The effect of Industry 4.0 revolution on the logistics sector was shortly analyzed. To fulfill the requirements of the future industry and also overcome the current challenges in the logistics, integration of CPS would be the key solution.

Structure of PhyNetLab and its nodes as a real physical testbed for evaluation of the future CPS nodes in the materials handling and warehousing application showed a strong basement for other solutions.

inBin and P-ink as two outcomes of the PhyNetLab experiment were explained in the context of the order picking application. Moreover, iCon as an outdoor asset tracking solution of the passive component was presented.

Acknowledgment. Part of the work on this paper has been funded by Deutsche Forschungsgemeinschaft (DFG) within the Collaborative Research Center SFB 876 "Providing Information by Resource Constrained Analysis", project A4.

References

1. Lasi, H., Fettke, P., Kemper, H.-G., Feld, T., Hoffmann, M.: Industry 4.0. Bus. Inf. Syst. Eng. **6**, 239–242 (2014)

2. Masoudinejad, M., Emmerich, J., Kossmann, D., Riesner, A., Roidl, M., ten Hompel, M.: A measurement platform for photovoltaic performance analysis in environments with ultra-low energy harvesting potential. Sustain. Cities Soc. **25**, 74–81 (2015)
3. Brettel, M., Friederichsen, N., Keller, M., Rosenberg, M.: How virtualization, decentralization and network building change the manufacturing landscape: an industry 4.0 perspective. Int. J. Mech. Ind. Sci. Eng. **8**, 37–44 (2014)
4. Jazdi, N.: Cyber physical systems in the context of Industry 4.0. In: 2014 IEEE International Conference on Automation, Quality and Testing, Robotics, pp. 1–4 (2014)
5. Macaulay, J., Buckalew, L., Chung, G.: Internet of Things in Logistics. DHL Trend Research, Cisco Consulting Services, Troisdorf (2015)
6. Lee, J., Bagheri, B., Kao, H.-A.: A cyber-physical systems architecture for industry 4.0-based manufacturing systems. Manuf. Lett. **3**, 18–23 (2015)
7. Meyer-Rühle, O. et. al.: Statistical coverage and economic analysis of the logistics sector in the EU. SEALS Consortium, Basel-Rotterdam-Nürnberg-Denzlingen (2009)
8. Fact-finding studies in support of the development of an EU strategy for freight transport logistics, Lot 1: Analysis of the EU logistics sector. Ecorys, Fraunhofer, TCI, Prognos and AUEB-RC/TRANSLOG (2015)
9. Masoudinejad, M., Emmerich, J., Kossmann, D., Riesner, A., Roidl, M., ten Hompel, M.: Development of a measurement platform for indoor photovoltaic energy harvesting in materials handling applications. In: 6th IEEE International Renewable Energy Congress, pp. 1–6 (2015)
10. Roidl, M., Emmerich, J., Riesner, A., Masoudinejad, M., Kaulbars, D., Ide, C., Wietfeld, C., ten Hompel, M.: Performance availability evaluation of smart devices in materials handling systems. In: IEEE ICCC Workshops on Internet of Things, pp. 6–10 (2014)
11. Lewandowski, M., Gath, M., Werthmann, D., Lawo, M.: Agent-based control for material handling systems in in-house logistics - towards cyber-physical systems in in-house-logistics utilizing real size. In: Proceedings of 2013 European Conference on Smart Objects, Systems and Technologies, SmartSysTech, pp. 1–5 (2013)
12. Kamagaew, A., Kirks, T., Ten Hompel, M.: Energy potential detection for autarkic smart object design in facility logistics. In: IEEE International Conference on Control System, Computing and Engineering, pp. 285–290 (2011)
13. Venkatapathy, A.K.R., Roidl, M., Riesner, A., Emmerich, J., ten Hompel, M.: PhyNetLab: architecture design of ultra-low power wireless sensor network testbed. In: IEEE 16th International Symposium on a World of Wireless, Mobile and Multimedia Networks, pp. 1–6. IEEE (2015)
14. Venkatapathy, A.K.R., Riesner, A., Roidl, M., Emmerich, J., ten Hompel, M.: PhyNode: an intelligent, cyber-physical system with energy neutral operation for PhyNetLab. In: Proceedings of Smart SysTech, European Conference on Smart Objects, Systems and Technologies, VDE-Verl, pp. 1–8 (2015)

Presented Paper

SHelmet: An Intelligent Self-sustaining Multi Sensors Smart Helmet for Bikers

Michele Magno[1,2(✉)], Angelo D'Aloia[1], Tommaso Polonelli[1], Lorenzo Spadaro[1], and Luca Benini[1,2]

[1] DIE, Università Di Bologna, Bologna, Italy
[2] D-ITET, ETH Zürich, Zürich, Switzerland
michele.magno@iis.ee.ethz.ch

Abstract. This paper presents the design of a wearable system to transform a helmet into a smart, multi-sensor connected helmet (SHelmet) to improve motorcycle safety. Low power design and self-sustainability are the key for the usability of our helmet, to avoid frequent battery recharges and dangerous power losses. Hidden in the helmet structure, the designed system is equipped with a dense sensor network including accelerometer, temperature, light, and alcohol gas level, in addition, a Bluetooth low energy module interfaces the device with an on-vehicle IR camera, and eventually the user's smart phone. To keep the driver focused, the user interface consists of a small non-invasive display combined with a speech recognition system. System architecture is optimized for aggressive power management, featuring an ultra-low power wake-up radio, and fine-grained software-controlled shutdown of all sensing, communication and computing subsystems. Finally, a multi-source energy harvesting module (solar and kinetic) performs high-efficiency power recovery, improving battery management and achieving self-sustainability. SHelmet supports rich context awareness applications; breath alcohol control; real time vehicle data; sleep and fall detection; data display. Experimental results show that is possible achieve self-sustainability and demonstrate functionality of the developed node.

Keywords: Wearable device · Sensors network · Energy harvesting · Power management

1 Introduction

According to the European Commission, in 2014 almost 25,700 road fatalities were reported in Europe, most of them involved motorcycles [1]. During recent years, road safety work throughout the European Union led to a considerable decreasing trend for road accidents. In fact, considering the 2010–2014 window, the annual number of road deaths decreased by 18% [1]. This means 5700 fewer deaths in 2014 than in 2010. However, there is still major room for improvement. In Europe, distraction (27.38%), and speeding (16.34%), combined with driving while intoxicated (14.6%), are the most important causes of death. For this reason, many efforts have been dedicated to help reduce these sources of danger.

© ICST Institute for Computer Sciences, Social Informatics and Telecommunications Engineering 2017
M. Magno et al. (Eds.): S-Cube 2016, LNICST 205, pp. 55–67, 2017.
DOI: 10.1007/978-3-319-61563-9_5

Technology advancements in integrated circuits, smart sensors and communication, allow the fabrication and integration of small form factor, light and ultra-low power sensing "smart" devices that they can be worn and completely "forgotten about" by users. Wearables, where the whole system it tightly coupled with the human body [1] are examples of these devices rapidly gaining in popularity. Many of them, from bracelets that monitor physical activity and sleeping patterns, to clothes with built-in sensors, or to smart glasses, may mark the next big technology wave well known as Internet of Things (IoT) [2–6]. Smart wireless sensors, have been recognised as a fundamental enabling technology for wide range of applications including automotive, healthcare, industrial and security [8]. With the same technologies today is it possible to design wearable devices that target the improvement of safety for drivers (i.e. integrated in helmets of glasses for bikers or other vehicles' drivers).

Sensing technologies are successfully used in biomedical and sports applications [3–7]. In fact, terms as multi sensors, sensors fusion, smart sensing, intelligent device, among others are very popular in the academic and industrial research [8]. Although wearable devices are very popular today, there is a big challenge that limits the success of these devices. This is the limited autonomy of the batteries that require too frequent recharges (every few hours or one day). Lifetime extension is aggressively pursued though low power design, the development of new battery technologies and other technologies [9–11].

Among others, harvesting energy technology achieved the right maturity to be exploited in several application scenarios to overcome the limited energy issue of batteries [12–16]. However, energy harvesting in a wearable context is still a very challenging scenario because of form factor constraints and usability concerns [17, 18]. Harvesting energy to power these small, always-on devices represents an exciting challenge, which needs particular design attention in the whole system and the combination of hardware and software.

In this paper we present SHelmet, a multi-sensor, intelligent, self-sustaining wearable helmet to increase the safety of motorcycle drivers. Every component of our SHelmet is designed to avoid fatalities and injuries on the road but also to increase awareness related to the driving experience. We analyzed the most common sources of road accidents to develop a wearable system aimed at reducing risks on the road [1]. Figure 1 shows the most common causes of road accidents and the solutions using sensors or other electronics implemented in our design to reduce the related risks.

As our smart helmet has been conceived to be worn as a normal helmet, it is designed as a self-sustainable system which the driver can always rely on, without the need for recharging. Due to the dual source (solar-kinetic) energy harvesting module, the user will be always supported by the SHelmet on the street. To achieve this goal, energy harvesting is supported also by aggressive hardware and software low power techniques to reduce the overall system power consumption. These features include a dynamic switch on the unused peripherals and wake-up radio technology embedded in the design, to increase the wireless communication energy efficiency. For example, when the helmet leaves the vehicle's area, it is forced into a deep sleep mode waiting for a radio signal from the on-board module.

Cause	Solution
Defect in vehicle	ECU data, Infrared camera, Buzzer feedback
Distractions (cellular, inputs to system)	GUI on helmet, speech recognition, bluetooth
Overspeeding	Accelerometer, Buzzer feedback
Driving under alcohol effect	Alcohol Gas Detection, Buzzer feedback
Drowsy driving	Eye Blink Detection, Buzzer feedback
Reduced visibility	Infrared Camera, Display
Lack of roadside assistance	Falls detection, auto-call via Bluetooth

Fig. 1. Causes of accidents and solution in SHelmet.

Recent literature on helmets using sensors and data processing is available especially targeting safety for workers [19–21]. In [19] the authors designed a helmet to monitor the air quality and to trigger the users in dangerous situation. In [20] other researcher developed a helmet to support mine-workers during their work while in [21] a helmet is equipped with a wireless interface (ZigBee) to enable voice communication between different workers. In [22] the authors present a helmet that continuously monitors brain and cardiac activity. This last system is designed as a helmet, however is not meant to be supplied by batteries but more as a data logger of the human parameters.

The above-presented works are all based on embedded electronics and sensors. They demonstrate the potential of use a smart helmet to give a feedback to the users and monitor human activities. In contrast with these works, in our smart helmet we focus on low power design and self-sustainability of the smart helmet in the motorbike safety application scenario. On the same application, a few examples of smart helmet were presented in literature. In [23] the authors designed a system with a camera to avoid collision. This work uses video processing to perform the classification of dangerous situations. Experimental results are based on a real helmet worn on the head. Finally in [24] the authors designed a system with GPS and ZigBee communication to geolocalize the drivers. Both works are presenting interesting implementation and in-field testing of the system, but they are not targeting low power design, multi sensing with novel sensors, Bluetooth low energy communication and especially self-sustainability as in our works.

2 System Overview

Figure 2 shows the overall architecture of the developed system that consists of two separate modules designed and developed (one for the Bike and one for the Helmet). The two modules host a microcontroller (MCU) to process sensors' data and take actions, and a Bluetooth Low Energy (BTLE) interface allows communication.

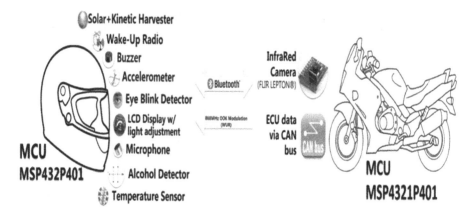

Fig. 2. System overview of the proposed solution. The system comprises of two separated wireless sensor node. The first node on the left is thought to be place into the helmet and it includes several sensors, and LCD display and a buzzer. The second node on the rights is placed on the motorbike including an infrared camera and the CAN communication. Both nodes are designed around the MSP432 microcontroller and CC2564 Bluetooth low energy module.

The microcontroller selected for both the modules is the *MSP432P401RIPZ* from Texas Instruments (TI). This choice has been made because the system needs both the computational performance to process on-board the data, and a low power profile to be self-sustainable. In fact, with 14-bit internal ADC, eight serial ports interface with 57 DMIPS and only 4.6 mA of power consumption were the perfect combination to achieve the goal of self-sustainability and to manage all the sensors and the embedded external peripherals (Bluetooth, LCD, etc.). For space reason only the module implemented in the smart helmet is presented and evaluated in this work in the following sections.

3   Helmet Wireless Sensor Node

Figure 3 shows the block diagram of the developed node that is mounted on the helmet. This node manages the sensor's acquisition and processing, as well as the user interface, which can be both graphical, using a LCD display and audio using a buzzer feedback and microphone. As one of main goal of the design is to have a device that does not need to recharge its batteries continuously, the node includes a dual source (solar and kinetic) energy harvesting circuit that provides continuous energy to supply the system and recharge the LiPo battery that is used as an energy buffer.

In terms of functionality the main aim of the developed node is to transform a standard motorbike helmet in a "smart helmet" to assist the driver in augmenting the probability of undertaking safe behaviour. To achieve this goal, we embedded a series of sensors (Figs. 1 and 2) to detect dangerous situations and a MCU to process the sensor data to alert the driver quickly. In the following subsections we present the sensors and the power supply subsystem that includes the dual source energy harvesting.

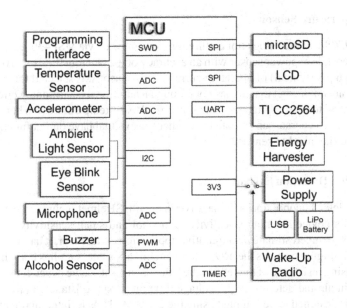

Fig. 3. Block diagram of the wireless sensor node developed to be place into the helmet. The node includes a rich set of sensors to increase the security of the driver, a Bluetooth wireless interface, an audio feedback and a power supply with battery that can be recharged by sola a kinetic energy harvesting. Finally, a wake up radio is used to reduce significantly the power consumption in sleep mode.

3.1 Accelerometer

The *Kionix KXTC9-2050* is a high-performance, tri-axis accelerometer with analog outputs, a factory-programmable low-pass filter and g-range from ±1.5 g to ±6 g. The sensor is directly connected with the MSP432 microcontroller through three channels of the Analog Digital Converter. This sensor provides very useful information on motion g-forces as well as fall detection, and the small packaging (3 × 3 × 0.9 mm 10-pin LGA) eases the tricky PCB layout needed for the board to fit in the helmet. Furthermore, it has low current consumption (5 µA in standby, 240 µA at full power) which is very important in terms of power management. With regards to safety, the system will wait for a user confirmation and, if that is not received, it will call ICE contacts with the phone connected via Bluetooth.

3.2 Ambient Light Sensor

The TI's *OPT3001* is a digital ambient light sensor (ALS) that measures the intensity of light as visible by the human eye. Its digital output is reported over an I²C serial interface; in addition, its low power consumption and low power-supply voltage capability enhance the device's self-sustainability. The main function of this sensor is to provide information about light levels in order to modify the system behaviour. For example, the LCD backlight is continuously adjusted by PWM depending on light measurements; thereby, useful power is saved and the user is not disturbed.

3.3   Temperature Sensor

The *MCP9700A* is an analog temperature sensor connected via MSP430 ADC channel. It is a low-cost, low-power sensor with an accuracy of ±2 °C from 0 °C to +70 °C while consuming 6 µA (typical) of operating current. This sensor was selected for low-power consumption and the fact that it does not require an additional conditioning circuit. This sensor is useful to detect dangerous situation linked to the temperature (too hot, too cold) but also to have accurate sensor date from other sensors that have output function of the temperature (i.e. alcohol sensor).

3.4   Alcohol Detection System

In order to detect alcohol traces in the driver's breath, SHelmet includes the *MQ-3 Gas Sensor*. This device has high sensitivity to alcohol and small sensitivity to benzene, which is not to underestimate in automotive applications. Moreover, it has a very simple drive circuit. Figure 6 shows the *MQ-3* drive circuit: a 5 V line supplies both the heating and the sensing resistance of the sensor, the latter changes its value depending on alcohol gas levels in air and determines the voltage drop on a load resistance. In the SHelmet, the MQ-3 is designed to be sampled using the 2.5 V MCU ADC internal reference both a 5 V supply line and an output de-amplification circuit were required.

Figure 4 shows the conditioning circuit for the MQ-3, including TI's *LM2622 Step-up DC/DC Converter* which generates the 5 V line from the 3.3 V and a TI's *OPA344 Low Power Operational Amplifier* used to reduce the output voltage swing from 0–5 V to 0–2 V. OPA344 (same of BOOSTXL-EDUMKII) was selected mainly for its low power consumption, compact package, and very low offset voltage. The MQ-3 acquisitions require 20 s of pre-heating time, this is necessary for the output to be stable. Then the signal rises or falls depending on alcohol concentration in air.

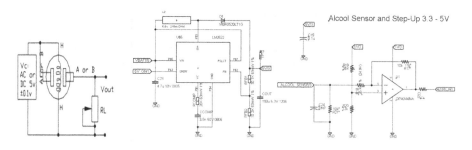

Fig. 4. Alcool sensor (left) and conditioning circuits schematics (right)

Figure 5 shows voltage trends for pre-heating (a), breath with alcohol (b) and breath with no alcohol (c). The voltage drops in (b) and (c) scenarios is due to the fact that the more you blow the more the heating resistance cools, causing its resistivity to rise. When the MCU detects a dangerous situation, an alert is sent to the motorbike module that prevents ignition of the motorbike.

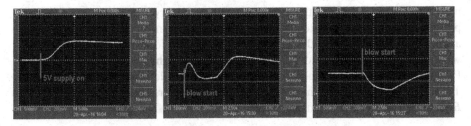

Fig. 5. MQ-3 voltage trends, in order, (a), (b) and (c)

3.5 Eye-Blink Detection

This feature has been included to avoid drowsy driving, by sending an alert to the driver when the eye is closed for too long. To enable the SHelmet with this capability, we used the **VL6180X Proximity Sensor**. This component is based on patented Flight Sense™ technology allowing absolute distance to be measured independent of target reflectance. Moreover, combining an IR emitter, a range sensor and an ambient light sensor in a three-in-one ready-to-use reflowable package, the VL6180X is easy to use as a one-dimension gesture detector. This is a digital sensor connected through I^2C directly to the MSP432. The pupil and the eyelid have different reflectance. Combining the ambient light sensor with a threshold in distance (time domain) and in amplitude (signal and noise), an algorithm that detects eye swipes is easily implemented. Figure 6 describes an eye pulse that can be processed to extract information about gesture detection (input commands to system) and driver alertness.

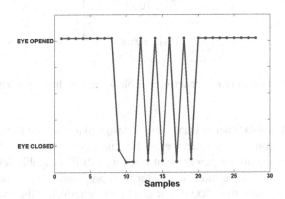

Fig. 6. Eye blink sampling

3.6 Energy Harvesting and Power Subsystem

The energy harvesting subsystem has been designed to achieve a self-sustainable system that can be fully embedded in a motorcycle helmet. This subsystem includes both a solar (or as further option thermal) and a kinetic path to exploit the combination for the two energy harvesting sources, and the recharging and power stags. The energy sources are used to recharge a single lithium-polymer (LiPo) battery that supplies the node as presented in Fig. 7. The adopted storage element is a 2000 mAh – 3.7 V LiPo re-chargeable battery. For supporting the energy harvesters, when for example the helmet is not worn for very long periods, to recharge this battery, a highly integrated Li-ion and Li-Pol linear charger device targeted at space-limited portable applications was included. The devices operate from either a USB port or AC adapter. This component is the TI's *BQ24093*. The block diagram is presented in Fig. 7.

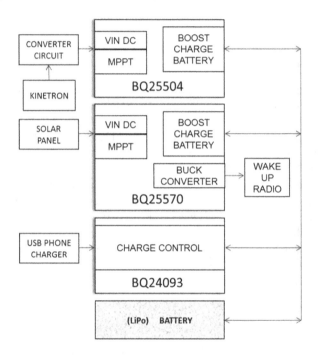

Fig. 7. Energy harvesting and battery management block diagram. In this paper the wake up radio is not presented.

Solar Energy: The solar energy harvesting is designed around the *BQ25570* ultra-low integrated circuit from Texas Instruments. For high efficient energy harvesting, the BQ25570 features maximum power point tracking (MPPT) capabilities. Moreover, it integrates an ultra-low power buck converter with programmable output voltage. The BQ25570 consumes less than 500 nA in active mode reducing the overall quiescent current of the whole system. The power source of our system is on the top of the helmet, which embeds four solar cells with a 40 cm^2 area. The developed systems providing a maximum power of 2mW under low room light conditions (250 lx) and 45 mW under sunlight (50000 lx).

Kinetic Energy: The kinetic harvester generator used is the Micro Generator System 26.4 (MGS26.4) produced by Kinetron [25] (shown in Fig. 8 on left); it is an electromagnetic generator with a 26.4 mm thickness and a 4.3 mm diameter. The kinetic energy harvesting has at its core the TI ***BQ25504***. It contains a Boost Converter with an ultra-low quiescent current of 330 nA. However, the Kinetron generates an alternating wave-form (AC), which is not directly accessible from the BQ25504, then a rectifier is needed. Figure 8 (right) shows the ac-dc doubler voltage converter (D3-D4-C43-C42) circuit we needed to insert before the BQ25504. The total efficiency of the whole circuit (AC-DC + BQ25504) has been measured to be 64%. We also tested the energy harvesting circuit in realistic condition when the driver is wearing the helmet and the energy acquired is reported in the following table.

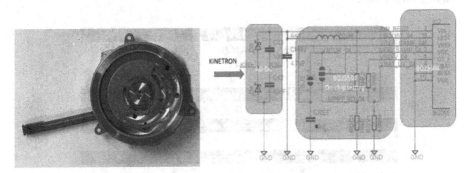

Fig. 8. Kinetic generator (on left) and kinetic energy harvesting circuits comprised by a AC-DC conversion stage connected with the DC-DC converter BQ25504.

4 Experimental Results

In order to evaluate the performance of the developed smart helmet module a prototype has been developed and test on the field (Fig. 9).

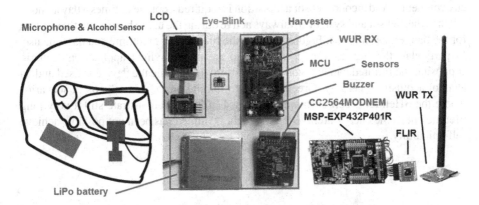

Fig. 9. Developed prototypes to test the functionalities and power performances.

All of the functions presented above have been tested, in particular: data acquisition from sensors, processing the data and testing the communication. Experimental measurements have also been conducted to evaluate the self-sustainability of the SHelmet under realistic circumstances. Figure 10 shows current consumption in the most used configurations of the device. When the system is in sleep mode with the harvester on and waiting for wake-up signal, the quiescent current consumption is ultra-low (3,7 µA). The second configuration is the standard one and only draws 17 mA current, with the context recognition sensors powered and analyzed, ensuring a fully operational user interface. It can be noticed that the alcohol sensor is a power hungry sensor consuming 270 mA@3,3 V, thus power management is important to use the sensor only when necessary (i.e. when the helmet is worn for the first time on the trip).

I_{sleep} @3.3V [µA]				
BQ24093	BQ25504	BQ25570	WUR	5 * LP5907
1	0,33	0,49	0,88	1
TOT		3,70		
$I_{MCU+MULTI-SENSOR+LCD+LED+BUZZER}$ @3.3V [mA]				
17				
$I_{MCU+MULTI-SENSOR+LCD+LED+BUZZER+BLUETOOTH}$ @3.3V [mA]				
58,2				
$I_{MCU+MULTI-SENSOR+LCD+ALCOHOL}$ @3.3V [mA]				
270				

Fig. 10. Current consumption of the developed wireless sensor node to be place on the helmet.

To evaluate the self-sustainability of the solution the power generated form the energy harvesting has been measured during 2 days of use of the developed prototype. To evaluate the lifetime and the self-sustainability of the system, we did some assumption on the application scenario, in particular. The Bluetooth module is on when the system requires infrared camera thermal images and that only happens in low light environments. And alcohol sensor acquisition is required a couple of times a day at most. All the other sensor and system are always active during the use to have a reactive system for the dangerous situation. Figure 11 show the lifetime for nighttime and daytime use. In particular, the Fig. 11 (up) is referred to an under-daylight application scenario supposing the infrared camera working for a third of the time the device is used and an alcohol acquisition per day. Green bars go to infinite on the "days" axis in scenarios where the SHelmet is self-sustaining. Figure 11 (down) demonstrate still a very long lifetime but as the energy archived in the night is limited has been not possible achieve self-suitability.

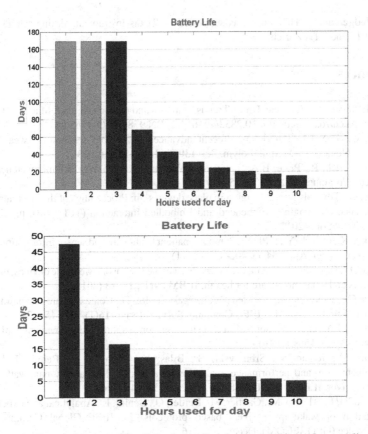

Fig. 11. Battery life during day light (up) and night (down). (Color figure online)

5   Conclusions

We presented SHelmet a smart helmet that results as a life-saving, self-sustainable, wearable device, which the user can always rely on during the driving experience. Context-aware sensors, in addiction to infrared camera, eye-blink detection, alcohol detection, on-board processing, and non-invasive user interface empower the driver to avoid dangerous situations. The wearable device has been thought with low power in mind and to be never recharged. To achieve this goal, it includes dual-source energy harvesting (solar and kinetic) to guarantee self-sustainability in the application scenario. Wireless communication trough Bluetooth Low Energy enables communication between vehicle and user guarantying fast alerts and flexibility of the solution. Experimental results on the developed prototype demonstrated both the functionality of the system and the self-sustainability when the helmet is worn on the motorbikes' head. Future work will focus in make a more accurate evaluation on the algorithms to detect dangerous situations and a long term in-field evaluation of the lifetime.

Acknowledgements. This work was supported by Texas Instruments during the TI Contest Europe 2016 and ETH Zürich.

References

1. Road safety in the European Union Trends, statistics and main challenges, March 2015. http://ec.europa.eu/roadsafety. doi:10.2832/404614. ISBN 978-92-79-45654-1
2. Pang, C., Lee, C., Suh, K.-Y.: Recent advances in flexible sensors for wearable and implantable devices. J. Appl. Polym. Sci. **130**(3), 1429–1441 (2013)
3. Rawassizadeh, R., Price, B.A., Petre, M.: Wearables: has the age of smartwatches finally arrived? Commun. ACM **58**(1), 45–47 (2014)
4. White, G.: Towards wearable aging in place devices. In: Proceedings of the 7th International Conference on Tangible, Embedded and Embodied Interaction (TEI 2013), pp. 375–376. ACM, New York (2013)
5. Prajakta, K., Ozturk, Y.: mPHASiS: mobile patient healthcare and sensor information system. J. Netw. Comput. Appl. **34**(1), 402–417 (2011)
6. Campo, E., Hewson, D., Gehin, C., Noury, N.: Theme D: sensors, wearable devices, intelligent networks and smart homecare for health. IRBM **34**(1), 11–13 (2013)
7. Perera, C., Zaslavsky, A., Christen, P., Georgakopoulos, D.: Context aware computing for the internet of things: a survey. IEEE Commun. Surv. Tutorials **16**(1), 414–454 (2014)
8. Mendes, J.J.A., et al.: Sensor fusion and smart sensor in sports and biomedical applications. Sensors **16**(10), 1569 (2016)
9. Magno, M., Jelicic, V., Srbinovski, B., Bilas, V., Popovici, E., Benini, L.: Design, implementation, and performance evaluation of a flexible low-latency nanowatt wake-up radio receiver. IEEE Trans. Industr. Inf. **12**(2), 633–644 (2016)
10. Ait Aoudia, F., Magno, M., Gautier, M., Berder, O., Benini, L.: Analytical and experimental evaluation of wake-up receivers based protocols. In: IEEE Global Communications Conference (GLOBECOM), December 2016
11. Magno, M., Marinkovic, S., Srbinovski, B., Popovici, E.M.: Wake-up radio receiver based power minimization techniques for wireless sensor networks: a review. Microelectron. J. **45**(12), 1627–1633 (2014)
12. Weddell, A.S., Magno, M., Merrett, G.V., Brunelli, D., Al-Hashimi, B.M., Benini, L.: A survey of multi-source energy harvesting systems. In: Design, Automation and Test in Europe Conference and Exhibition (DATE), 2013, pp. 905–910, March 2013
13. Mauriello, M., Gubbels, M., Froehlich, J.E.: Social fabric fitness: the design and evaluation of wearable E-textile displays to support group running. In: Proceedings of the 32nd Annual ACM Conference on Human Factors in Computing Systems. ACM (2014)
14. Magno, M., Boyle, D., Brunelli, D., O'Flynn, B., Popovici, E., Benini, L.: Extended wireless monitoring through intelligent hybrid energy supply. IEEE Trans. Industr. Electron. **61**(4), 1871–1881 (2014)
15. Magno, M., Tombari, F., Brunelli, D., Di Stefano, L., Benini, L.: Multimodal video analysis on self-powered resource-limited wireless smart camera. IEEE J. Emerg. Sel. Top. Circ. Syst. **3**(2), 223–235 (2013)
16. Magno, M., Jackson, N., Mathewson, A., Benini, L., Popovici, E.: Combination of hybrid energy harvesters with MEMS piezoelectric and nano-watt radio wake up to extend lifetime of system for wireless sensor nodes. In: Proceedings of 2013 26th International Conference on Architecture of Computing Systems (ARCS), pp. 1–6, 19–22 February 2013

17. Mitcheson, P.D.: Energy harvesting for human wearable and implantable bio-sensors. In: 2010 Annual International Conference of the IEEE Engineering in Medicine and Biology Society (EMBC). IEEE (2010)

18. Thielen, M., Sigrist, L., Magno, M., Hierold, C., Benini, L.: Human body heat for powering wearable devices: From thermal energy to application. Energy Convers. Manag. **131**, 44–54 (2016)

19. Behr, C.J., Kumar, A., Hancke, G.P.: A smart helmet for air quality and hazardous event detection for the mining industry. In: 2016 IEEE International Conference on Industrial Technology (ICIT), Taipei, pp. 2026–2031 (2016)

20. Pirkl, G., et al.: Smart helmet for construction site documentation and work support. In: Proceedings of the 2016 ACM International Joint Conference on Pervasive and Ubiquitous Computing: Adjunct. ACM (2016)

21. Geetha, A.: Intelligent helmet for coal miners with voice over zigbee and environmental monitoring. Middle-East J. Sci. Res. **16**(12), 1835–1837 (2013)

22. von Rosenberg, W., Chanwimalueang, T., Goverdovsky, V., Mandic, D.P.: Smart helmet: monitoring brain, cardiac and respiratory activity. In: 2015 37th Annual International Conference of the IEEE Engineering in Medicine and Biology Society (EMBC), Milan, pp. 1829–1832 (2015)

23. Rupanagudi, S.R., et al.: A novel video processing based smart helmet for rear vehicle intimation & collision avoidance. In: 2015 International Conference on Computing and Network Communications (CoCoNet). IEEE (2015)

24. Kulkarni, C., Talole, M., Somwanshi, R.: Safety using Road Automated Wireless Communicating Smart Helmet Application (SURACSHA). Int. J. Eng. Res. Technol. **3**(9), 1046–1050 (2014). ESRSA Publications

25. Magno, M., Spadaro, L., Singh, J., Benini, L.: Kinetic energy harvesting: toward autonomous wearable sensing for internet of things. In: 2016 International Symposium on Power Electronics, Electrical Drives, Automation and Motion (SPEEDAM), Anacapri, pp. 248–254 (2016)

iHouse: A Voice-Controlled, Centralized, Retrospective Smart Home

Benjamin Völker$^{(\boxtimes)}$, Tobias Schubert, and Bernd Becker

Chair of Computer Architecture, Faculty of Engineering,
Institute of Computer Science, Albert-Ludwigs-University Freiburg,
79110 Freiburg, Germany
{voelkerb,schubert,becker}@informatik.uni-freiburg.de

Abstract. Speech recognition in smart home systems has become popular in both, research and consumer areas. This paper introduces an innovative concept for a modular, customizable, and voice-controlled smart home system. The system combines the advantages of distributed and centralized processing to enable a secure as well as highly modular platform and allows to add existing non-smart components retrospectively into the smart environment. To interact with the system in the most comfortable way - and in particular without additional devices like smartphones - voice-controlling was added as the means of choice. The task of speech recognition is partitioned into decentral Wake-Up-Word (WUW) recognition and central continuous speech recognition to enable flexibility while maintaining security. This is achieved utilizing a novel WUW algorithm suitable to be executed on small microcontrollers which uses Mel Frequency Cepstral Coefficients as well as Dynamic Time Warping. A high rejection rate up to 99.93% was achieved, justifying the use of the algorithm as a voice trigger in the developed smart home system.

Keywords: Smart home · Retrospective home · Offline speech recognition · Wake-up-word recognition · Distributed speech processing

1 Introduction

Smart homes in general are habitats that provide their owners comfort, efficiency, security and convenience even if they are not at home. The provided support is achieved by incorporating common devices into smart objects to be able to control several features of the home like the lighting or heating automatically and more intelligent. Even though, this concept as well as corresponding open and commercial solutions are already available ([1–3] and many more), only minor households have adopted to this hype yet. According to [4], only 14% of all households in Germany for instance used at least one smart home component in 2014, leaving 86% of households not using any type of smart components. As reported, the reason for the actual quite low acceptance of smart homes is the missing compatibility between several providers of smart components as well as a high effort required to install these systems. Furthermore, a (new) smart

© ICST Institute for Computer Sciences, Social Informatics and Telecommunications Engineering 2017
M. Magno et al. (Eds.): S-Cube 2016, LNICST 205, pp. 68–80, 2017.
DOI: 10.1007/978-3-319-61563-9_6

home solution requires the purchase of equipment most people typically already own and which is still working. As an example, most aging HiFi systems or televisions can not be controlled with a smartphone or by voice. However, this is not a sufficient reason for most people to buy new systems. It should be possible to retrospectively update the existing systems at low cost to interact as smart components within the smart home system.

Another apprehension related to smart home systems is security. People are afraid that using these systems might help other people to spy on them. Since the own home is a hideaway from the outside world, it should not be vulnerable to any kind of attack. Therefore, smart home systems should be highly secure and should not allow, for example, that the neighbour could turn off or on devices accidentally or intentionally.

An additional issue of existing smart home concepts is the lack of user-friendliness and ease of use. These systems often require a lot of maintenance and are either too complex or do not offer sufficient adjustment options. To control these systems, most providers offer smartphone or web apps. Indeed, the use of smartphones simplifies the tasks of changing settings and controlling several devices. But this simplification is restricted to situations where a person already holds the smartphone in his or her hand. To increase the ease of use, an interface should be used which works everywhere in the house and is carried around by everyone all the time. Thus, the perfect interface is voice. To switch on the light, a user could simply express the command *"House, turn on the light"*. Another benefit of using voice commands is that they can be personalized easily. As an example, the light could be also turned on by the command *"House, it's too dark"*.

The idea of using speech as an input technique for smart home systems is not novel. In [5] a remote speech interaction system to control entertainment devices using beam-forming and speaker-verification techniques has been proposed. More recently, [3] implemented a smart home system using contextual information and the human speech. However, it is not pointed out how the microphone data is acquired and how their systems can be expanded to a multi-room setup. Commercial systems like *Amazon's Echo* [7] or the just announced *Google Home* [6] exist as well. However, the speech interaction is limited to the room in which the system is installed. Furthermore, these devices are continuously listening for fixed, not personalizable WUWs like *"Alexa"* or *"Ok Google"* and require a connection to external servers for continuous speech processing. This implies that a device connected to the internet is always listening regardless of whether a person in the house is speaking towards the system or privately communicating. Due to the "always online state", these systems are of high risk for the leakage of personal information. Regarding a more secure system, it should be guaranteed that voice data is processed completely offline.

In order to approach the stated issues of existing smart home solutions, the *iHouse* smart home system was developed which is highly customizable, user-friendly and handles sensitive voice data as secure as possible by distributing the task of Wake-Up-Word spotting and continuous speech recognition. Compared to e.g. approaches from Amazon and Google, the system presented here can be used totally offline, avoiding in particular the "always online state" discussed before. To introduce the iHouse system in more detail, the remainder of this paper is structured as follows: In Sect. 2 an overview of the developed smart home system is given. The developed hardware and how existing devices are controlled (by means of some examples) is explained in Sect. 3. More details about the implementation of the software is depicted in Sect. 4, in which the server application is presented. Details and test results of the novel WUW spotting algorithm are further explained in Sect. 5. Concluding remarks and future work are provided in Sect. 6.

2   iHouse System Overview

The iHouse smart home system was developed to provide its users support and convenience during everyday's tasks. The **i** in the name of the system refers to the fact that the provided support is done as 'intelligent' as possible. Therefore, several devices like the lighting, heating or the television can be controlled and sensor data such as the energy consumption of a device or the room temperature can be monitored in a convenient way. Speech recognition is build on top, so that voice commands can be expressed to trigger certain actions like switching on the ceiling light or getting access to several information like the current temperature in a certain room. An overview of the system's workflow is shown in Fig. 1. If the user expresses a custom voice trigger like *"Ok House"*, the system responds with a certain sound indicating that it is now continuously listening for commands. Each utterance or sentence spoken afterwards, like *"Lights on"* or *"Room temperature"*, will be treated as a command. If such a command is recognized, the system will either execute an action or answer accordingly. Furthermore, the system automatically adds context information by triggering certain sensor measurements or by making use of past events and spatial information. The spatial information is obtained by evaluating in which room the command was triggered. Thus, one does not need to point out, for example, which specific light should be turned on. Furthermore, rules or scenarios can be set, so that for example all lights will be switched off automatically at midnight.

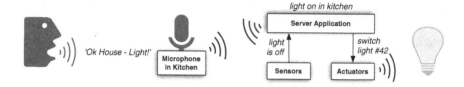

Fig. 1. Working principle of the iHouse smart home system for the example of switching on a light in the kitchen.

Several sensors can be added dynamically to the system to get information about the current temperature, humidity and brightness level. The system is not limited to switching lights on and off, since other modules can be added as well. For example, one might add thermostats to the system so that the heating can be controlled as well or metering devices to be able to record and monitor the energy consumption of certain devices like the refrigerator. Each of these modules can be added, removed or replaced dynamically in order to provide a highly customizable setup comprising both decentral and central components.

2.1   Central vs. Decentral Processing

A smart home environment itself is distributed by its nature. It consists of several spatially separated places, each of them with multiple sensors and actuators like temperature sensors or thermostats. To connect with these devices, a centralized approach with a server application was selected. The centralized processing and execution simplifies dependent tasks and the interconnection between different rooms as well as the maintenance of the entire system. The server therefore acts as the central brain of the smart home with knowledge of past and present sensor data and user events. This information is then used to select the most suitable action to support the user. As an interface to the system, a server application by itself is not appropriate since it lacks fast remote access and portability. For this reason, decentral access to the system is provided by either using a smartphone application or voice. However, the arrangement of a home with its multiple distributed rooms hampers the use of speech recognition, since either the user must be equipped with a microphone or every room. If the user is equipped with a microphone, a device with a portable power supply is needed which - like a smartphone - lacks portability and, thus, also accessibility during recharging. If, on the other hand, every room is equipped with a microphone, a portable power supply would not be essential since power sockets are typically available in every room. The decentralization of these devices into multiple rooms leads to different possible approaches. Each microphone module can either independently evaluate and execute a given voice command by itself or has to stream the speech signal to the centralized server which further recognizes the command. Each of the two methods has its benefits and drawbacks. If the devices would recognize commands by their own, each of them needs to have enough computational power to perform speech recognition on a large vocabulary. However, devices with sufficient computational power are typically pretty expensive. The centralized approach requires only one device with enough power to perform speech recognition which is the server. But this approach also requires that the voice data is transmitted to this server over a potential insecure wireless channel. Additionally, receiving and processing voice data from multiple microphone modules is a high overhead even for high-end devices. For the stated reasons, a combination of both approaches is used by distributing the task of voice controlling to decentral WUW recognition on microphone modules and central command detection on a server. The microphone modules recognize any WUW recorded in advance. This recognition is done directly on the module without streaming any audio data to a server. Only if a WUW is recognized, audio data is continuously streamed to the server application. This ensures, that the potentially insecure wireless channel for streaming is only used if the user wants to express a command and, thus, is aware of it. To minimize eavesdropping, audio data may also be encrypted before it is sent to the server application. Additionally, the outsourcing of the WUW detection to the microphone modules reduces the overhead for the receiving and processing of audio data on the server. Moreover, the microphone modules have to compute less complex speech recognition tasks which reduces the requirements for their hardware.

3   Hardware Components

The main components of the system are the microphone modules placed in every room, the receiver station attached to the server and the server application. The microphone modules serve to recognize spoken WUWs and transmit the speech signals spoken afterwards to the receiver station. The receiver station handles the incoming speech data as well as the transmission of audio back to a certain microphone module for audio feedback. The server application handles the recognition of voice commands and executes them. The overall data flow of the audio data between a microphone module and the server is sketched in Fig. 2.

Fig. 2. An overview of the audio data flow between microphone module and server application. The most important hardware components and their connection are shown.

An *ARM Cortex M4* microcontroller is used as the main processing unit for the microphone modules and the receiver station since it offers just enough computational power to sample and process the audio data. Moreover, it features a build in *Analog-to-Digital-Converter*, a *Digital-to-Analog-Converter*, and an *SPI*-bus. SPI is needed for communication with the wireless interface which is a *nRF24L01* from *Nordic Semiconductor*. To be compatible to common PCs, the audio data connection between the receiver station and the server application is achieved over the standard analog soundcard's line in and line out plugs. Furthermore, a USB connection is required for communicating with the server application.

As mentioned, the retrospective use of existing systems in the home like the television or lighting is preferred by most people instead of buying new devices. Therefore, additional modules are used to update these systems so that they can interact as smart components with the iHouse smart home system. To switch and meter lights or generic devices with a power plug, off-the-shelf switchable sockets are used, which communicate via 433 MHz. Existing infrared-light based systems are controlled with a self-build module featuring an IR-receiver to record commands and an IR-sender to control systems like the TV. The overall connections between the main components and some additional modules is shown in Fig. 3.

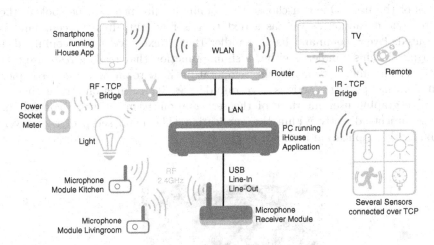

Fig. 3. Schematic overview of the connection of several hardware components in the iHouse smart home system.

4   Server Application

The server application is the centerpiece of the entire system. Commands are extracted from the voice stream, data of all sensors is collected and actuators are controlled. A graphic user interface makes it possible to add, remove and setup modules as well as to control them. In general, each device has a name, a picture and a device type. While the name and the picture are only for identification and further highlighting, the device type decides which kind of sub-device it is and what smart object it actually represents and, thus, what actions can be performed and what states can be queried. Furthermore, different graphic user interfaces for controlling the device or changing its settings are displayed depending on the device type. One example for such a sub-device is a switchable socket. The available actions for this sub-device are *switching on* and *switching off* the socket, while the available state is whether the socket is currently turned *on* or *off*. The sub-device stores ID information of the physical device in order to establish a physical connection. Such a connection is done either using *TCP* or a more rudimentary protocols via e.g. 433 MHz depending on the smart object. Data collection is achieved using a hierarchic star network structure with the server as the main data sink. If data can not be exchanged with the target platform directly because specialized communication hardware is needed, communication-bridge modules are added to the network which represent the data sink for all devices communicating with this specialized hardware. These modules further send the data to the server application over standardized protocols such as TCP. As an example, a TCP to infrared-light-bridge is used to be able to control existing television or HiFi-systems.

Voice commands are build on top and can be customized to the personal needs of the user. One can choose the command that needs to be spoken, the corresponding action as well as a text that is read out after the command is executed. Every command has a handler that is executed if the command is recognized. This handler is either a simple function that reads a response text with certain information like the temperature in a room or a more complex function that performs actions of certain devices like turning on the heating.

The graphic user interface of the server application allows to control the smart objects directly within the application. The main setup of the server, running the application is shown in Fig. 4.

Fig. 4. The iHouse smart home server application running on a PC connected to the receiver module over USB, Line in and Line out. A microphone module is shown on the right side. On the left side of the app, the room of interest can be selected. In the center, all available devices in this selected room are shown and can be controlled.

Voice controlling can be activated by either speaking the WUW in a room equipped with a microphone or by triggering a specific keystroke at the desktop computer. The application will automatically display a view showing all recognized commands as well as textual and graphical answers.

In order to add time or action based rules to a device, information and sensor data of other devices need to be accessed, too. If, for example, the heating should automatically adapt to the temperature in the room or to the time of day, those information must be accessible to the heating object. This information propagation is achieved by a *publish* and *subscribe* model. If a new temperature sensor reading is available, this data is *published* by the sensor object. Other objects interested in the room temperature can now *subscribe* this value and get notified on each new reading. The server application can be seen as a modular platform that can be further optimized and extended according to the preferences of a particular user.

5 The Wake-Up-Word Spotting Algorithm

To enable voice controlling from a specific room of the house, a microphone module needs to be installed as described in Sect. 3. After detecting a pre-recorded WUW, speech data is transmitted to the server for continuous command detection. The detection of the WUW is, however, task of the microphone module itself. To reduce the cost and size of these modules, only inexpensive microcontrollers with limited resources are used, which provide only a small amount of computational power and internal memory (see Sect. 3). Therefore, they are not capable of handling the high load of traditional speech recognition techniques. Optimized algorithms to detect keywords on low-level microcontrollers are proposed in literature but are not suitable for real-time applications. In [8] *Linear Prediction Coefficients* with *Hidden Markov Models* are implemented on an 8 bit, 16 MHz microcontroller resulting in an average recognition time of 15 to 17 s. Another approach using *Linear Prediction Cepstral Coefficients* on an 8 bit MCU, clocked at 40 MHz with a specialized *Dynamic Time Warping* (DTW) algorithm is used in [9]. However, the authors do not give any hint whether their system can be applied to real-time applications or not.

For small vocabulary speech recognition systems such as keyword spotting systems, the template matching approach is widely used ([9,10]). The specially developed WUW spotting algorithm adopts this approach but makes it suitable for real-time applications on low-level microcontrollers. An overview of the realized approach is shown in Fig. 5, in which additional as well as optimized stages (compared to the traditional flow) are highlighted in orange.

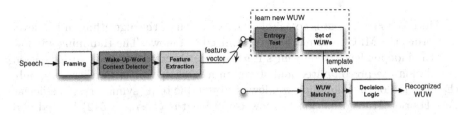

Fig. 5. An overview of the proposed WUW-spotting algorithm. Blocks in orange are added to the standard template matching pipeline while blocks in light orange show highly optimized implementations to maintain real-time behavior for low-level systems. (Color figure online)

To evaluate the dynamic process speech, the simplifying assumption is made that speech is statistically stationary on short time scales. Therefore, features are extracted and evaluated on a frame by frame basis over a specific time interval called window. For the algorithm, a frame length of 10 ms with a window length of 20 ms and a sampling frequency of 16 kHz is used. Discussion about proper frame and window durations for speech processing can be found in [11]. A WUW Context Detector is developed to distinguish speech directed towards the system from speech that is not. Humans usually get the attention of other people by hyper-articulating their names or by using interjections like *"excuse me"*. This is often coherent with a preceding and succeeding silence to highlight the spoken utterance even more. By applying this human behaviour to a more general model, the WUW context is defined as a preceding voiceless segment followed by a voiced segment in the length of a stored WUW succeeded by an additional voiceless segment. The WUW Context Detector uses a Voice Activity Detector (VAD) [12] to decide whether voice is present or not and thresholds to evaluate the length of each segment.

The feature extraction is optimized for the calculation of *Mel Frequency Cepstral Coefficients* (MFCCs) with 26 filter banks linear distributed in the mel-scale between 100 Hz and 8000 Hz to model the speaker and the spoken WUW. MFCC features have successfully been applied to speech recognition tasks since their introduction in the 70's [14]. An overview of the steps done to compute the MFCCs is shown in Fig. 6.

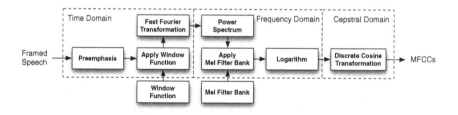

Fig. 6. An overview of the extraction of Mel Frequency Cepstral Coefficients.

Since the major goal is to enable the execution of the algorithm on low-level platforms, the MFCC calculation is optimized as follows. The Hamming window and the independent cosine values used for the Discrete Cosine Transformation calculation are precomputed and stored in a LookUp Table. Furthermore, only the first half of the Hamming window is stored due to its symmetry. An efficient Fast Fourier Transformation for power-of-2 lengths ($N_{FFT} = 512$) is used and the mel filter banks are optimized by only calculating the relevant values for each triangular filter. In the WUW matching block, a sequence of extracted feature vectors is tested consecutively against each stored template. If strong deviation is found between the length of the template and the test sequence, a mismatch is assumed and further matching is canceled. This reduces the computational complexity and improves the systems response time. If no strong deviation is found, further analysis using an optimized DTW algorithm with a *Euclidean Distance* measure is applied to both sequences. DTW has successfully been applied to speech recognition problems ([8,13]). However, its computational complexity is $\mathcal{O}(n \cdot m)$, with n and m being the lengths of two sequences to compare. Depending on the frame duration and the length of the WUW, the extracted sequence of feature vectors can get quite large resulting in a huge matrix that needs to be explored. This exploration is not only computational complex for an embedded device but might also become a memory problem depending on the underlying hardware platform. In order to solve this problem the *Sakoe-Chiba band* [14] with distance r is used to reduce the search space. The complexity is even further reduced by using a sub-word matching technique: Each feature vector sequence is divided into k subsequences of equal length. The corresponding subsequences of the test and template sequence are successively matched with DTW and the distance of each match is stored. The total distance is finally estimated by the mean of the distances of all subsequences. Therefore, the complexity is decreased to

$$n \cdot r + m \cdot r - k \cdot r^2 \rightarrow \mathcal{O}\left(r \cdot \max\left(n, m\right)\right). \tag{1}$$

If the total distance of a test sequence drops below an empirically defined threshold, the sequence and, thus, the utterance said, is classified as a WUW. If the system is in the learning state, an Entropy Test ensures that the template recording is suitable to be used as a WUW by requiring its length to be greater 0.2 s and smaller 2 s and the environment in which it is recorded to be almost noise-free.

With the performed optimizations in the template matching and feature extraction pipeline, the average recognition time is 300 ms for a single stored WUW of 1.3 s length. The recognition time scales according to Eq. 1 with the length of the WUW and linear with the total number of stored WUWs.

5.1 Experimental Setup and Results

To evaluate the proposed system, a database of 11 different speakers - two female and nine male - and two different scenarios (WUW and continuous speech) was recorded for three different distances (1, 3 and 5 m) between the microphone and speaker. Two WUWs were chosen by each subject individually and were recorded in a noiseless environment at a distance of 1 m to the microphone. In the WUW scenario several utterances are spoken successively with a 1 s silence interval between each utterance to ensures that the WUW Context Detector assumes it to be spoken in the WUW context during evaluation. Both WUWs occur at least three times in this scenario. The purpose of this scenario is to evaluate the performance of the feature extraction and matching block of the proposed algorithm. In the continuous speech scenario the subjects were reading texts from a book to simulate a regular conversation. The purpose of this scenario is to test the WUW Context Detector which should reject all speech not spoken in a WUW context. The performance of the system was measured in terms of *correct acceptance* (CA) and *correct rejection* (CR) rates [12], since WUW or keyword spotting systems need a measure of rejection. Rejection is the ability of the system to detect and reject *Out Of Vocabulary* utterances. CA and CR rates can be obtained by

$$CA = \frac{TP}{TP + FN}, \qquad CR = \frac{\#\,\text{words} - FP}{\#\,\text{words}}, \qquad (2)$$

where TP is the number of *true positives*, FN is the number of *false negatives* and FP is the number of *false positives*. As Table 1 shows, the CR rate is as high as 99.69% for a CA rate of 100% in the speech scenario. In the WUW scenario, however, the CR rate drops to 89.66%. Depending on the application of the system, a large CR rate is more important than a high CA rate. Therefore, the system was re-evaluated by omitting the WUW with the largest distance measure to the corresponding template recording. In other words, the worst pronunciation of each WUW was deleted for every person. This leads to an overall CA rate of 67.86%, meaning that approximately two out of three WUW would still be recognized correctly. This reduction causes that the CR rate increases to 99.93% in the speech scenario and to 96.91% in the WUW scenario. 99.93% is equivalent to one erroneously trigger around 1400 words.

Table 1. System performance depending on the scenario evaluated for two CA rates.

Scenario	# Words	# WUW	CA rate	# TP	# FP	# TN	# FN	CR rate
Speech	4149	0	100%	0	13	4136	0	99.69%
			67.86%	0	3	4146	0	**99.93%**
WUW	1392	282	100%	282	144	1248	0	89.66%
			67.86%	192	43	1067	90	**96.91%**
Total	5541	282	100%	282	157	5102	0	97.17%
			67.86%	192	46	5213	90	**99.17%**

6   Conclusion

This paper proposes a modular and expandable smart home solution, which is user-friendly in installation and usage. Additionally, it is secure by processing all data offline. The system consists of external microphones and a central server application which interacts with different smart components like light switches, the heating, or the TV. To improve the ease of use, voice controlling was added to the smart home system as the main interface. This enables the interaction with the system through voice commands that, unlike existing systems, are processed completely offline and can be customized to the personal needs of the user. To be able to interact with this system from every room of the house, microphone modules were designed which can be installed easily into existing households since all communication to the server is done wireless. To separate speech directed to the system from speech not directed to the system, a novel WUW algorithm was developed which recognizes predefined WUWs spoken in an alerting context of getting attention. Thus, all voice commands directed to the system must be spoken with a leading WUW like *"Hey House [pause] light on!"*. Speech data is only transmitted to the server if the leading WUW is recognized by the embedded platform. The WUW algorithm was improved in terms of computational complexity to enable the execution on embedded platforms with less computational power. An evaluation was done on a speech database of 11 different speakers. The algorithm achieved an overall correct rejection ratio of 99.17% for a correct acceptance rate of 67.86%. The rejection of speech not expressed in the WUW context is up to 99.93%. Future work for the smart home system will focus on extending its scope and smartness. This will be achieved by utilizing the implemented publish and subscribe model to make the system even more context aware and, thus, to provide additional convenience and aid for the user. Nevertheless, first feedback obtained from test users and other participants indicates that voice controlling is a key feature and will enhance smart homes to bring them into more households any time soon.

References

1. Nest Labs - Nest. http://www.nest.com
2. FHEM: A perl server for house automation. http://www.fhem.de
3. Han, Y., Hyun, J., Jeong, T., Yoo, J., Hong, J.: A smart home control system based on context and human speech. In: 18th IEEE International Conference on Advanced Communication Technology, pp. 165–169. IEEE Press, PyeongChang (2016)
4. Illek, C.P.: Smart home in Deutschland. Survey, Bitkom Research GmbH (2014). http://www.bitkom.org/Publikationen/2014/Studien/ Smart-Home-in-Deutschland-Praesentation/Praesentation-Smart-Home.pdf
5. Potamitis, I., Georgila, K., Fakotakis, N., Kokkinakis, G.K.: An integrated system for smart-home control of appliances based on remote speech interaction. In: 8th International Conference on Speech Communication and Technology, pp. 2197–2200. ISCA, Geneva (2003)
6. GoogleHome. http://home.google.com
7. Amazon Echo. http://www.amazon.com
8. Thiang, D.W.: Limited speech recognition for controlling movement of mobile robot implemented on atmega162 microcontroller. In: 1st IEEE International Conference on Computer and Automation Engineering, pp. 347–350. IEEE Press, Bangkok (2009)
9. Yuanyuan, S., Jia, L., Runsheng, L.: IdentificationSingle-chip speech recognition system based on 8051 microcontroller core. IEEE Trans. Consum. Electron. **47**, 149–153 (2001)
10. Barakat, M.S., Ritz, C.H., Stirling, D.A.: Keyword spotting based on the analysis of template matching distances. In: 5th IEEE International Conference on Signal Processing and Communication Systems, pp. 1–6. IEEE Press, Honolulu (2011)
11. Picone, J.W.: Signal modeling techniques in speech recognition. Proc. IEEE **81**, 1215–1247 (1993)
12. Këpuska, V.Z., Klein, T.B.: A novel wake-up-word speech recognition system, wake-up-word recognition task, technology and evaluation. Nonlinear Anal. Theor. Methods Appl. **71**, e2772–e2789 (2009)

13. Zehetner, A., Hagmuller, M., Pernkopf, F.: Wake-up-word spotting for mobile systems. In: 22nd IEEE European Conference on Signal Processing Conference, pp. 1472–1476. IEEE Press, Lisbon (2014)
14. Sakoe, H., Chiba, S.: Dynamic programming algorithm optimization for spoken word recognition. IEEE Trans. Acoust. Speech Signal Process. **26**, 43–49 (1978)

PackSens: A Condition and Transport Monitoring System Based on an Embedded Sensor Platform

Marc Pfeifer[(✉)], Tobias Schubert, and Bernd Becker

Chair of Computer Architecture, Institute of Computer Science,
Faculty of Engineering, Albert-Ludwigs-University Freiburg,
79110 Freiburg, Germany
{pfeiferm,schubert,becker}@informatik.uni-freiburg.de

Abstract. As a consequence of the growing globalization, transports which need a safe handling are increasing. Therefore, this paper introduces an innovative transport and condition monitoring system based on a mobile embedded sensor platform. The platform is equipped with a variety of sensors needed to extensively monitor a transport and can be attached directly to the transported good. The included microcontroller processes all relevant data served by the sensors in a very power efficient manner. Furthermore, it provides possible violations of previously given thresholds through a standardized Near Field Communication (NFC) interface to the user. Since falls are one major cause of damages while transportation, the presented system is the first one that not only detects every fall but also analyses the fall height and other parameters related to the fall event in real-time on the platform. The whole system was tested in different experiments where all critical situations and in particular all fall situations have been detected correctly.

Keywords: Embedded system · Condition monitoring · Transport monitoring · Low power · Sensor platform

1 Introduction

Due to the growing globalization especially in the last 20 years the local and international markets have moved close together. It is for example common today that one product is produced at different sites and that all necessary components for a particular product arrive for the final assembly "just-in-time". One aspect this example and many others have in common, is that more and more goods need to be transported from one place to another which has caused a big rise in goods traffic in recent years. For example, only the German courier-, express- and parcel-services have seen a rise of 74% in the transport volume since 2000 [1].

With the rise in goods traffic also the transports of goods with special needs like fresh or fragile products increased. For these products an incorrect transport or incorrect transport conditions like too warm or too rough environments could

© ICST Institute for Computer Sciences, Social Informatics and Telecommunications Engineering 2017
M. Magno et al. (Eds.): S-Cube 2016, LNICST 205, pp. 81–92, 2017.
DOI: 10.1007/978-3-319-61563-9_7

lead to big damages and (financial) problems. To overcome these issues it is quite common (at least for almost all industrial facilities) that goods are extensively checked directly after receiving them. Unfortunately, such a check is often not possible if one receives a private parcel since it could not be opened directly. And even if a damage has been detected during the incoming check it is often not possible to identify the initiator.

Modern embedded systems could provide a perfect solution for the above mentioned problems. Through the combination of a microcontroller with small Micro-Electro-Mechanical-System-sensors (MEMS-sensors) it is possible to create compact, mobile and universal sensor platforms. These platforms could be transported directly with the good to monitor the transport conditions in real-time. If a violation like an interruption of the cooling chain or a drop is detected, it is stored on the platform and the receiver is able to read out the event in less than a second during the incoming check. Obviously, this saves time and resources in industrial facilities and also enables reliable checks for private persons directly at the door. An additional advantage is that the exact time at which a violation occurred could be stored. Together with the tracking information this provides relevant information about the initiator of a possible damage. This paper introduces such an intelligent platform and highlights all components needed to build up the entire transport and condition monitoring system called *PackSens*.

The remainder of the paper is structured as follows: In Sect. 2 existing condition monitoring systems are introduced before a general overview of the *PackSens* system is given. Section 3 deals with the hardware used for the sensor platform, while the corresponding low-power concept is described in Sect. 4. In Sect. 5 the innovative fall detection and analysis algorithms are explained. The results of different experiments for the evaluation of the entire system are shown in Sect. 6. Section 7 concludes the work and gives some hints for future research.

2   Existing Systems and System Overview

Only one transport monitoring system developed by the MIT has been proposed in the scientific field yet [2]. The sensor platform of this system consists of a microcontroller, a 2.4 GHz wireless module and different analog sensors like a shock sensor, a light sensor, and a temperature sensor. With special wake-up mechanisms the platform consumes little energy but due to the simple analog sensors nearly no precise measurements are possible. Another drawback is the need for a special configuration and read-out device which increases the application costs. In the commercial field a few transport monitoring systems are available specialized for big shipment boxes like sea containers. There are the *EDR-3C* and the *Shock Timer Plus 3Dv2* from *Instrumented Sensor Technology* [3] and the *Container Security Tag ST-675* from *Savi Technology* [4], to mention only a few. All systems can monitor a variety of parameters and are very robust. But they are also huge, heavy, and expensive which makes them unsuitable for the use in smaller and in particular private transportation. A system which provides similar features but is small enough that it could be used in smaller transportation scenarios is the *SenseAware* from *FedEx* [5]. However, this system is apparently only available to companies. There are, to our best knowledge, only two systems which are potentially also designed for the demands of the private sector, namely *DropTag* from *Cambridge Consultants* [6] and *Pakkcheck* [7]. But both systems are not yet available on the market and their final functionality still remains unclear. Finally, there are also several systems that are specialized in the monitoring of just one certain parameter like temperature [8] or shock [9].

Our novel *PackSens* system combines all advantages of the above mentioned systems and adds some new functions which no other system yet provides: It is very small and lightweight however robust so that it could be used in both, private transportation and big industrial containers for instance. The platform also implements a sophisticated low-power concept to enable a long autonomous operating time. Since not all components are needed in every use case, the entire platform is build in a modular way. Components could be turned off or omitted also physically with no effect on the remaining functions. Another novel feature is the on-board detection and analysis of drop events. Even if drop events are a major cause for damages while transportation, it seems that no system yet performs a deeper detection and analysis. The standardized communication module which is based on NFC is also an innovative feature as it enables the configuration and read-out through a standard NFC-capable smartphone or computer without any complex linking.

Figure 1 sketches the entire *PackSens* system. The main part is the sensor platform itself which will be transported with the good that should be monitored. The heart is a microcontroller which connects all components, in particular all "monitoring" sensors. To provide a non-volatile storage of critical events together with precise timestamps a flash memory and a real-time clock module are included. The power supply is realized with the help of a single-cell Lithium-Polymer-battery. The size and capacity of this battery could be chosen arbitrarily and by this adjusted to different needs. The power supply also includes a charging circuit for the battery which uses the upcoming QI-standard to provide external charging power to the platform without the need for any cable connection. For the communication with the configuration and read-out

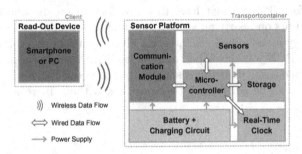

Fig. 1. Overview of the entire *PackSens* transport and condition monitoring system.

device a NFC-based interface is included. This allows a quick and easy to link communication even through a completely closed transport box. Moreover, any NFC-capable smartphone or PC equipped with an appropriate app can be used as a configuration and read-out device.

3   Hardware

The *PackSens* sensor platform is equipped with a variety of sensors which allow the precise monitoring of all important parameters while the transportation of a good. As already mentioned before, the occurrence of a drop is one very important parameter, which is also closely related to shocks (=high accelerations) and vibrations. All three parameters are monitored with the help of two accelerometers, one providing a high resolution for lower accelerations (low-g accelerometer *ST - LIS3DH*) and one offering a high measuring range (high-g accelerometer *ST - H3LIS200DL*). Other important parameters, at least for some transportation goods, are temperature, humidity and pressure. As a consequence the sensor platform includes a *NXP - PCT2075* temperature sensor, a *ST - HTS221* humidity sensor and a *ST - LPS25HB* pressure sensor. Additionally, an ambient light sensor (*LiteOn - LTR-303ALS-01*) is included that serves for two purposes: On the one hand it could be used to detect high light intensities on light sensitive goods, on the other hand it could be used to detect unauthorized openings of a transport container.

All chosen sensors not only had to be as cheap, as small, and as power-saving as possible but they also had to provide a digital output and if possible a threshold interrupt output that is fired if the measured value goes above or below a given threshold. These requirements help to reduce the demands for the microcontroller and are a key part of our low-power concept. Another mandatory requirement all sensors had to fulfil are low-power modes in which the sensor is turned off and consumes almost no energy. This is also helpful to decrease the power consumption through the deactivation of sensors which are currently not needed.

All components discussed so far together with the passive NFC- and QI-interface are connected to a *SAMD20G15* microcontroller from *Atmel*. This Cortex-M0+ controller is cheap but provides enough computational power and memory for all tasks that have to be performed on the platform. It also provides interrupts on nearly all I/O-pins and offers a deep sleep mode in which almost no energy is consumed. To integrate all components in a robust and compact manner a PCB was developed and enclosed with a custom-made case (see Fig. 2). The final sensor platform is smaller than a credit card and with a weight of about 50 g it can be add to any transport box without increasing the weight significantly.

Fig. 2. The *PackSens* sensor platform. PCB dimensions: 68 mm × 41 mm. Outer case dimensions: 71 mm × 50 mm × 19 mm. Weight of the whole platform: 52 g.

4   Low-Power Concept

Since the costs and the size of the battery, the run-time and many other important parameters of the condition monitoring system are influenced by the power consumption, a special effort has been put in its reduction. While it would be the easiest way to just choose the cheapest sensor for each parameter and then always monitor the corresponding output with the microcontroller, this concept is very energy consuming. Besides other issues, the biggest problem with this straightforward concept is the continuous monitoring which must be performed by the microcontroller. To achieve this the controller always has to be in its normal operation mode in which it consumes quite a lot of energy (in case of the *Atmel SAMD20* about 3.1 mA). A big energy saving can be achieved by reducing the time the microcontroller is in this power consuming operation mode. So the monitoring is sourced out to the sensors and the microcontroller is put into a deep sleep mode most of the time where it consumes almost no energy (in case of the *Atmel SAMD20* about 4 μA). Fortunately, many modern sensors support this outsourcing through a threshold monitoring directly on the sensor's IC. If the current output of such a sensor is above or below a previous given threshold the IC provides an interrupt. This interrupt is used to wake up the microcontroller from its sleep. The controller then checks, computes, and stores a possible violation before it is put in the deep sleep mode again. With this interrupt-driven concept the microcontroller is only activated in case of a possible important event which saves a lot of energy. The concept is also illustrated in Fig. 3 and it underlines the special requirements for the component selection as discussed in the previous section.

Another problem in terms of energy consumption are critical events that last for a longer time. These events would trigger the threshold interrupt and by this wake up the microcontroller every time a measurement is taken. To overcome this issue the threshold interrupts are changed after the first violation of a threshold in such a manner that if a sensor output has triggered an upper threshold the next interrupt is only triggered if the output is again below this threshold and vice versa.

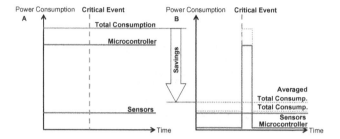

Fig. 3. Schematic comparison of the energy consumption with the straightforward concept (A) and the interrupt-driven concept (B). The real power consumption values of the *PackSens* highly depend on the configuration (see Sect. 6).

5   Fall Detection

Falls are a major cause of problems and damages while transportation. Therefore, a special fall detection was developed which not only detects falls but also tries to analyze different fall parameters. As already introduced, accelerometers are used to detect falls which is done through a characteristic pattern of the resulting acceleration. Such an ideal pattern is shown as the red line in Fig. 4. It could be divided into four parts: In the pre-fall phase before the start of the fall the normal acceleration of 1 g due to gravity acts on the good. Then after the fall start the good is in free fall and no acceleration is measurable. It becomes faster until it hits the ground or something similar. This is called the impact. Here, a very high acceleration is detected since the good is stopped immediately and the kinetic energy gained in the free-fall phase is converted. After the fall, in the post-fall phase, again the normal acceleration due to gravity acts on the good while it lays on the ground. Especially through the characteristic and large peak in the impact phase this pattern could be easily spotted. Unfortunately, an acceleration measurement during a real drop like it is shown as the dots in

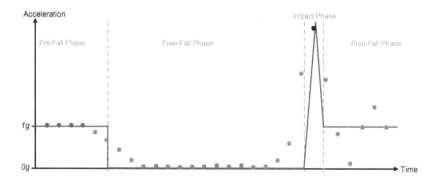

Fig. 4. Red line: ideal acceleration on an object during a fall. Dots: schematic representation of the measured acceleration during a real fall. (Color figure online)

Fig. 4 does not provide such a perfect pattern. In particular the transitions from one phase to another cannot be clearly spotted anymore and the post-fall phase is not as smooth and steady as in the ideal case because of rebounds from the impact surface. The fluctuations also vary with every measurement.

For the pure detection of a fall the literature provides in general three different concepts: pattern recognition [10], subsequence matching [11] and the threshold concept ([10,12]). While the first two methods are unsuitable for the presented system due to the required training set and the required computational power, the threshold concept suits very good and is the base for the algorithm in this work. In this concept the acceleration measurement has to cross one or more different thresholds which characterize the fall pattern before a drop is detected. To fit to the low-power concept the detection of the first threshold is outsourced to the low-g accelerometer. It provides an interrupt as soon as the acceleration on all three axis is below 0.375 g for at least ten samples which corresponds to a free fall of 10 ms and is a good first hint for a fall. After this trigger every sample is analyzed in real-time and it is checked whether its magnitude is above a value of 9.6 g. In this case it corresponds to the impact peak and a fall is detected that has to be analyzed. If the value is not reached no fall happened or the fall had a very soft impact. The thresholds used for the detection as well as all following thresholds were chosen empirically.

In the following analysis the fall height is determined first. For its calculation two methods are known in general: The impact-based method [13] uses the impact measurements and different specific information about the drop for the height calculation. Some of the required information, in particular about the impact surface, are not accessible by the presented system which is the main reason why the second method based on the free-fall time [14] is used for the analysis. To gain the free-fall time, the measured samples which belong to the free-fall phase had to be determined in a first step. While a coarse estimation of the amount of these samples and the corresponding fall height is simple and has been done already in some works (e.g. in [14]), this is not sufficient for the proposed system. Since the outcome of the system should serve as a proof in case of damages, it has to be very precise and especially respect the mentioned imperfections appearing in a real fall measurement. This is the reason why a more sophisticated algorithm was developed to find the samples in the free-fall phase and why the system not only outputs one fall height, but a lower and an upper bound. For the lower bound only the samples are taken into account which are part of the free-fall phase with absolute certainty (in Fig. 4 these samples are marked in green). For the upper bound all samples starting from the last one in the pre-fall phase (last violet dot in Fig. 4) until the peak sample (black dot in Fig. 4) are considered. With the number of samples for each bound and the sampling rate, the free-fall times are calculated. Since the good was accelerated with the known acceleration due to gravity g between these times (t) a lower and higher bound for the fall height h could be calculated with Eq. 1.

$$h = \frac{1}{2} \cdot g \cdot t^2 \qquad (1)$$

There are many special cases that can occur during a fall which could falsify the fall height or which are interesting for the user. Examples are that the good could be thrown or that the good could fall down some stairs which leads to many successive impacts. Since it is impossible to detect all possible special cases directly on the platform, the main focus is on detecting each and every fall independent of a potential special case. After that the fall height is estimated as described above and all known special cases are checked with different methods. In the current version potential throws, the occurrence of a second impact and the occurrence of an intermediate peak in the free-fall phase are detected. Of particular interest is a throw upwards since in this special case the free-fall phase is detected from leaving the hand until the impact and so the calculated fall height would be estimated far too high. Since the detection methods are not completely safe, the outcome is given to the user only as a hint and all raw acceleration data of every fall is additionally stored and also made accessible to the user. So the user can, in case of a damage, follow the hints and perform a detailed analysis afterwards.

Another parameter that is analysed after a fall is the impact strength. This is an interesting information because it could be for example possible that a good is thrown or dropped on purpose which is no problem if it is caught afterwards. The caught then equals a soft landing with a low impact strength. One simple way to gain the impact strength is an analysis of the height of the acceleration peak in the impact phase. However, since this peak normally exceeds the measuring range of standard accelerometers, we came up with a new and different way for the evaluation: By looking at the dominating frequencies in the post-fall phase a good estimation can be made on the impact strength. If the dominating frequencies are low the good has landed on a probably soft and elastic surface. If the dominating frequencies are high the impact surface is probably hard and inelastic. Thus, for the detection of the impact strength at least 64 samples after the peak of the fall are additionally stored and fed into a frequency analysis routine where frequencies around 1.5 Hz and 3 Hz are analyzed. The result of this analysis directly corresponds to the impact strength.

6   Experiments and Results

6.1   Fall Detection

Since it is an important but complex part of the system the fall detection and analysis was tested first. Therefor the sensor platform was fixed in different transport boxes out of cardboard and then dropped from different heights with the help of a drop tester. The first box was a small one (outer dimensions: $19\,cm \times 18.5\,cm \times 13\,cm$) made out of thin 1-layer cardboard with a total weight of about 145 g, the second one was a bigger box (outer dimensions: $31\,cm \times 23.5\,cm \times 12\,cm$) made out of thick 1-layer cardboard with a total weight of about 500 g. During the tests different special cases were simulated and their detection was checked, too. In total 90 test falls with fall heights between 0.3 m and 1.5 m were performed and the results are summarized in Table 1. As one can

Table 1. Test results for the fall detection and analysis.

	True positives	False positives	False negatives
Fall detection	100% (90)	0% (0)	
Fall height	91.1% (82)	8.9% (8)	
Impact strength	82.1% (64)	17.9% (14)	
Second impact	58% (7)	2.2% (2)	42% (5)
Throw	100% (12)	0% (0)	0% (0)

see the main goal of detecting each and every fall was achieved. Moreover, the fall height detection provides very good results. The only cases where the lower bound of the fall height was wrong are the special cases with a throw upwards. But since the throw detection worked in every tested case these false results could be filtered out effectively. For the check of the impact strength detection every fall, except the 12 which had a second impact, was categorized as a fall with a soft or a hard landing. Afterwards, it was checked whether the frequency analysis provides the same result. While this achieved quite good results the detection of the second impact had some issues. Only about one half of the falls with a second impact were detected correctly and also about 2% of all tested falls were incorrectly classified as falls with a second impact. As a consequence the impact strength detection as well as the second impact detection still need some improvement but they already provide a good hint for the user, exactly as intended.

6.2 Energy Consumption

Since the energy consumption is a critical parameter of the sensor platform it was also tested extensively. The results are shown in Table 2. Here, the measured power consumption is shown for every component on the sensor platform in two different configurations. For the ground consumption the component is configured to be active but all parameters are set in such a way that the minimal power is consumed. This means in case of a sensor that for example the resolution and the measuring rate are set to the minimal possible value. In the worst-case configuration every parameter of the certain component is configured in such a way that it consumes the maximum power. The most interesting results are the total power consumptions of the sensor platform in the last row. If the platform is activated the ground consumption adds up to about 17 µA which is mainly characterized by the flash storage, the real-time clock and the "sleeping" microcontroller and corresponds to an uptime of about 1.2 years using a small 180 mAh battery. Depending on the settings of the user the power consumption of the activated sensors additionally adds up to the platforms ground consumption. The total consumption in the active mode is between 17 µA and 2 mA depending on the number of activated sensors and their settings. In case of a threshold violation the consumption is shortly increased by about 3.1 mA

Table 2. Energy consumption of the different components of the *PackSens* sensor platform. Measuring conditions: about 23 °C, about 400 LUX.

Component	Ground consumption	Worst-case consumption
Flash storage	11.1 μA	11.1 μA
Real-time clock	0.7 μA	0.7 μA
Temperature sensor	about 98.5 μA	about 109.5 μA
Light sensor	400 μA	535.5 μA
Pressure sensor	about 6 μA	705 μA
Accelerometer - low G	21 μA	21 μA
Accelerometer - high G	about 25 μA	401 μA
Humidity sensor	10 μA	218 μA
Microcontroller	about 4 μA (sleep)	3.1 mA (active)
Sensor platform (in sleep mode)	about 17 μA	2 mA (everything monitored)

through the active consumption of the microcontroller. But since this is normally only the case for a very short amount of time (compared to the whole running time), the overall power consumption does not really change. This leads to an uptime of around 3.75 days with a small 180 mAh battery if all sensors are active and configured with the worst-case configuration. For a rather typical configuration like it is used in the next section (see Table 3 for the configuration details) the sensor platform draws about 770 μA which leads to an uptime of around 9.7 days with the same battery. Even if the calculated runtimes should be enough for every normal transport the uptime can always be easily increased by using a larger battery.

6.3   Condition Monitoring System

To finally evaluate the entire condition monitoring system, different transport scenarios had been tested in the laboratory. This kind of tests had been preferred to actual shipments since the real conditions and violations would have been completely unknown and an evaluation of the system would not be possible. In all tests the system was used exactly as a user would do it. The platform was fixed inside a transport box out of cardboard, configured through a specially developed Android app from outside and while the incoming check the data was read out again with the app. During the tests, different likely scenarios like a normal transport with falls and an opening or a transport with critical temperature and humidity phases (here the platform was used without a box) had been simulated. Exemplary, the outcome of the normal transport scenario is shown in Table 3. On the left hand side one can see the tested events and on the right hand side the output of the system is shown. Each event was detected immediately and all shown events are exactly as expected. It is remarkable that often two shock events for the same acceleration peak were detected. The reason

Table 3. Results for the tests of a normal transport with falls and an opening event. Active parameters: Fall, light (upper/lower threshold: 100 LUX/20 LUX, sampling rate: 2 s), shock (threshold: 15.625 g, sampling rate: 400 Hz).

Test		System output	
Time	Action	Time	Event
19:40	Fall, about 1 m, caught	19:40	Fall event: 0.47 m - ?[a], Soft landing
		19:40	Shock event: x: 21.9 g
19:41	Opening	19:41	Light event: 129 LUX
19:42	Closing	19:42	Light event: 0 LUX
19:43	Hit against box	19:43	Shock event: y: −89 g
19:44	Throw upwards	19:44	2x Shock event: y: −43.8 g, z: −15.6 g
		19:44	Fall event: 2.33 m–2.98 m, Soft landing, Throw
19:45	Fall, about 1 m	19:45	Fall event: 0.94 m - ?[a], Hard landing
		19:45	2x Shock event: y: −15.6 g, y: −20.3 g

[a]If the transition between the pre-fall and the free-fall phase is very unclear the system does not output an upper bound for the height.

for this is the high sampling rate of the high-g accelerometer which leads to a double detection of large peaks[1] or to a detection of the rebouncing after a fall. Also in the other tests all events were detected and the outcome was as expected. However, in the test results of different critical temperatures and humidities a delayed event detection was observed. While a certain delay is normal for these parameters these delays could probably be nevertheless reduced by an improved positioning of the sensors within the custom-made case (see Fig. 2).

7 Conclusion

In this paper we introduced an innovative transport monitoring system called *PackSens*. The system consists of a mobile embedded sensor platform and a configuration and read-out device. While the configuration and read-out device could be any NFC-enabled smartphone or PC with a custom-made software, the sensor platform is a highly specialized design. It uses a variety of carefully selected sensors to monitor violations of given thresholds for all relevant parameters during transportation. To guarantee a long run-time a highly adapted low-power concept was implemented, which outsources the threshold monitoring to the sensors and exploits the sleep modes of the microcontroller. Tests showed that even with a small battery run-times between 4 days and about 1.2 years are possible. A unique feature of the *PackSens* system is a newly developed fall detection and

---

[1] In the case of the shock detection the method described in Sect. 4 for detecting only the start and end of a critical event is not used since shock events are by nature always very short.

analysis. With the help of different successive thresholds every fall of a monitored good is detected and the fall height is estimated. Through methods like a special frequency analysis also the impact strength and other parameters of the fall are analyzed. While the fall detection and the fall height estimation showed very good results, the detection of additional fall parameters and in particular the detection of certain special cases still need some improvement. Also the position of the temperature and humidity sensor should be optimized. Nevertheless, the *PackSens* system is already an effective transport and condition monitoring system which could provide huge advantages in the area of transports and logistics.

References

1. Bundesverband Paket und Express Logistik e.V. (BIEK): KEP-Studie 2016: Analyse des Marktes in Deutschland. Study, Germany (2016)
2. Malinowski, M., Moskwa, M., Feldmeier, M., Laibowitz, M., Paradiso, J.A.: CargoNet: a low-cost micropower sensor node exploiting quasi-passive wakeup for adaptive asychronous monitoring of exceptional events. In: 5th ACM Conference on Embedded Networked Sensor Systems, pp. 145–159. ACM, New York (2007)
3. Instrumented Sensor Technology - Products. http://www.isthq.com/Products.aspx
4. Savi Technology - Container Security Tag ST-675. http://www.savi.com/wp-content/uploads/Hardware_Spec_Sheet_ST_6751.pdf
5. Fedex - Senseaware. http://www.senseaware.com/
6. Cambridge Consultants - Droptag. http://www.cambridgeconsultants.com/droptag
7. Pakkcheck. http://pakkcheck.com/
8. DHL - SmartSensor. http://www.dhl.com/smartsensor
9. ShockWatch - Impact Indicators. http://shockwatch.com/products/impact-and-tilt/impact-indicators
10. Luštrek, M., Gjoreski, H., Kozina, S., Cvetković, B., Mirchevska. V., Gams, M.: Detecting falls with location sensors and accelerometers. In: 23rd Innovative Applications of Artificial Intelligence Conference, pp. 1662–1667. AAAI Press, Menlo Park (2011)
11. Lan, M., Nahapetain, A., Vahdatpour, A., Au, L., Kaiser, W., Sarrafzadeh, M.: SmartFall: an automatic fall detection system based on subsequence matching for the SmartCane. In: 4th International Conference on Body Area Networks, pp. 8:1–8:8. ICST, Brussels (2009)
12. Bourke, A.K., O'Brien, J.V., Lyons, G.M.: Evaluation of a threshold-based tri-axial accelerometer fall detection algorithm. Gait Posture **26**(2), 194–199 (2007)
13. Luan, J.E., Tee, T.Y., Pek, E., Lim, C.T., Zhong, Z.: Modal analysis and dynamic responses of board level drop test. In: 5th Electronics Packaging Technology Conference, pp. 233–243. IEEE Press, New York (2003)
14. Kionix: Free-fall sensing for drop-force modeling using Kionix MEMS tri-axis accelerometer (application note no. 001). Application Note (2016)

Smart LED Lights Control Using Nano-Power Wake Up Radios

Tommaso Polonelli[1] and Michele Magno[1,2]($\boxtimes$)

[1] DIE, Università Di Bologna, Bologna, Italy
[2] D-ITET, ETH Zürich, Zürich, Switzerland
michele.magno@iis.ee.ethz.ch

Abstract. Wireless sensor networks (WSNs) are widely employed today in real world applications. Smart homes and smart cities are the most promising application currently exploiting WSN. Smart lighting with WSN in particular is promising to achieve a low cost, wireless, easily installed, adaptable system to automatically adjust the light intensity of LED panels, with the aim of saving energy and maintaining user satisfaction. However, lifetime and power consumption of wireless devices are still the most critical challenge that limits the success of this technology. This issue is especially critical when wireless sensor nodes are powered by limited energy storage devices (i.e. small batteries or supercaps). To overcome this issue, major research efforts focus on reducing power consumption, particularly communication, as the radio transceiver is one of the highest power consumers. In this work we present the design and development of a highly efficient wireless system targeting indoor control of lights using ultra low power wake up radio technology. Thanks to the wake up radio the energy efficiency of the communication is improved and this significantly increases the lifetime of the solution. We design the sensor and control devices for a smart light controlling system that can be retrofitted and maintain a long lifetime even when supplied by batteries. Measurements of current and power consumption of both the designed system confirm the ultra-low power of the nodes and the benefits to use the energy efficient power communication implemented with the wake up radio.

Keywords: Sensors network · Energy harvesting · Power management · Smart devices · Light control · LED system

1 Introduction

Today residential lighting systems represents one of the most energy consumption item in buildings even with modern lighting solutions. This is confirmed by a recent study that claims that 25% of energy consumption in residential and commercial buildings in United States of America is spent to supply lights [1]. In recent years, the trend for academic and industrial research is to try to reduce lights energy consumption and many results has been achieved (i.e. introducing LED lights instead of fluorescent light). However, there is still a lot of room to further improve the energy efficiency, especially reducing the energy waste. Thus, a lot of effort has been invested in autonomous system with distributed intelligence. This effort results in many solution

© ICST Institute for Computer Sciences, Social Informatics and Telecommunications Engineering 2017
M. Magno et al. (Eds.): S-Cube 2016, LNICST 205, pp. 93–104, 2017.
DOI: 10.1007/978-3-319-61563-9_8

that uses sensors and wireless communication to minimize the energy waste (i.e. switching off the light when nobody is around). In the previous solutions, the main aim was try to improve the system from an energy efficiency point of view, often without caring of the users' comfort (i.e. light switched off also if the user is inside). However, users' comfort has an enormous impact on human mood and it for example in working environment an reduce the employees' productivity, creating less than optimal working conditions, especially for focus intensive, problem-solving activities. Thus, new challenges in energy efficiency need to consider that lights do not just illuminate a building, but they affect also the mood and efficiency of users and eventually improve their sense of comfort [1].

New advance in technology, i.e. Wireless Sensors Networks (WSN), can bring improvements also to lighting solution. WSN is a popular technology that cover a wide range of applications from structural health monitoring to health care, from building and home automation to agriculture monitoring, and many other [6–11]. WSN are well-know to cover a large number of application as well as they are well known to suffer of limited lifetime when they are supplied by batteries. The most power hungry subsystem of a WSN device is typically the radio transceiver. For this reason, one of the most effective way to improve the lifetime is improve the energy efficiency of the communication. As well documented in literature, it is possible reduce the power consumption of the radio with adaptive duty cycling that limit the radio activity turning periodically the radio on ("idle listening or transmitting mode") and off ("power save mode") [1]. On one hand, duty-cycling is the most popular technique to reduce the overall power consumption of the communication; on the other hand, duty cycling has to stringent drawbacks: the radio still consumes power to listen the medium periodically also when there is no message for the receiver (called idle-listening). In the period where the radio is switched off, it is not possible receive messages, so it is important evaluated the latency of the communication and evaluate the trade-off between the reactiveness of the communication and energy saved. In fact, as it is obvious, more the radio stays in power save mode, more it is the power saved, however the communication latency will be increased. To overcome these two drawbacks, asynchronous communication has been investigated and it is recently raising a lot of interest. With the recent asynchronous techniques it is possible achieve energy efficient communication never achieved before [1] and this makes asynchronous an emerging technology in energy efficient communication. This is due to the fact, that with asynchronous mechanisms both the energy wasted for the idle-listening energy waste is eliminated and the latency of communication the communication is improved. Today, many protocols are exploiting wake-up radios (WUR) to achieve pure-asynchronous communication in WSN [2]. WUR are ultra-low power radios, in the order of microwatts or even nano-watts, which are always on listening the radio channels ready to receive short messages [3]. WUR are usually working in combination with main transceiver or more rarely are used alone or integrated into the transceiver self. The ultra-low power feature of the WUR allows the main radio and rest of the node to go into a sleep mode (consuming significantly less), however, the whole system can be woken up by the WUR using interrupts only when radio messages, called often wake up beacons, are received. Although only few years ago, wake up radio was a simple receiver to trigger when "something" was detected on the medium, today they are becoming more complex system with computational capability to process messages to implement part of the medium access protocols [4]. In this paper, we present the design and implementation of a micro-power wake up radio receiver that embeds an ultra-low System on Chip (SoC) with an integrated transmitter. Due to the presence of the SoC, the WUR can efficiently process the received data (i.e. enabling the addressing), implement part of the MAC directly on the WUR and eventually retransmit information without waking up the main radio. The designed wake up radio has been implemented and evaluated in-field in terms of power consumption, sensitivity and range.

In this work, we present a solution that exploits the ultra-low power nature of WUR and the transmission with On Off Keying modulation to achieve energy efficient communication. We designed and developed a smart light system where the two main devices have the WUR as a communication subsystem. The developed system has been implemented and developed in field to evaluate the solution's functionality and lifetime when the sensor node is supplied by batteries. In fact, the main goal of the proposed solution is to allow the designed devices to be supplied with long-lifetime Li-Ion batteries (i.e. several months or even years).

The remainder of this paper is organized as follows: Sect. 2 presents recent related work in the area. Section 3 presents the smart lighting proposed approach, describing the communication protocol and the developed nodes. Section 4 describes the experimental results including a comparative evaluation with the ZigBee network and Sect. 5 concludes the paper.

2 Related Works

Controlling lighting applications has been a widely explored topic in the last decade and many solutions have been presented in literature from academic and industrial researchers. Many commercial solutions are using wired systems that control the monitored area to increase the energy efficiency of the building [22]. The main drawback of the wired solutions is the high cost of the installation and the limited capability to retrofit existing lights in buildings. For this reason, wireless technology is increasingly used as a solution for demand-side energy management, monitoring and control in buildings. Wireless sensor network is the enabling technology for building energy control, as it is much easier and flexible to install and implement than wired networks. By using the combination of advanced wireless control systems and the energy efficiency of the LED lights, it is now possible to achieve a more energy efficient building [23]. WSN have recently been successfully applied to improving energy efficiency, especially controlling lights [1, 5]. Recently, WSNs were presented in many industrial and academic works that demonstrated how they can achieve better energy efficiency in light control applications for buildings [1, 2, 5, 13–20] or also for other application scenario [4, 6, 12]. The authors in [5] present an interesting study to evaluate the trade-off between the power consumption of building and the user satisfaction when a smart lighting system is used. In [5] the proposed solution the dimming and the switch on of the light is performed with the users' location to minimize the power consumption and to maximize the total utilities. However, the presented system has a fixed luminosity level for all the people and room, without take in count that the users need different light in different activities (i.e. cooking, reading, watching TV). In other previous work, the intelligent control for the light is done measuring the room-light intensity, using light-sensitive sensors [14]. This is a similar approach of our system and it demonstrate the benefits to use it in intelligent control. The authors in [15] present another interesting work where different users' requirements and cost functions are combined to maximize the overall energy efficient of the according to the cost of the energy. In [15] the results are demonstrated only for an entertainment and media production system rather than for lights in a building. A system baes on WSN to control the lights to improve the energy efficiency of the building is presented [16]. Unfortunately the authors did not give details of the control algorithm, especially it is not possible know if the system is base on centralized or distributed intelligence. It is interesting to notice that all these previous works demonstrate the benefits to use motion sensors and lights sensors to adjust the automatically the luminosity of the light in order to save energy in buildings. This is the approach that is to the base of our solution.

The previous literature showed several example of wireless sensors networks to lighting building control. One of main challenge when WSN are designed is to their energy consumption to achieve long-lifetime. In the recent years, many solutions have been proposed to improve the energy efficiency of the communication. Between others wake up radios shows impressive results in energy efficiency. Design of wake up radio that achieve high sensitivity (-55 dBm) with low power (nanoWatts) are presented in the following works [3, 21, 24, 25]. Other recent works [26, 27] show the benefits in terms of energy efficient when WUR are used in-field with optimized protocols.

In this paper, we focus on the development of an intelligent sensor network that achieves long-life time exploiting a novel wake up radio coupled with a SoC with a transceiver to improve the energy efficiency of the communication. The main features of the proposed design is the possibility to work years with a small battery, thus, to cut installation costs improving the flexibility. Our solution is also suitable for retrofitting existing light installations. In fact, the designed nodes have the capability to be supplied only with battery and then, they can be placed anywhere in the buildings to control the lights. The system includes also an automatic light control using an infrared sensor (PIR) and a light sensor, to improve both the building energy efficiency, dimming the lights in the optimal way, and increasing user satisfaction by allowing them to set users' preferences. In-field experimental results have been demonstrated that our wireless solution achieve low lower and long lifetime. We compared this novel solution with the results of a previous work [2]. The benefits of this solution in terms of building energy efficiency have been thoroughly demonstrated.

3 Smart Lighting Proposed Approach

The proposed wireless controlling system is shown in Fig. 1. The whole system is comprised of several groups of LED panels controlled by sensor nodes that embed both a pyroelectric infrared sensor and a light sensor. Both the *sensor nodes* and *driver nodes* have a wireless interface to exchange data and commands. In particular, each LED driver, which supplies the LED panel with DC current and controls the light

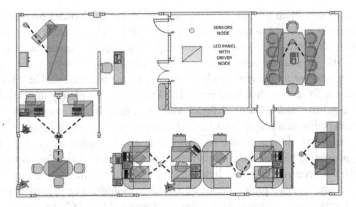

Fig. 1. Typical application scenario of smart lighting with the topologies of devices used: (i) coordinator of network connected to a host device; (ii) router to monitor the environment with light and motion sensors, (iii) end device connected to the panel to adapt the light intensity to save energy achieving the optimal level of brightness in the area.

intensity, is directly connected to a wireless *driver node*, designed in this work to provide the wireless interface. Figure 2 shows the power consumption measurement of a LED panel according to the dimming PWM signal to reduce the light intensity. As the figure shows, dimming the light can significantly reduce the power consumption of the LED panel and avoid energy waste if full light intensity is not needed. Thus, the *driver node* is directly connected to the LED driver through a pulse-width modulation (PWM) port. Using a PWM signal to encode the level of the LED brightness is the most common interface for commercial LED driver. In our solution, a microcontroller on the *driver node* sets the PWM value according to the command received by the *sensor node*; this is explained in more detail in next subsection. Due to the standard PWM, control port it is possible to retrofit many existing installations. On the other hand, each *sensor node* processes its sensor data on-board to evaluate the optimal intensity level according with the users' preferences. The main goal of the sensor node

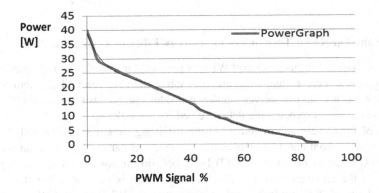

Fig. 2. Power consumption measurement of the PWM control signal to adapt the light intensity [2].

algorithm is to minimize the energy consumption of the LED panel by automatically adapting the light intensity to match the user preferences. The wireless interface allows the reduction of the installation costs and the deployment of the sensors node in the best position in the monitored area. This network configuration uses only two node topologies in various applications, which allows a scalable, extendable, and easy to deploy solution. In fact, each sub-group of LED panels is completely independent, and needs only a *sensor node* to control them. More precisely, each *sensor node* is able to control an adaptable number of associated *driver nodes* and LED panels. All the LED panels of the same subgroup can be controlled same conditions or with different luminosity according to the policy implemented on the *sensor node*. Due to this feature, it is possible to control different lights and areas with optimal intensity of lights according to the users' preferences. The entire systems can be managed by a higher-level super node that acts as a gateway connected to a PC or to another device (laptop, wall embedded devices, Wireless Lan/Bluetooth devices, and so on), to enable human interaction.

As in this work the primary goal is to build a system with devices that can achieve the best wireless communication efficiency to achieve long life time also when supplied by batteries, the two nodes topologies use an ultra-low power wake up radio technology. In next subsection, an overview of this technology and how the designed nodes exploit it to exchange data will be explained.

In the proposed smart lighting system the most important elements are:

- The LED panel with a dimmable commercial driver that is able to be controlled trough a PWM signal.
- The wake up radio technology used as energy efficiency communication based on the PIR ultra low power microcontroller with transmission capability.
- Light and PIR sensors, used by the wireless sensor node to control the brightness and the movement in the area and decide the right dimming level.
- The wireless driver node that is connected with the commercial LED driver to set the dimming level of each LED panel.

In the following subsection the two nodes' architectures and the efficient communication are presented.

3.1   Wake Up Radio Technology for Energy Efficient Communication

The block diagram of the developed WUR is presented in Fig. 4. The node incorporate a wake up radio received and a transmission sub-system built around a system on chip (SoC) that has a radio transceiver integrated inside. The SoC is the main transmission block and it can also process the data received by the wake up radio. The whole node consists of three main sub-systems: (1) the receiving subsystem is basically a radio frequency (RF) front-end that demodulate the received data and generate an interrupt for the SoC when a data is received. (2) The processing subsystem (all around the SoC) that parses the received data. (3) The last sub-system is the transmitter that is also integrated into the SoC but it shares the antenna with the WUR trough a RF switch. The SoC is the core of the node allowing data processing directly on the WUR and makes

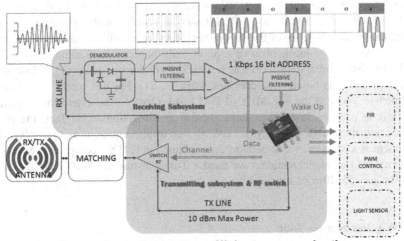

WURX+ Transmistter for energy efficient communication

Fig. 3. Block diagram of the developed wake up radio with addressing and retransmission capability used as main block for both the wireless *sensor node* and the LED panel *driver node*

the decision and further actions. In fact, according to the protocol implemented it is possible to send: commands, wake up beacons, or addresses to only wake up the Main Node. With the computational capabilities of the microcontroller of the SoC is possible for a communication protocol to optimize the energy consumption (i.e. performing semantic addressing [21] to reduce the number of false positive wake ups (Fig. 3).

To achieve low power consumption the SoC has to consume very low power in sleep and active mode. For this reason, the Microchip PIC16LF1824T39 has been selected for the hardware implementation. This SoC has very low power consumption in low power mode of only 350 nW@1.8 V and in running mode achieve 80 µW at 1 MHz. The SoC integrates an 868 MHz transmitter so it is not needed to use other external chips and it is possible keep the power low. The power consumption in transmission (either using OOK or FSK modulation) is also very low compared with

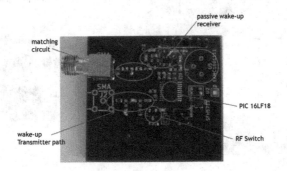

Fig. 4. Prototype of the wake up radio used for evaluations.

similar transmitter on the market. We measured a power consumption of only 20 mW@1.8 V when a message of 16 bit was transmitted with an output power of 0 dBm. Due to the presence of the transmitter, MAC protocols can leverage this novel WUR to acknowledge mechanism or support multi-hop communication.

The receiving subsystem works as a demodulator for on-off-keying (OOK) communication and it is based on a previous work [3, 21]. For this work, we tuned the implemented WUR at the 868 MHz of ISM band. One of most interesting feature of the WUR is its very low power consumption in always-mode. In fact, the power consumption measured was only 1.3 µW in our implementation, as the only active component is a low power comparator. As explained in [21] the comparator affects the sensitivity for our implementation we used a Texas Instruments LPV7215 that guarantees up to −55 dBm of sensitivity.

3.2   Wireless Sensor Node

The *wireless sensor node* has as its core the PIC microcontroller and the wake up radio presented in the previous subsystem. The main role of the sensor node is to take decisions on the light intensity using its sensor data, and to send the intensity level to each wireless driver under its control. The block diagram of the node architecture is presented in Fig. 5. The architecture includes an infrared sensor (PIR) and a light sensor which are directly interfaced with the PIC microcontroller. A Panasonic EW-AMN34111J has been selected to guarantee fast and accurate interrupt for any moving object in the range of 10 m. When a movement is detected the motion sensors generate an interrupt that is connected with a general purpose pin of the PIC microcontroller. On the other hand, the light sensor SSFH 5711 from Osram is connected to an Analog input of the PIC processor to detect the intensity of the light in the monitored area. The PIC evaluated both the

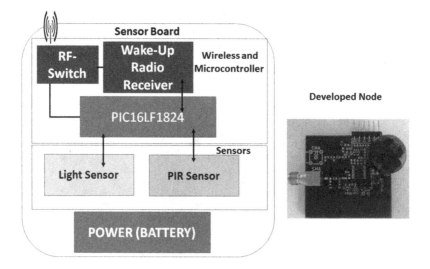

Fig. 5. Block diagram and developed wireless sensor node

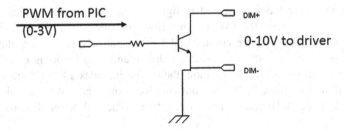

Fig. 6. Control circuits to convert PWM from PIC to 0–10 V for commercial drivers.

movement and the light intensity to decide the dimming level of its associated devices. If the dimming level is different from the previous one, the wireless node sends the new value via the integrated radio the OOK generated message to the *wireless driver nodes*.

3.3   Wireless Driver Node

The main goal of *wireless sensor node* is to provide an ultra-low power always-on wireless interface to receive the dimming level, and to control by PWM the driver LED when commands are received. The architecture of the wireless driver node is presented in Fig. 7. The *wireless sensor node* is designed to allow the power to be supplied by either commercial LED drivers or a battery. For this reason the power stage is able to cover a wide range of input voltage from 3 V to 42 V using an ultra-low power DC-DC converter which exploits the integrated circuit TLV70433 from Texas Instruments. Each designed *wireless node* can retrofit existing commercial LED drivers that are controlled by a PWM signal or be embedded inside the LED driver-self. Thus, each *wireless node* is associated with each LED panel and connected through the PWM port and eventually the power supply.

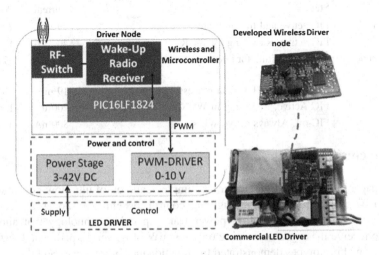

Fig. 7. Block diagram and developed control node.

The PWM-Driver block presented in figure is one of the most critical designed subsystems, as it converts the PWM signal from the microcontroller (1.8–3 V) to a 0–10 V signal needed to drive commercial LED panel drivers. In fact, the 0–10 V control is the standard control for such as driver and its support is mandatory for flexibility and retrofitting. In our solution, the design includes a P-MOS transistor that is connected in Common Collector configuration using the PWM signal from the microcontroller and 0–10 control input from the commercial driver (Fig. 6).

4   Experimental Results

The system has been designed, implemented and deployed in a real office testbed to evaluate the benefits in terms of energy saving. Both device topologies, *Wireless Sensor node and Wireless driver node,* were tested in terms of power consumption.

The current consumption of both designed and developed nodes in different states has been measured and are presented in Table 1. The supply voltage during the measurements was 3.7 V, typical for a Li-Ion battery, so the power consumption is taking into account the DC-DC conversion losses. In the experimental setup, we clocked the PIC microcontroller with 1 MHz, each node was in one of the three configurations presented in the following table. The table shows the very low quiescent current of only 4 µW and 0.5 mW of the sensor node and driver node respectively. The quiescent current also includes the power for the wake up radio, thus, both nodes can continuously listen the medium in this mode. As expected, the quiescent current of the sensor node is higher as this includes also the PIR sensor quiescent current and the circuits to generate an interrupt when movement is detected. Finally, the PIC in transmission has a much higher power consumption due to the activation of the radio to transmit the commands or other data.

Table 1. Nodes' current and power characteristics

Device/Mode	Consumption		
	State	Current	Power
Sensor node	PIC active and transmitting	19 mA	70 mW
	PIC active, Receiving by WUR	400 µA	1.4 mW
Driver node	PIC off, Waiting for interrupts from PIR or Wake-up radio	101 µA	375 µW
	PIC on, Radio TX, data processing	19 mA	70 mW
	PIC Active, Receiving in WUR	200 uA	1 mW
	PIC-off, Always active WUR	800 nA	4 uW

5   Conclusions

In this paper, we presented the design and implementation of ultra-low power sensors node to be employed in a smart lighting control system. The nodes are designed exploiting an ultra-low state-of-art power wake up radio technology that allow the nodes to receive messages consuming only few uW of power. Experimental results on the developed prototypes demonstrated the functionality of the nodes and the ultra-low power achieved. With this power consumption it is possible to achieve long lasting devices that can live continuously several years with small size batteries.

Acknowledge. This work was supported by "Transient Computing Systems", a SNF project (200021_157048), by SCOPES SNF project (IZ74Z0_160481).

References

1. Caicedo, D., Pandharipande, A.: Distributed illumination control with local sensing and actuation in networked lighting systems. IEEE Sensors J. **13**(3), 1092–1104 (2013)
2. Magno, M., Polonelli, T., Benini, L., Popovici, E.: A low cost, highly scalable wireless sensor network solution to achieve smart LED light control for green buildings. IEEE Sensors J. **15**(5), 2963–2973 (2015)
3. Magno, M., Jelicic, V., Srbinovski, B., Bilas, V., Popovici, E., Benini, L.: Design, implementation, and performance evaluation of a flexible low-latency nanowatt wake-up radio receiver. IEEE Trans. Ind. Inform. **12**(2), 633–644 (2016)
4. Ait Aoudia, F., Magno, M., Gautier, M., Berder, O., Benini, L.: Analytical and experimental evaluation of wake-up receivers based protocols. In: IEEE Global Communications Conference (GLOBECOM), December 2016
5. Singhvi, V., Krause, A., Guestrin, C., Garrett, J.H., Matthews, H.S.: Intelligent light control using sensor networks. In: Proceedings of ACM International Conference Embedded Networked Sensor Systems, SenSys 2005, San Diego, CA, USA, pp. 218–229, 2–4 November 2005
6. Kerhet, A., Leonardi, F., Boni, A., Lombardo, P., Magno, M., Benini, L.: Distributed video surveillance using hardware-friendly sparse large margin classifiers. In: IEEE Conference on Advanced Video and Signal Based Surveillance, AVSS 2007, pp. 87–92, 5–7 September 2007
7. Niklaus, P., et al.: StoneNode: a low-power sensor device for induced rockfall experiments. In: 2017 IEEE Sensors Applications Symposium (SAS). IEEE (2017)
8. Murphy, F.E., et al.: Development of an heterogeneous wireless sensor network for instrumentation and analysis of beehives. In: 2015 IEEE International Instrumentation and Measurement Technology Conference (I2MTC). IEEE (2015)
9. Jeličić, V., et al.: An energy efficient multimodal wireless video sensor network with eZ430–RF2500 modules. In: 2010 5th International Conference on Pervasive Computing and Applications (ICPCA). IEEE (2010)
10. Conti, F., et al.: Accelerated visual context classification on a low-power smartwatch. IEEE Trans. Hum. Mach. Syst. **47**(1), 19–30 (2017)
11. Magno, M., Spagnol, C., Benini, L., Popovici, E.: A low power wireless node for contact and contactless heart monitoring. Microelectron. J. **45**(12), 1656–1664 (2014)
12. Jeličić, V., Magno, M., Paci, G., Brunelli, D., Benini, L.: Design, characterization and management of a wireless sensor network for smart gas monitoring. In: 2011 4th IEEE International Workshop on Advances in Sensors and Interfaces (IWASI), pp. 115–120. IEEE, June 2011
13. Magno, M., et al.: Adaptive power control for solar harvesting multimodal wireless smart camera. In: Third ACM/IEEE International Conference on Distributed Smart Cameras, ICDSC 2009. IEEE (2009)

14. Wen, Y.J., Granderson, J., Agogino, A.M.: Towards embedded wireless-networked intelligent daylighting systems for commercial buildings. In: Proceedings of the IEEE International Conference on Sensor Networks, Ubiquitous, and Trustworthy Computing, SUTC 2006, Taichung, Taiwan, 5–7 June 2006

15. Park, H., Srivastava, M.B., Burke, J.: Design and implementation of a wireless sensor network for intelligent light control. In: Proceedings of the 6th International Symposium on Information Processing in Sensor Networks, IPSN 2007, Cambridge, MA, USA, 25–27 April 2007

16. Hong, S.H., Kim, S.H., Kim, J.H., Kim, Y.G., Kim, G.M., Song, W.S.: Integrated BACnet-ZigBee communication for building energy management system. In: 39th Annual Conference of the IEEE on Industrial Electronics Society, IECON 2013, pp. 5723–5728, 10–13 November 2013

17. Baronti, P., Pillai, P., Chook, V.W., Chessa, S., Gotta, A., Hu, Y.F.: Wireless sensor networks: a survey on the state of the art and the 802.15.4 and ZigBee standards. Comput. Commun. 30(7), 1655–1695 (2007)

18. Popovici, E., Magno, M., Marinkovic, S.: Power management techniques for wireless sensor networks: a review. In: 2013 5th IEEE International Workshop on Advances in Sensors and Interfaces (IWASI), pp. 194–198, 13–14 June 2013

19. Jelicic, V., Magno, M., Brunelli, D., Bilas, V., Benini, L.: Benefits of wake-up radio in energy-efficient multimodal surveillance wireless sensor network. IEEE Sensors J. 14(9), 3210–3220 (2014)

20. Le, T.N., et al.: Ultra low power asynchronous MAC protocol using wake-up radio for energy neutral WSN. In: Proceedings of the 1st International Workshop on Energy Neutral Sensing Systems. ACM (2013)

21. Magno, M., Benini, L.: An ultra low power high sensitivity wake-up radio receiver with addressing capability. In: 2014 IEEE 10th International Conference on Wireless and Mobile Computing, Networking and Communications (WiMob), pp. 92–99, 8–10 October 2014

22. Lu, J.K., Birru, D., Whitehouse, K.: Using simple light sensors to achieve smart daylight harvesting. In: Proceedings of 2nd ACM Workshop Embedded Sensing Syst. Energy-Efficiency Building, Switzerland (2010)

23. Erol-Kantarci, M., Mouftah, H.T.: Wireless sensor networks for cost-efficient residential energy management in the smart grid. IEEE Trans. Smart Grid 2(2), 314–325 (2011)

24. Del Prete, M., et al.: Optimum excitations for a dual-band microwatt wake-up radio. IEEE Trans. Microwave Theory Tech. 64(12), 4731–4739 (2016)

25. Polonelli, T., Le Huy, T., Lizzi, L., Ferrero, F., Magno, M.: A wake-up receiver with ad-hoc antenna co-design for wearable applications. In: 2016 IEEE Sensors Applications Symposium (SAS), Catania, pp. 1–6 (2016)

26. Ait Aoudia, F., Gautier, M., Magno, M., Berder, O., Benini, L.: A generic framework for modeling MAC protocols in wireless sensor networks. IEEE/ACM Trans. Netw. 25(3), 1489–1500 (2017)

27. Magno, M., et al.: WULoRa: an energy efficient IoT end-node for energy harvesting and heterogeneous communication. In: IEEE/ACM Design, Automation and Test in Europe Conference and Exhibition (DATE) (2017)

Monitoring Approach of Cyber-Physical Systems by Quality Measures

Pedro Merino Laso[1(✉)], David Brosset[1,2], and John Puentes[1,3]

[1] Chair of Naval Cyber Defense, École navale - CC 600, 29240 Brest Cedex 9, France
{pedro.merino,david.brosset}@ecole-navale.fr
[2] Naval Academy Research Institute, École navale - CC 600,
29240 Brest Cedex 9, France
[3] Département ITI - Institut Mines-Telecom, Telecom Bretagne Lab-STICC UMR
CNRS 6285 Équipe DECIDE, CS 83818, 29238 Brest, France
john.puentes@telecom-bretagne.eu

Abstract. Modern cities, industrial plants, cars, trucks, and vessels, among others, make extensive use of cyber-physical systems and sensors. These systems are very critical and contribute to assist decision making. Large data streams are thus produced and analyzed to extract information that allows building knowledge through a set of principles called wisdom. However, because of multiple imperfections, as well as intrinsic, contextual, and extrinsic conditions that alter data, the quality of the generated streams must be evaluated, to determine how relevant they are for decision support. This paper presents a methodology to monitor cyber-physical systems by quality estimation, which defines suitable evaluation characteristics for pertinent analysis. Quality assessment is defined for data imperfections, information dimensions, knowledge factors, and wisdom aspects. The case study of a cyber-physical network of a liquid container training platform is presented in detail, to show how the approach can be applied. Obtained measures are multidimensional, heterogeneous, and variable.

Keywords: Monitoring · Sensor data processing · Multi-source sensor network · Cyber-physical system · Data quality · Information quality

1 Introduction

Cyber-physical systems have become necessary in many realms like transport, manufacturing, home, and cities automation. These systems are composed of sub-systems, which process information and support decision making based on different data sources as sensors, control, and communication systems. Increasingly, multiple systems assist human operators to accomplish efficiently and safely their tasks. To this end, critical monitoring data and information are continuously generated. These fundamental systems are cyber-physical as they interact with the environment making sensor measurements and executing responses

Funded and supported by École navale, Télécom Bretagne, Thales and DCNS.

© ICST Institute for Computer Sciences, Social Informatics and Telecommunications Engineering 2017
M. Magno et al. (Eds.): S-Cube 2016, LNICST 205, pp. 105–117, 2017.
DOI: 10.1007/978-3-319-61563-9_9

using actuators. Usually, in order to perform external control and monitoring, these systems are also connected to networked stations.

Infrastructure governance is as a consequence completely based on decision-aided or automatic responses, defined by the obtained information, according to a so-called wisdom. Moreover, cyber-physical systems are being developed to improve their performance, conceive new functionalities, or simplify their use. Given the fact that a growing number of these systems are currently deployed, voluminous data streams are permanently produced.

An emerging problem created by such enlarged scale and diversity of systems is the complexity to analyze generated data, taking into account specific operational contexts. Numerous factors can alter collected data and extracted information changing the expected impact on decision support, from innocuous to catastrophic. Therefore, methodologies and models of quality estimation emerge as a possibility to determine, if collected data and extracted information are relevant for decision support.

Our work proposes to address this issue, defining a quality evaluation methodology, identifying which analysis elements are the most pertinent to provide suitable system's streams quality characterization. This evaluation is intended to support decision makers responsible for the corresponding cyber-physical systems. Therefore, if the quality of data, information, knowledge, and wisdom are evaluated with respect to a given operational objective, an adapted response is likely to be given. On the other hand, quality evaluation has several implications. For example, it can be used to discover potential evidence of suspicious anomalies to be further examined by cyber-security tools. It can also permit to identify malfunctions in information systems, or sources that after a qualification, can be trusted and integrated for decision aid, in spite of such imperfections. To provide suitable analyses, quality evaluation must be carried out according to the same functional constraints of the examined system.

Data and information quality have been widely studied in other domains like Management Information Systems (MIS), Web Information Systems (WIS), and Information Fusion Systems (IFS) [11]. However, none of the developed methods can be directly and fully applied to cyber-physical systems. The main reason is that those approaches have been developed for specific data and a particular application. Moreover, the definition of data and information quality assessment is not obvious in cyber-physical streams, given the significant differences in measurement's times and test points. Few other initiatives have conceived automatic quality evaluation methods applied to particular cyber-physical systems, like sensors data for personal health records [9] and wireless sensor networks [4], adapted to very specific user needs.

The proposed contribution relies on three principles. First, quality evaluation of data, information, knowledge, and wisdom are dynamic and derived from intrinsic, contextual, and extrinsic dimensions related to each examined subsystem. Second, quality evaluation is independent of the associated functional task carried out by the sub-system components. Finally, some of the quality evaluation concepts studied by the MIS, WIS, and IFS methods are adapted to cyber-physical systems. The rest of the paper is organized as follows. A definition of the proposed methodology is presented in Sect. 2. To illustrate how the proposed method could be applied, the case of a liquid tank prototype is studied in Sect. 3. Discussion and conclusions are presented in Sect. 4.

2 Quality of Sensor Streams

This section defines the main components of the proposed quality evaluation method. The key entities are introduced in Sect. 2.1, explaining the difference between data, information, knowledge, and wisdom quality evaluation. Subsections 2.2, 2.3, 2.4 and 2.5 are dedicated to describe separately each quality evaluation approach. In Sect. 2.6, a global quality measurement method is defined integrating the previously defined components.

2.1 Data, Information, Knowledge, and Wisdom

To avoid a well known general confusion regarding the concepts of data, information, and knowledge [14], we consider essential representation notions of the well known DIKW - Data, Information, Knowledge, and Wisdom - pyramid. Its definition can be summarized as know-nothing, know-what, know-how, and know-why, respectively [13].

Accordingly, in cyber-physical systems: data are the streams of bits with no comprehensible sense (know-nothing), including single values, multidimensional signals, and text; information is data with a semantic sense in a context (know-what); knowledge is how this information can be used in a particular case depending on wisdom (know-how); and wisdom is the set of principles, usually created by progressive learning from experiences to explain how information can be transformed into knowledge (know-why). Figure 1 illustrates how these entities interact in the context of the proposed quality evaluation methodology.

Taking into account contextual factors, data and information definitions can be adapted to cyber-physical systems applying:

$$Information = Data + Context_{sub\text{-}system} \qquad (1)$$

where the context is formally defined by the corresponding sub-system and system specifications, to be represented as follows:

$$Context_{sub\text{-}system} = Sub\text{-}system_{specs} + System_{specs} \qquad (2)$$

The context is defined by the sub-system specifications available in one or several data-sheets and the characteristics of the whole system. Besides, the environment is considered as a variable of the system specifications, *i.e.* where and how it is installed, besides which are its attributes (fixed or variable).

Knowledge is the result of a principle - called wisdom - applied to information. This principle can be for example a mathematical expression, a physical law, or a predefined rule. When knowledge is not fully compatible with the studied context, it requires to be adapted to preserve coherence. In general, multiple information streams inputs are necessary to create knowledge, represented by:

$$Knowledge = Wisdom(Information) \qquad (3)$$

The proposed method defines a quality evaluation for each one of the described entities. These quality evaluations are presented in the next sections.

2.2 Data Quality

Studies on data quality have been carried out focusing on various application domains. Multiple categories of dimensions identified by data consumers were used in Total Data Quality Management (TDQM) to define what is data quality [12]. The Cost-effect Of Low Data Quality (COLDQ) examined a data quality approach according to some enterprises' needs [6]. Several quality metrics were proposed by the Data Quality Assessment (DQA) [8]. Data Quality in Cooperative Information Systems (DaQuinCIS) was introduced to assist collaborative data quality evaluation [10]. In financial information systems, the Quality Assessment on Financial Data (QAFD) studied how to improve the quality of relevant data [2]. Also, for other types of organizations and businesses, the Comprehensive methodology for Data Quality management (CDQ) searched to enhance efficiency and effectiveness by increasing data quality [1].

On the other hand, from an information processing point of view, data quality can be measured by a characterization of key imperfections as follows [7]:

- **Error** (i_{err}): Data are erroneous when values are different from the true data.
- **Incomplete** (i_{inc}): Data are not totally supplied.
- **Imprecision** (i_{imp}): Data denote a set of possible values and the real value is one of the elements of this set.
- **Uncertainty** (i_{unc}): Data cannot be stated with absolute confidence.
- **Unavailable** (i_{una}): The system cannot obtain a value because of its limitations or due to missing measurements.

Erroneous data affect the integrity of the system and it should be discarded when detected. As a result, all information obtained from wrong data is also erroneous and its quality evaluation has no sense. Data affected by the other four imperfections preserve its integrity and can still supply valid information.

In some cases, observations should complete identified imperfections to ameliorate quality estimation. For example, data are frequently supplied with correction codes. Corrected data are not imperfect, although corrections may have an impact on quality, depending on the context. Similarly, unavailable data can also be detected when needed environment properties are provided (a condition to point out whenever possible).

2.3 Information Quality

Related specialized studies on information quality are less diverse than those on data quality. For example: the information quality evaluation proposed by the Total Information Quality Management (TIQM) searched to improve business data warehousing and raise benefits [3]; and a methodology for Information Quality Assessment (AIMQ) evaluated and benchmarked information quality [5]. It is nevertheless important to note that studies cited in the previous section, also handle partially the corresponding questions about information quality. Yet, none of them is directly applicable to cyber-physical systems in general.

To specify our information quality evaluation approach, two considerations are underlined. Instead of placing humans as just data consumers and despite the existence of a wide range of automatic processes, cyber-physical networks relate to humans as decision-makers. Besides, given that any information can be part of different tasks, quality evaluation should be task-independent. For this reason, several parameters are necessary to define tasks' quality requirements.

In the absence of a global consensus on basic methodological elements to measure information quality, we concentrate on the most known approaches to define an adapted method for cyber-physical systems. The proposed method consists of customized components of the previously cited TDQM, COLDQ, DQA, DaQuinCIS, QAFD, CDQ, TIQM, and AIMQ approaches. Note that in these works quality dimensions were structured in four groups: intrinsic, contextual, representational, and accessibility. In our case however, the basic quality view relates to sub-systems, which are rarely affected by the representational characteristics. As a consequence, only three groups of quality dimensions are applied. Intrinsic dimensions are defined when sensors are examined separately, without connections. Contextual dimensions are assessed when it is known where the sub-system is installed and what it is measuring. Extrinsic dimensions appear when the sub-system connections are identified.

We define therefore three groups of information quality dimensions, convenient for cyber-physical sub-systems, to manage the lack of specifically designed dimensions in the literature. Namely, the **Intrinsic** category is the group of quality dimensions defined for an isolated sub-system (Table 1). The **Contextual** category includes the quality dimensions that study a sub-system as part of a full system (Table 2). The **Extrinsic** category contains the dimensions that permit to evaluate streams quality considering interconnected sub-systems (Table 3).

2.4 Knowledge Quality

The subjects of knowledge and wisdom quality for networked cyber-physical systems have not been treated in the literature. We propose therefore the corresponding definitions, factors, and aspects, required in the framework of our study. Knowledge is produced by the direct application of wisdom to information. This implies that the quality of knowledge is considerably influenced by both, information quality and wisdom quality. Moreover, in the case of cyber-physical systems some particular factors should also be taken into account:

Table 1. Intrinsic information quality dimensions in cyber-physical systems

ID	Name	Description
id_{sp}	Source precision	The extent to which every information under unchanged conditions show the same results due to the source acquisition
id_{acc}	Accuracy	The extent to which extracted information is close to the true information
id_{obj}	Objectivity	The extent to which information is unbiased, unprejudiced, and impartial
id_{rep}	Reputation	The extent to which information is highly regarded in terms of its source or content
id_{obs}	Obsolescence	The extent to which information is valid through time
id_{fre}	Freshness	The extent to which information is new
id_{tru}	Trust	The extent to which information is trustworthy
id_{acq}	Acquisition cost	The cost to acquire the information
id_{rea}	Readable	The extent to which data used to obtain information are noiseless and intelligible
id_{res}	Resolution	The extent to which data used to obtain information are distanced in sampling
id_{itg}	Integrity	The extent to which information is complete and the provider sub-system is fully available
id_{cns}	Consistency	The extent to which information is presented in the same format
id_{uni}	Uniqueness	The extent to which information is not repeated

Table 2. Contextual information quality dimensions in cyber-physical systems

ID	Name	Description
cd_{rp}	Real precision	The extent to which every information under unchanged conditions shows the same results due to the use of the sub-system
cd_{cla}	Clarity	The extent to which information is comprehensible through other information
cd_{val}	Value-added	The extent to which information is beneficial and provides advantages from its use
cd_{tim}	Timeliness	The extent to which information is expected by the system
cd_{cmt}	Completeness	The extent to which information is know in a complete context
cd_{cnc}	Concision	The extent to which information is compactly represented
cd_{vol}	Volume	The extent to which the volume of information is appropriate for the task at hand
cd_{bel}	Believability	The extent to which information is regarded as true and credible

Table 3. Extrinsic information quality dimensions in cyber-physical systems

ID	Name	Description
ed_{acc}	Accessibility	The extent to which information is available, easily, and quickly retrievable
ed_{sec}	Security	The extent to which access to information is restricted appropriately to maintain its security
ed_{eu}	Ease of utilization	The extent to which information is easy to use and apply to different tasks
ed_{man}	Manipulation	The extent to which an information link is easy to manipulate
ed_{int}	Interpretability	The extent to which information is in appropriate languages, symbols, and units, and the definitions are clear
ed_{cmp}	Compatibility	The extent to which information is comprehensible for different sub-systems
ed_{for}	Format	The extent to which information respects a specific format
ed_{und}	Understandability	The extent to which information is easily comprehended
cd_{red}	Redundancy	The extent to which other sub-systems provide the same information
ed_{coh}	Coherence	The extent to which information is logical with respect to other information

- **Completeness** (f_{com}): The extent to which information sources needed by wisdom are available.
- **Error cost** (f_{err}): The potential cost produced by erroneous knowledge.
- **Relevancy** (f_{rel}): The extent to which knowledge is applicable and helpful for the task at hand.

2.5   Wisdom Quality

Depending on the type of wisdom - mathematical principle, physical law or predefined rule (based on experience) - as well as the related source, attributes, and pertinence, among others, the confidence on wisdom changes. Hence, to evaluate wisdom quality six aspects should be examined:

- **Experience** (a_{exp}): The extent to which wisdom is verified through a defined knowledge put in practice.
- **Confidence** (a_{con}): The extent to which wisdom is highly regarded in terms of its source or content.
- **Accessibility** (a_{acc}): The extent to which wisdom is available, easily retrievable, and modifiable.

- **Interpretability** (a_{int}): The extent to which wisdom is clearly defined in appropriate languages, symbols, and units.
- **Security** (a_{sec}): The extent to which access to wisdom is restricted appropriately to maintain its security.
- **Completeness** (a_{com}): The extent to which wisdom takes into account the variables that influence it.

2.6 Quality Assessment

The proposed quality evaluation methodology (Fig. 1) regulates the transformation of data streams into information and knowledge, depending on the measured quality of each entity. Quality evaluations of DIKW are individual, in order to handle appropriately a large scope of qualification conditions. For instance, a data-set containing several different information elements, which depending on the availability of multiple wisdom principles, can potentially generate various knowledge streams. Therefore, the separate quality evaluation of each particular DIKW sequence contains four unique vectors, specifically: **DQV** (Data Quality Vector), **IQV** (Information Quality Vector), **KQV** (Knowledge Quality Vector), and **WQV** (Wisdom Quality Vector), encompassing previously defined properties related to imperfections, dimensions, factors, and aspects, respectively. Since the evaluation of these properties is rarely exhaustive because of variable unavailability of one or several elements, the proposed method intends to define a complete quality evaluation framework that can be applied according to changing practical conditions.

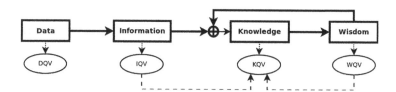

Fig. 1. Entities interactions in the proposed evaluation method.

Depending on the evaluated sub-system, units of quality vectors are likely to vary, depending on the reference system of measurement and the declared attributes' types (Boolean, string, char, word from a dictionary, integer, real, etc.). This fact makes necessary to represent separately the imperfections, dimensions, factors, and aspects, in the evaluation vectors. For instance, to evaluate the quality of a sub-system on which a data stream with K data imperfections (I_i), produces information requiring to examine L dimensions (D_i), leads to the definition of the following **DQV** and **IQV** vectors:

$$\mathbf{DQV} \in \{I_1...I_K\} \tag{4}$$

$$\mathbf{IQV} \in \{D_1...D_L\} \tag{5}$$

By definition, knowledge quality is related to information quality (**IQV**) and wisdom quality (**WQV**). Hence, for a knowledge stream created with M information streams and assessed with N factors (F_i) and **KQV** is defined as:

$$\mathbf{KQV} \in \{IQV_1...IQV_M, WQV, F_1...F_N\} \tag{6}$$

Similarly, wisdom quality formed by P aspects (A_i) defines the following **WQV** vector:

$$\mathbf{WQV} \in \{A_1...A_P\} \tag{7}$$

Additionally, specific constraints identified on the system components should be applied to evaluate quality. These constraints include limitations of the analyzed sub-system, restrictions inherited from other connected sub-systems, or derived from the main system. Whenever different constraints are identified for a given dimension characteristic, quality evaluation is carried out assuming that the sub-system should respect the most restrictive ones (usually related to the need for responses in real time and computational limitations).

3   Simple Case Study

To test the proposed quality evaluation approach we use a cyber-physical platform representing a liquid container subsystem. Such platform commonly used for training on networked control infrastructure, can be found at different scales in cities, homes, industrial plants, or vehicles, to contain liquids like water or fuel. It is composed by two tanks (cisterns): a main tank (Cistern B) and a secondary tank (Cistern A). While the secondary tank fills the main tank using Pump 2, the main tank (smaller than the secondary) provides the liquid to the system. Consumption is simulated by a valve placed at the bottom. To simulate when the main tank is filled, the secondary tank can transfer the liquid contained in the recovery tank by means of Pump 1.

This platform is controlled by a Schneider programmable logic controller (PLC), accessible from a touch screen and through Modbus[1] network commands. Two types of sensors generate data: four discrete sensors (in Cistern A) and one ultrasonic sensor (in Cistern B). Discrete sensors are switches activated when the liquid makes them float. The level of liquid present on the main tank is measured by the ultrasonic sounder. All these components are connected in a local network, which can be linked to remotely monitor and control the whole system. The network schema is shown in Fig. 2, including transmitted information and used protocol for the main connections.

Analysis of system performance is done at a control and monitoring machine connected to the platform network. The system receives **data**, a binary sequence used by communication protocols that is not directly comprehensible.

---

[1] Modbus is an open OSI level 7 protocol developed by Scheinder Electric in 1979 and largely used in SCADA (Supervisory Control and Data Acquisition) systems (http://modbus.org/docs/PI_MBUS_300.pdf).

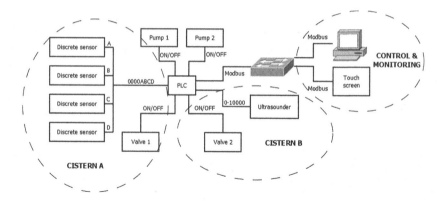

Fig. 2. Training platform network.

This sequence initializes the quality evaluation process. **Information** is defined when a protocol decodes the data and the context gives a meaning to values, making use of the sensors' data specifications and tank size. The resulting information is the measured level of liquid, represented by a comprehensible value (*e.g.* 30 L of liquid). To obtain this information a measure of distance obtained by the ultrasonic sensor is transformed to a measure of volume, according to the tank dimensions. Furthermore, knowing the liquid consumption of the system, its autonomy can also be determined defining related **knowledge** (*e.g.* 20 min). This principle is associated to **wisdom**, specifically the consumption per hour, *i.e.* a vehicle fuel consumption as a function of speed, distance, or type of engine. Once wisdom is defined (*e.g.* 1.5 L/min), knowledge about the autonomy of the system can be calculated. Wisdom will be updated and improved depending on experience, or modified if it does not agree with expected values.

In Table 4, an example of quality evaluation on four contexts, applying the proposed model, is shown. Only the most representative quality elements are indicated to evaluate DQV and IQV. Data quality measures include: Erroneous data marked as true when the CRC (code of cyclic redundancy) provided by the stream cannot be verified; incompleteness detects lost messages using the ID sequence and indicates how many packages are lost. At the information quality level measures take into account: Source precision calculated with the parameters indicated on the data-sheet of the sensor; integrity as the percentage of the sub-system that works properly; uniqueness as a Boolean that indicates if the information is unique for an instant of time; real precision identified as the noise filtered from the signal; timeliness as the difference between the expected and the real time of arrival of the information; format as a Boolean that evaluates if the format is valid; and coherence as the difference between a theoretical behavior of the system calculated knowing the state of pumps and the observed one.

Table 4. Quality evaluation for ultra-sounder

Anomaly	DQV $\{i_{err}, i_{inc}\}$	IQV		
		Intrinsic $\{id_{sp}, id_{itg}, id_{uni}\}$	Contextual $\{cd_{rp}, cd_{tim}\}$	Extrinsic $\{ed_{for}, ed_{coh}\}$
Normal	{false, 0}	{4, 100, true}	{5, 2}	{true, 2}
Foreign objects	{false, 0}	{3, 100, true}	{35, 1}	{true, 2}
DoS attack	{false, 11}	{3, 100, true}	{3, 120}	{true, 5}
Leak	{false, 0}	{1, 100, true}	{15, 0}	{true, 1/35}

An example of a normal behavior is described in the first row: $DQV = \{i_{err} = \text{false}, i_{inc} = 0 \text{ messages}\}$; $IQV = \{\text{intrinsic } \{id_{sp} = 4 \text{ u.}, id_{itg} = 100\%, id_{uni} = \text{true}\}$, contextual $\{cd_{rp} = 5 \text{ u.}, cd_{tim} = 2 \text{ ms}\}$, extrinsic $\{ed_{for} = \text{true}, ed_{coh} = 2 \text{ u.}\}\}$, where '$u.$' are the units used by the system, that is, 1 of the 10000 uniformed steps of a full tank. Examples of three different anomalies that deteriorate some dimensions of quality are analyzed in the next three rows. When foreign objects are floating on the liquid, measure precision worsens significantly, e.g. contextual $IQV = \{cd_{rp} = 35 \text{ u.}\}$. A DoS (Denial-of-Service) network attack produces the lost of network packages, affecting data incompleteness and increasing information timeliness, e.g. $DQV = \{i_{inc} = 11 \text{ messages}\}$ and $IQV = \{cd_{tim} = 120 \text{ ms}\}$. Finally, when a leak is produced the measure of coherence decreases, e.g. $IQV = \{cd_{coh} = 1/35 \text{ u.}^{-1}\}$.

Knowledge quality can be defined making use of - $\{f_{err}, f_{rel}\}$ - as: $KQV = \{2, 2\}$, $KQV = \{4, 4\}$, $KQV = \{3, 3\}$, and $KQV = \{3, 3\}$, for the indicated cases respectively, adding relevant factors to previously obtained IQV, as defined in Eq. (6). Completeness is not considered in this case because knowledge is created from a unique source. Defined levels - from 1 to 5 - based on the tank capacity, represent error cost and relevancy. In this particular case, errors' cost make knowledge more relevant and directly related. On the other hand, WQV is static when the system is functioning e.g. $WQV = \{a_{exp}, a_{com}\} = \{38, 1\}$ - i.e. based on 38 previous cases, only considering the liquid level. Potential costs of wrong decisions resulting from ignoring quality evaluations could be, for instance: blocked pipes if foreign objects are not removed; significant amount of missing values that are not updated if the DoS attack is not detected; and wrong system autonomy previsions if a leak is not fixed.

4 Discussion and Conclusion

Quality evaluation in cyber-physical systems appears as an alternative to monitor systems' operations and adjust if necessary the behavior of sub-systems, as well as to reduce potential risks and costs resulting from wrong decisions. We have proposed a methodology to completely evaluate data, information, knowledge, and wisdom quality. Following an analysis of existing quality measurements in other domains, the proposed approach identifies the most suitable elements of quality evaluation for cyber-physical systems. Defined knowledge factors and wisdom aspects for quality measurement, not previously conceptualized in the literature, enhance the evaluation to take into account complementary quality evaluation elements. All imperfections, dimensions, factors, and aspects, do not need to be systematically examined to evaluate the quality of a networked cyber-system. Since each element can be separately qualified, dynamic quality evaluations are applied according to the available elements in a given context.

A schematic simplified application of the proposed approach was presented, taking the case study of a cyber-physical system sensor network. It illustrates how the defined quality evaluation components are analyzed. Despite the apparent simplicity of this experiment, obtained results reveal the complexity of evaluating the complete system quality from data to wisdom, at normal and three different possible functioning stages. Resulting measures are multidimensional, heterogeneous, and variable. We also observe the need to encode considerable prior knowledge to facilitate system quality assessment. On the other hand, the interest of global quality measures to monitor cyber-physical systems remains unknown. It is unclear what a single qualification obtained from multiple heterogeneous elements could mean to a decision maker. Further work will consist on extending the proposed approach to other cyber-systems in operational conditions.

References

1. Batini, C., Scannapieco, M.: Data Quality: Concepts, Methodologies and Techniques. Data-Centric Systems and Applications. Springer, New York (2006)
2. De Amicis, B.: A methodology for data quality assessment on financial data. Stud. Commun. Sci. **4**, 115–136 (2004)
3. English, L.P.: Improving Data Warehouse and Business Information Quality: Methods for Reducing Costs and Increasing Profits. Wiley, New York (1999)
4. Guo, J., Liu, F.: Automatic data quality control of observations in wireless sensor network. IEEE Geosci. Remote Sens. Lett. **12**(4), 716–720 (2015)
5. Lee, Y.W., Strong, D.M., Kahn, B.K., Wang, R.Y.: AIMQ: a methodology for information quality assessment. Inf. Manag. **40**(2), 133–146 (2002)
6. Loshin, D.: Enterprise Knowledge Management. The Data Quality Approach. Academic Press, San Diego (2001)
7. Motro, A., Smets, P.: Uncertainty Management in Information Systems: From Needs to Solutions. Springer Science & Business Media, New York (1996)
8. Pipino, L.L., Lee, Y.W., Wang, R.Y.: Data quality assessment. Commun. ACM **45**(4), 211–218 (2002)
9. Puentes, J., Montagner, J., Lecornu, L., Lähteenmäki, J.: Quality analysis of sensors data for personal health records on mobile devices. In: Bali, R., Troshani, I., Goldberg, S., Wickramasinghe, N. (eds.) Pervasive Health Knowledge Management. Healthcare Delivery in the Information Age, pp. 103–133. Springer, New York (2013)
10. Scannapieco, M., Virgillito, A., Marchetti, C., Mecella, M., Baldoni, R.: The DaQuinCIS architecture: a platform for exchanging and improving data quality in cooperative information systems. Inf. Syst. **29**(7), 551–582 (2004)

11. Todoran, I.-G., Lecornu, L., Khenchaf, A., Le Caillec, J.-M.: Information quality evaluation in fusion systems. In: 16th International Conference on Information Fusion (FUSION), pp. 906–913, July 2013

12. Wang, R.Y., Strong, D.M.: Beyond accuracy: what data quality means to data consumers. J. Manag. Inf. Syst. **12**(4), 5–33 (1996)

13. Zeleny, M.: Human Systems Management: Integrating Knowledge, Management and Systems. World Scientific Publishing Co., Pte. Ltd., London (2005)

14. Zins, C.: Conceptual approaches for defining data, information, and knowledge. J. Am. Soc. Inform. Sci. Technol. **58**(4), 479–493 (2007)

Energy Consumption and Data Amount Reduction Using Object Detection on Embedded Platform

Boris Snajder[(⊠)], Zoran Kalafatic, and Vedran Bilas

Faculty of Electrical Engineering and Computing,
University of Zagreb, Zagreb, Croatia
boris.snajder@fer.hr

Abstract. High resolution image handling often results with high energy burden for battery-powered devices, such as sensor nodes in WSN. Motivation for this study is assessment of energy consumption of the sensor node with high-resolution camera, featuring image processing. We present a selection of object detection algorithms and evaluate their efficiency. To verify applicability of those algorithms, we acquired image sequence that correspond to applications of pests detection in agriculture. We verified considered algorithms' performances: recall, precision and expected reduction of the data amount. Energy required to execute considered algorithms was measured on ARM processor based platform. Our results show that object extraction on a node can provide reduction of the data amount by up to three orders of magnitude. While simple algorithms can lead to lower overall energy consumption of the node, the more complex algorithm provides better performances, but at a cost of prohibitively high energy consumption.

Keywords: Wireless sensor networks · Energy efficiency · Image processing · Object detection · Data amount reduction

1 Introduction

Wireless sensor networks (WSN) are widely used in environmental monitoring, where sensor nodes acquire information from their surrounding and route them to a server or a user, Fig. 1. Appearance of small and affordable CMOS image sensors, that can be easily used in embedded devices, provides opportunity for WSN usage in visual inspection and monitoring of environment [1, 2]. As the sensor nodes are usually battery-powered embedded devices, they have limited energy budget, that ultimately limits their lifetime. Thus, in WSN research field there is big emphasis on power management methods [3, 4]. Also, as wireless communication is an energy intensive task, wireless protocols targeted for use in WSN, such as a ZigBee, incorporates various means to reduce sensor node energy consumption [5]. However, data intensive operations, such as image acquisition, processing and transmission, can result with significant increase in energy consumption [6].

© ICST Institute for Computer Sciences, Social Informatics and Telecommunications Engineering 2017
M. Magno et al. (Eds.): S-Cube 2016, LNICST 205, pp. 118–129, 2017.
DOI: 10.1007/978-3-319-61563-9_10

In available literature [7,8] description of several sensor nodes with image sensors can be found. However, as a consequence of limited energy and computing resources, all of those sensor nodes feature relatively low resolution image sensor. In some applications, such as pests detection, it is necessary to use a high resolution image sensor [9]. As camera resolution increases, an increase in energy consumption can be expected, as the sensor nodes have to handle even more data. High energy consumption of the node with high resolution image sensor can be met with solar cells [10]. Alternatively, image processing on the nodes can be used to reduce the data amount to be transferred and consequently to lower energy consumption [11]. The data amount reduction in WSN can be achieved either by image compression or by object detection and extraction, where only fragments of the image containing objects of interest, are sent [12]. Depending on the data amount, that the nodes have to send, different wireless protocols provide lower energy consumption [13].

Thus, the goal of our research is an evaluation of several object detection and extraction algorithms, including assessment of their energy consumption in applications that require high resolution image sensors. The remainder of the paper is organized as follows. Section 2 gives an overview of considered algorithms for object detection and extraction. Description of methods and measurement setups, based on low cost embedded platforms, is presented in Sect. 3. Section 4 presents the results and Sect. 5 concludes the paper.

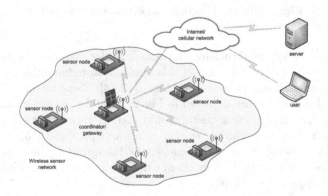

Fig. 1. Illustration of WSN in environmental monitoring application.

2   Object Detection Algorithms

Required resolution of the camera is application driven. For example, in pests detection applications spatial resolution of approximately $50\,\mu m \times 50\,\mu m$ is required [9]. To achieve that spatial resolution, if camera field of view is $10\,cm \times 10\,cm$, a 5 MPix image sensor should be used. Lossy image compression is not a suitable option for data amount reduction in this application, since size of some anatomy details of pests will be just a few pixels. Thus, focus will be on the algorithms for object detection and extraction.

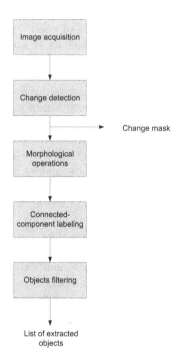

Fig. 2. Objects detection and extraction flowchart

In pests detection applications, the sensor nodes acquire images of sticky traps. Static nature of background in this application reduces the object detection problem to a change detection problem [12,14]. Steps required for objects detection and extraction are depicted in Fig. 2, with change mask estimation as the first step. As change mask contains information about changed pixels, this step will define overall performance, i.e. recall and precision [15], of the algorithms. In the case of static and homogenous background, the appearance of objects can be detected by various change detection algorithms. We considered three typical approaches [14,16]:

– Background subtraction,
– Color change detection,
– Difference of Gaussians.

Morphological operations, connected component labeling and size filtering are used for objects extraction from change mask. Result of objects extraction is a list of objects, defined by their positions and sizes. As the expected size of pests is known *a priori*, filtering can be applied to discard objects that are either too big or too small.

2.1   Background Subtraction

Except possible changes in scene illumination, background is static and homogenous, while trapped pests appear as objects of lower intensity. Thus, they can be detected by subtracting pixels intensity of current image $I_N(\mathbf{x})$ from reference background image $I_0(\mathbf{x})$:

$$I_{DIFF}(\mathbf{x}) = I_0(\mathbf{x}) - I_N(\mathbf{x}). \tag{1}$$

As subtracting is done on pixels intensity, firstly conversion to grayscale image is done. To eliminate small changes, that are result of noise and variances in illumination conditions, a threshold operation is applied and a change mask $C_N(\mathbf{x})$ is obtained:

$$C_N(\mathbf{x}) = \begin{cases} 1, & \text{if } I_{DIFF}(\mathbf{x}) > \tau \\ 0, & \text{otherwise,} \end{cases} \tag{2}$$

where τ is value of threshold. If pixel intensity values are in interval $[0, 1]$, difference $I_{DIFF}(\mathbf{x})$ and τ values are in interval $[-1, 1]$. Usually, threshold value is empirically chosen. This is the most simple method in determining that some pixel has changed. As variations in illumination conditions change intensity of pixels, it can be expected that this method will be sensitive to changes in illumination [14].

2.2   Color Change Detection

Typical color of sticky traps used in pests monitoring is yellow. Thus, color information of each pixel can be used to detect change. Color image sensors usually provide color information in RGB or YUV color spaces, while the hue of color, and thus deviation from the expected value, is easily defined in HSV color space. Hue component $H(\mathbf{x})$, that carries color information, can be converted from RGB color space using expression:

$$H(\mathbf{x}) = \begin{cases} \frac{G-B}{max(R,G,B)-min(R,G,B)} \cdot 60°, & \text{if } max(R,G,B) = R \\ \frac{B-R}{max(R,G,B)-min(R,G,B)} \cdot 60° + 120°, & \text{if } max(R,G,B) = G \\ \frac{R-G}{max(R,G,B)-min(R,G,B)} \cdot 60° + 240°, & \text{if } max(R,G,B) = B, \end{cases} \tag{3}$$

where R, G, B are values of pixel color components in RGB color space. Values of the hue component are in interval $[0°, 360°]$, while hue value of yellow pixel is around $60°$. Thus, the change mask can be found by thresholding all pixels whose hue component differ from background for more than threshold value τ:

$$C_N(\mathbf{x}) = \begin{cases} 1, & \text{if } H(\mathbf{x}) < (C - \tau) \text{ or } H(\mathbf{x}) > (C + \tau) \\ 0, & \text{otherwise.} \end{cases} \tag{4}$$

In comparison to the background subtraction approach, color change detection does not require reference image.

2.3   Difference of Gaussians

Difference of two low-pass Gaussian (DoG) filters can be used show local changes in pixel values, thus it can be used for object detection [16]. Difference of Gaussians $D(\mathbf{x}, \sigma, k)$ can be expressed as:

$$D(\mathbf{x}, \sigma, k) = (G(\mathbf{x}, k\sigma) - G(\mathbf{x}, \sigma)) * I_N(\mathbf{x}), \tag{5}$$

where σ is standard deviation of the first Gaussian filter, $k\sigma$ is standard deviation of the second Gaussian filter. If there is big enough local change in pixel intensity, such as pest on sticky trap, there will be increase in value of $D(\mathbf{x}, \sigma, k)$. As pests size is known, it is possible to run only one DoG, with predetermined values of standard deviation that maximizes DoG response for the targeted application. The values of σ and k, that provide the best object detection performance, are found empirically. To provide better energy efficiency, the Gaussian filters were implemented using 1-D filters. Before filtering, the image is converted to grayscale.

3   Methods and Experimental Setups

Delivery of reliable information is as much important as energy consumption of the node. Thus, it is necessary to verify performance of objects detection algorithms. For that purpose algorithm performances were evaluated on image sequences, including measurement of energy consumption.

3.1   Image Acquisition

To be able to verify object detection algorithms in different conditions, an image sequence containing more than hundred images was acquired using a measurement setup depicted in Fig. 3. The measurement setup is consisted of a mechanical mounting, a yellow sticky trap, a Raspberry Pi and a 5 MPix OV5640 camera. A software run on the Raspberry Pi acquired a new image every hour during daylight. A result is acquisition of images in different illumination conditions, ranging from direct sunlight on the sticky trap, to the illumination conditions of cloudy days. When the sticky trap is mounted to the setup, the software was restarted triggering immediate image acquisition. Thus, the first image in the sequence does not contain any objects and can be used as the background reference image. All acquired images were stored without compression in RGB color space and indexed to ease algorithms evaluation, resulting with image size of approximately 14.4 MB.

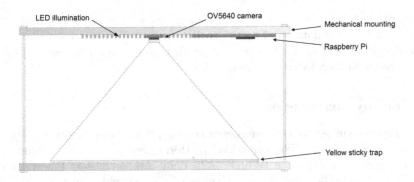

Fig. 3. Illustration of setup for image acquisition

3.2 Algorithms Performance Evaluation

For the purpose of performance evaluation, the considered algorithms were implemented in MATLAB, while recall, precision and F-measure were used for the algorithms performance evaluation. To reduce run time, assessment of influence of threshold and standard deviation values on algorithms performance was done a smaller subset consisted of four images. On the each test image at least a dozen objects were present, while size and position of all objects were manually labeled. Thus, for every test image there was associated labeled list with bounding boxes of all objects used as the ground truth. A list of extracted objects from the test images is then compared to the list of labeled objects. Recall R and precision P are calculated using expressions:

$$R = \frac{TP}{TP + FN}, \tag{6}$$

$$P = \frac{TP}{TP + FP}, \tag{7}$$

where TP is number of true positives, FN is number of false negatives and FP is number of false positives. Extracted object is considered as true positive if its center is located within area defined by some object from labeled list. Number of false positives FP equals to the number of extracted objects that do not match any object from labeled list, while number of false negatives FN is number of objects in labelled list that weren't matched by any extracted object.

Threshold value τ, and values of σ and k in case of DoG, affect recall and precision. Typically, selection of parameters that leads to increase in precision will result with lower recall, and *vice versa*, while in ideal scenario both values would be equal to one. Thus, to ease comparison of algorithms F-measure can be used:

$$F_{meas} = 2\frac{R \cdot P}{R + P}. \tag{8}$$

After algorithms parameters that provide the best performance on the test images set are determined, each algorithm was run on the whole image sequence to evaluate its performances in different illumination conditions.

As primary goal is to lower overall energy consumption of the node, the expected amount of data required to describe extracted objects is estimated for each algorithm. Expected amount of data then can be used for estimation of energy required for wireless communication.

3.3   Energy Consumption

The measurement setup used for energy consumption during algorithms execution is shown in Fig. 4. The embedded platform used for energy consumption measurement is based on AllWinner A20 dual core processor. Power supply voltage was 5 V. The current consumption of the embedded platform is measured over a shunt resistor and a National Instruments NI USB-6221 acquisition card [17], with the sampling rate of 100 ksps and the resolution of 16 bits. Processor executed algorithms implemented using OpenCV 3.0 library [18]. To ensure maximal performance, OpenCV library was compiled with NEON instructions support enabled. Start and completion of each step in object detection and extraction was signaled using GPIO lines. Energy consumption of algorithms' each step was calculated by integration of power supply voltage and measured current product. Algorithms were run on 5 MPix images and each measurement was repeated 15 times.

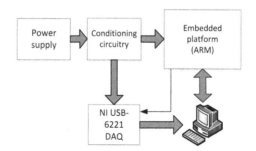

Fig. 4. Setup for measuring energy consumption of embedded platform during algorithms execution

4   Results

One of the acquired images is shown in Fig. 5. As expected, the background of the image is yellow, while pests show as darker objects on the background. Typical size of trapped pests range from 10 to 30 pixels. Also, nonuniform illumination of the scene, caused by surrounding vegetation, can be observed.

Fig. 5. A representative image acquired with the set-up given in Fig. 3. (Color figure online)

4.1 Performance of the Algorithms

Performances of the considered algorithms and their dependence on threshold value is evaluated through a recall-precision curve, Fig. 6. As expected, with threshold value selection each algorithm can be adjusted towards achieving higher recall or higher precision. The background subtraction algorithm can achieve recall $R = 1$, but at the same time precision drops to $P \approx 0.7$. Maximal value of F-measure the background subtraction algorithm achieves is $F_{meas} = 0.85$ for the threshold value $\tau = 0.25$. Decreasing threshold value results with higher recall and lower precision. While the color change detection algorithm achieves almost the same maximal value for F-measure $F_{meas} = 0.84$, its overall performances are lower compared to the performance of the background subtraction algorithm. Maximal value of F-measure is achieved for $\tau = 7.5°$. As in the case of the background subtraction algorithm, increase of threshold value decreases recall and increases precision. The best performance on the test images achieves DoG algorithm with precision $P = 1$, recall $R = 1$ and $F_{meas} = 1$, thus ideal detection. This is achieved for the threshold value of $\tau = 0.05$. The value of standard deviation was set to $\sigma = 10$ and $k = 4$, as those settings provided the best performance on the test images.

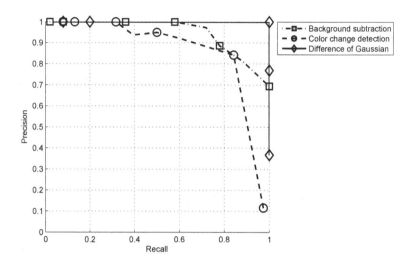

Fig. 6. Precision-recall curve of considered algorithms run on the test images

Based on the performance evaluation on the test images, the parameter for each algorithm were set and the algorithms were evaluated on the whole image sequence. The results show that DoG performs best in all illuminations conditions, although for some of the images it does not achieve values of recall or precision equal to 1. The DoG achieves recall higher than $R > 0.8$ on all images. As the background subtraction is susceptible illumination variations, change in illumination causes recall and precision to drop as low as 0.6. The color change detection algorithm is much more susceptible to illumination changes, so we observed a significant drop in recall and precision with non-homogeneous illumination, where for some images precision was lower than $P < 0.1$.

The average data required to describe detected objects with the considered algorithms are given in Table 1. If all extracted objects are sent as detected, the average data amount, depending on the used algorithm, is in the range between 26 kB and 52 kB. The average data amount to be sent can be further reduced by sending only newly detected objects. In that case the DoG and the background subtraction algorithms result with approximately 4.5 kB of data. As uncompressed full resolution image was more than 14 MB in size, data reduction in all cases is significant. Higher average data amount that the color change detection generates is result of its lower precision. Blurring of objects' edges due to low-pass filtering results with overestimated objects size and the higher data amount that the DoG algorithm generates compared to the background subtraction algorithm.

4.2   Energy Consumption

Measured energy consumption required for execution of each step of the considered algorithms is shown in Fig. 7. The background subtraction algorithm achieves

Table 1. Average amount of data

Algorithm	Average amount of data in list of extracted objects	Average amount of data in difference between lists of current and previous image
Background subtraction	26.217 kB	4.576 kB
Color change detection	52.186 kB	32.045 kB
Difference of Gaussians	45.887 kB	4.514 kB

the lowest energy consumption of $E_{BS} = 3.783 \pm 0.029$ J, while the execution time is approximately 2 s. The step of change mask estimation takes only 68 ms to execute and it consumes approximately 125 mJ of energy. Steps that are required to extract objects from the change mask consume around 3.33 J, while conversion from RGB color space to grayscale image consumes additional 326 mJ.

More complex operation required for the estimation of change mask using the color change detection algorithm results in higher energy consumption. The change mask estimation in this case consumes 1.73 J. As the color change algorithm does not require conversion to grayscale image and the steps required for objects extraction from the change mask are the same as in the case of the background subtraction algorithms, total energy consumption of the color change algorithm is $E_{CC} = 5.270 \pm 0.032$ J.

As the standard deviation used in the DoG has to reflect the expected size of objects to be detected, using 3σ rule results with a kernel size of 60×60 pixels. This results with a long execution time for the change mask estimation, and consequently with high energy consumption of approximately 70 J. Total energy consumption for the object extraction using the DoG algorithm is $E_{DoG} = 73.487 \pm 0.784$ J, while the execution time is approximately 43 s.

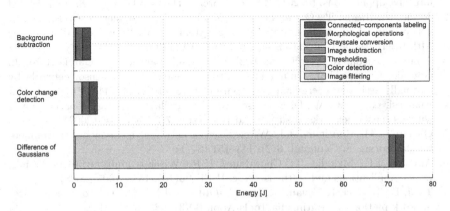

Fig. 7. Measured energy consumption for execution of each step of the considered algorithms.

5 Conclusion

Presented results show that considered algorithms are suitable for detecting objects on static background, while the DoG achieved the best performance. However, when run on the representative image sequence, all algorithms show drop in performance due to nonhomogeneous illumination conditions. As the DoG algorithm is sensitive to local changes in illumination, it achieves the best performance even in those conditions, while the color change detection performs poorly. Further, a lower data amount that the DoG achieves when comparing extracted objects from current and previous image, suggest more robust object detection compared to the background subtraction algorithm.

Better performance of the DoG algorithm comes at cost of significantly higher energy consumption. According to energy consumption analysis of wireless transfer presented in [13], transmission of 10 MB of data using ZigBee requires around 60 J of energy, while Wi-Fi requires around 9 J. Thus, image processing on the node can provide lower overall energy consumption when the background subtraction or the color change detection algorithms are used. However, energy consumption of DoG algorithm is higher than energy required to transfer whole 5 MPix image. Thus, when considering usage of image processing as means for node energy consumption reduction, it is required to take into account the energy constraint of the node, efficiency of the wireless communication, expected amount of data and required reliability of object detection.

Further, as results suggest lower performance in nonhomogeneous illumination conditions, in future we will assess possibility of using LED illumination.

References

1. Pham, C.: Communication performance of low-resource sensor motes for data-intensive applications. In: 2013 IFIP on Wireless Days (WD), pp. 1–8. IEEE (2013)
2. Jeličić, V., Ražov, T., Oletić, D., Kuri, M., Bilas, V.: Maslinet: a wireless sensor network based environmental monitoring system. In: MIPRO: Proceedings of the 34th International Convention, pp. 150–155. IEEE (2011)
3. Asorey-Cacheda, R., García-Sánchez, A.J., García-Sánchez, F., García-Haro, J., González-Castano, F.J.: On maximizing the lifetime of wireless sensor networks by optimally assigning energy supplies. Sensors **13**(8), 10219–10244 (2013)
4. Anastasi, G., Conti, M., Di Francesco, M., Passarella, A.: Energy conservation in wireless sensor networks: a survey. Ad Hoc Netw. **7**(3), 537–568 (2009)
5. Oliveira, L.M., Rodrigues, J.J.: Wireless sensor networks: a survey on environmental monitoring. J. Commun. **6**(2), 143–151 (2011)
6. Akyildiz, I.F., Melodia, T., Chowdhury, K.R.: Wireless multimedia sensor networks: applications and testbeds. Proc. IEEE **96**(10), 1588–1605 (2008)
7. Tavli, B., Bicakci, K., Zilan, R., Barcelo-Ordinas, J.M.: A survey of visual sensor network platforms. Multimedia Tools Appl. **60**(3), 689–726 (2012)
8. López, O., Rach, M., Migallon, H., Malumbres, M., Bonastre, A., Serrano, J.: Monitoring pest insect traps by means of low-power image sensor technologies. Sensors **12**, 15801–15819 (2012)

9. Boissard, P., Martin, V., Moisan, S.: A cognitive vision approach to early pest detection in greenhouse crops. Comput. Electron. Agric. **62**(2), 81–93 (2008)

10. Fukatsu, T., Watanabe, T., Hu, H., Yoichi, H., Hirafuji, M.: Field monitoring support system for the occurrence of leptocorisa chinensis dallas (hemiptera: Alydidae) using synthetic attractants, field servers, and image analysis. Comput. Electron. Agric. **80**, 8–16 (2012)

11. Ferrigno, L., Marano, S., Paciello, V., Pietrosanto, A.: Balancing computational and transmission power consumption in wireless image sensor networks. In: IEEE International Conference on Virtual Environments, Human-Computer Interfaces, and Measurement Systems (VECIMS), Giardini Naxos, Italy, 18–20 July 2005

12. Aziz, S.M., Pham, D.M.: Energy efficient image transmission in wireless multimedia sensor networks. IEEE Commun. Lett. **17**(6), 1084–1087 (2013)

13. Snajder, B., Jelicic, V., Kalafatic, Z., Bilas, V.: Wireless sensor node modelling for energy efficiency analysis in data-intensive periodic monitoring. Ad Hoc Netw. **49**, 29–41 (2016)

14. Radke, R., Andra, S., Al-Kofahi, O., Roysam, B.: Image change detection algorithms: a systematic survey. IEEE Trans. Image Process. **14**(3), 294–307 (2005)

15. Powers, D.M.: Evaluation: from precision, recall and F-measure to ROC, informedness, markedness and correlation (2011)

16. Kong, H., Akakin, H.C., Sarma, S.E.: A generalized Laplacian of Gaussian filter for blob detection and its applications. IEEE Trans. Cybern. **43**(6), 1719–1733 (2013)

17. DAQ M Series NI USB-621 x User Manual, National Instruments (2009). http://www.ni.com/pdf/manuals/371931f.pdf

18. Bradski, G., Kaehler, A.: OpenCV Library: Computer Vision with the OpenCV Library. O'Reilly Media Inc., Sebastopol (2008)

Reconfigurable and Long-Range Wireless Sensor Node for Long Time Operation

Nabil Islam[1], Fabien Ferrero[2(✉)], Leonardo Lizzi[2], Christophe Danchesi[1], and Stephane Boudaud[1]

[1] Abeeway, Sophia Antipolis, France
[2] Université Cote d'azur, CNRS, LEAT, Bâtiment forum,
Campus SophiaTech, 06903 Sophia Antipolis Cedex, France
fabien.ferrero@unice.fr

Abstract. This paper presents a low-power wireless sensor node platform with long-range communication capabilities based on LoRa technology. A frequency reconfigurable antenna is integrated to compensate effects from the environment. The platform integrates an accelerometer and a temperature sensor and it can monitor and transmit the device activity and temperature during more than 7 years.

Keywords: Wireless sensor network · Reconfigurable antenna · Low-power electronics

1 Introduction

During last decades, a large effort has been devoted to provide wireless connectivity to any type of object. Several disruptive technologies as Low-Power Wireless Area Network (LP-WAN) and ultra-low power electronics are now giving the possibility to connect almost any object almost anywhere [1]. The design of Wireless Sensor Networks (WSNs) for long time operation is very challenging. Power consumption has to be optimized on the radiofrequency, sensing and digital parts [6,7]. In literature, ZigBee and Bluetooth technologies have been mainly used because of the easy integration and wide availability [2,3]. However, wireless communication range is usually limited due to the weak propagation capabilities at 2.4 GHz. Recently, several long-range and low power wireless technologies have been proposed, mainly based on sub-GHz bands, where better propagation characteristics can be found [4]. One of the main issues for miniaturization of sub-GHz communication systems concerns the miniaturization of the antenna. The reduction of the antenna size causes the decrease of the radiation efficiency and the increase of the sensibility to the environment [5].

WSN nodes are usually placed in a-priori unknown environments and therefore smart systems with the capability to adapt to the context is strongly desired. Reconfigurability on the antenna directivity has already been proposed to improve WSN network efficiency [8]. However, this technique cannot compensate the close effect of the environment on the antenna. Proximity effects on

© ICST Institute for Computer Sciences, Social Informatics and Telecommunications Engineering 2017
M. Magno et al. (Eds.): S-Cube 2016, LNICST 205, pp. 130–136, 2017.
DOI: 10.1007/978-3-319-61563-9_11

antennas have been studied for both dielectric and metallic environments. For magnetic antennas, like in RFID applications, the metallic environment causes the frequency resonance to shift towards higher frequency [10]. On the other hand, metallic sections can also be used as a technique to miniaturize the size of antennas. Metallic planes performs a capacitance loading of the antenna so that the frequency resonance is shifted toward lower frequencies [11–13]. Examples of capacitance loading of inverted-F antennas (IFAs) and Planar Inverted-F antennas (PIFAs) using a metallic plane have been proposed in [14,15]. Finally, dielectrics can also cause down-shift in the resonance frequency [9].

A possible solution to compensate the resonance frequency shifting consists in the design of a frequency reconfigurable antenna and successively to re-tune the antenna resonance frequency depending on the close environment of the device.

In this paper, we present a low-power wireless sensor node platform with long-range communication capabilities based on LoRa technology, integrating a reconfigurable antenna to compensate environment effect.

2   Wireless Sensor Node Platform

The proposed WSN platform is based on a LoRa radio system working at 868 MHz, which makes it ideal for low-power small size device trackers. The device fits in a 120 mm long cylinder with a diameter of 20 mm. The system is powered by one AA lithium battery as shown in Fig. 1. In order to provide an optimal radiation performance in any operation context, a reconfigurable antenna has been designed. Thanks to the ability to compensate the environment effect, the WSN platform can be fixed on any type of equipment to efficiently monitor its activity and position.

2.1   Reconfigurable Antenna

In order to compensate the environment effect, a Digital Tunable Capacitor (DTC) connected to the antenna is adopted. We have selected the PE64906 from Peregrine with a capacitance tuning range from 0.9 to 4.6 pF with 32 different states. In order to accurately tune the frequency range of the reconfigurable antenna, an inductor of 15nH is placed in parallel to the DTC (Fig. 1). The typical power consumption of this component is 140 uA for 2.75 V, which is negligible compared to the transceiver power consumption (33 mA for 3.3 V).

LoRa communications are performed at 868 MHz and, considering the small size of the antenna compare to the wavelength, only a reduced bandwidth of 10 MHz can be covered instantaneously (for a reflection coefficient criteria of −6 dB). When the antenna is placed near a dielectric or a metallic part, the resonance frequency is shifted. As an example, for an antenna resonating at 868 MHz in free space, the resonance frequency will shift to 700 MHz when the antenna is placed on a metallic plate. Due to un-matching effect, the transmitted power is reduced by a 12 dB. With the reconfigurable antenna, the frequency shift of the antenna resonance can be compensated by changing the DTC value.

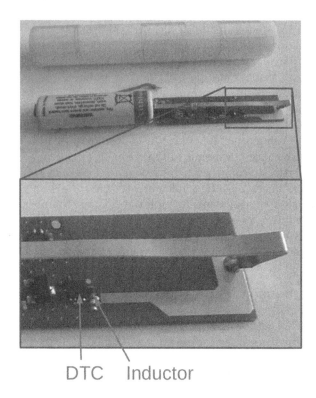

Fig. 1. Picture of the proposed WSN device

2.2   Electronic Components

Long time operation mainly depends on the power consumption of the electronic components. An ultra low power Gecko 32-bit microcontroller (MCU) from Silicon Labs (EFM32G200F64) has been selected. It consumes 2 mA in active mode and only 3 uA in stand-by mode with interrupt inputs enable. The design is based on the LoRa modem using the SX1272 from Semtech with 14 dBm output power. The different power consumptions of the MCU and the transceiver are described in Table 1.

2.3   Sensors

Several sensors are integrated in the device. The most important one is the accelerometer because it will strongly contribute to the power consumption reduction. An ultra-low power 3-axis component from Freescale has been selected (MMA8652FC). The output date rate is set to 12.5 Hz for reducing the power consumption (6.5 uA on 2.5 V). The process of the x, y and z accelerations is described in Fig. 2. The square sum of the accelerations is performed. Then, a highpass filter is used to get rid of the static (gravitational) acceleration value.

Table 1. Power budget of the WSN platform

Components	Current consumption	Duty cycle(%)	Average current
LoRa (active)	38 mA	0.03	10uA
LoRa (sleep)	0.1 uA	99.97	10uA
MCU (stand-by)	3 uA	99	
MCU (active)	2 mA	1	23uA
Accelerometer (LP mode)	6.5 uA	100	6.5uA
DTC	500 uA	0.03	0.15uA
Total		100	40uA

Battery	Power	Autonomy
AA lithium battery	2.6A.h	7.42 years

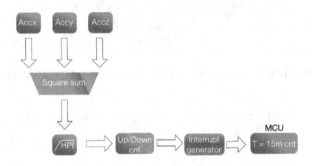

Fig. 2. Accelerometer processing

From this result, a counter is incremented when the output value of the HP filter is higher than a threshold. For a determined period of time (15 min for our model), we count the number of detected accelerations. Since the firmware of the WSN platform is optimized to make as less wireless LoRa uplinks as possible, the system only send an uplink with the count number of detected accelerations every 15 min (if some activity has been detected). The MCU also integrates a temperature sensor.

2.4 Power Budget

Based on a representative scenario, the average power consumption of the device can be extracted from Table 1. The WNS is transmitting each hour with no activity or each 15mn in case of detected activity. The average duration for a LoRa communication can be estimated to 300 ms. Based on a lithium AA battery, an autonomy larger than 7 years can be expected. This calculation do not include the self-discharge of such a battery and the influence of the temperature. As it can be observed from the average current distribution in Fig. 3, most of the power consumption is due to the MCU, and the accelerometer and communication part are consuming almost a quarter of the whole power. It can be also noticed that the power consumption of the DTC, for adding the antenna reconfigurability, is negligible in the overall power budget.

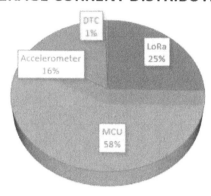

Fig. 3. Average current distribution in a standard scenario

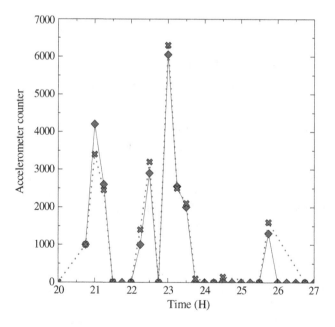

Fig. 4. Comparison between a reference accelerometer (blue) and the device (red) fixed on the same tool. (Color figure online)

3   In-Field Sensing Testing

The first presented test is the comparison between a reference accelerometer and the WSN platform placed on the same object. The result presented in Fig. 4 shows a good agreement between the activity monitored with the reference accelerometer and the WSN node.

The second test evaluates the joint use of the accelerometer and the temperature sensor. The temperature sensor from the MCU is used for the monitoring. The WSN platform has been placed in a tree during 10 days, transmitting temperature and activity detected every 15 min. The results are presented in Fig. 5. The test had been started on July 7, 2016. As expected, the temperature curve exhibits a periodic trend that corresponds to the day/night cycle. The activity counter do not report any accelerations until the 6th day (corresponding to 150 h), which was particularly windy.

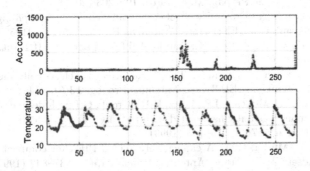

Fig. 5. Activity and temperature monitored on the WSN platform during 10 days

4   Conclusion

This paper presents a reconfigurable wireless sensor platform for long-time and long-range applications. In-field tests have confirmed a communication range in open environment up to 10 km. Autonomy up to 7 years is expected.

References

1. Lazarescu, M.T.: Design of a WSN platform for long-term environmental monitoring for IoT applications. IEEE J. Emerg. Sel. Top. Circ. Syst. **3**(1), 45–54 (2013)
2. Nair, K., et al.: Optimizing power consumption in iot based wireless sensor networks using bluetooth low energy. In: 2015 International Conference on Green Computing and Internet of Things (ICGCIoT), pp. 589–593, Noida (2015)
3. Chou, J.C., et al.: Wireless sensing system for flexible arrayed potentiometric sensor based on XBee module. IEEE Sens. J. **16**(14), 5588–5595 (2016)

4. Petajajarvi, J., Mikhaylov, K., Roivainen, A., Hanninen, T., Pettissalo, M.: On the coverage of LPWANs: range evaluation and channel attenuation model for LoRa technology, In: 2015 14th International Conference on ITS Telecommunications (ITST), pp. 55–59, December 2015

5. Ferrero, F., Lizzi, L., Danchesi, C., Boudaud, S.,: Environmental sensitivity of miniature antennas for IoT devices. In: IEEE APS 2016 Proceedings, Fajardo, Porto Rico, July 2016

6. Dietrich, I., DresslerSmith, F.: On the lifetime of wireless sensor networks. ACM Trans. Sens. Netw. **5**(1), 5:15:39 (2009)

7. Yang, J., Li, X.: Design and implementation of low-power wireless sensor networks for environmental monitoring in wireless communications. In: IEEE International Conference on Networking and Information Security, pp. 593–597 June 2010

8. Le, T.N., et al.: Improving energy efficiency of mobile WSN using reconfigurable directional antennas. IEEE Commun. Lett. **20**(6), 1243–1246 (2016)

9. Babar, A.A., Ukkonen, L., Elsherbeni, A.Z., Sydnheimo, L.: Wall-proximity effects on the performance of small antennas for UHF wireless applications [wireless corner]. IEEE Antennas Propag. Mag. **53**(6), 190–203 (2011)

10. Qing, X., Chen, Z.N.: Proximity effects of metallic environments on high frequency RFID reader antenna. IEEE Trans. Antennas Propag. **55**(11), 3105–3111 (2007)

11. Seeley, E., Burns, J., Welton, K.: Cap-loaded folded antenna. IRE Int. Convention Rec. **6**, 133–138 (1958)

12. Gangi, A., Sensiper, S., Dunn, G.: The characteristics of electrically short, umbrella top-loaded antennas. IEEE Trans. Antennas Propag. **13**(6), 864–871 (1965)

13. Francavilla, L.A., McLean, J.S., Foltz, H.D., Crook, G.E.: Mode-matching analysis of top-hat monopole antennas loaded with radially layered dielectric. IEEE Trans. Antennas Propag. **47**(1), 179–185 (1999)

14. Rowell, C.R., Murch, R.D.: A capacitively loaded PIFA for compact mobile telephone handsets. IEEE Trans. Antennas Propag. **45**(5), 837–842 (1997)

15. Loizou, L., Buckley, J., Belcastro, M., Barton, J., O'Flynn, B., O'Mathuna, C.: Miniaturized inverted-f antenna with capacitive loading. In: 7th European Conference on Antennas and Propagation, pp. 3213–3216 (2013)

Comparative Analysis of Simulation and Real-World Energy Consumption for Battery-Life Estimation of Low-Power IoT (Internet of Things) Deployment in Varying Environmental Conditions Using Zolertia Z1 Motes

Ashutosh Bandekar, Akshay Kotian, and Ahmad Y. Javaid[✉]

EECS Department, The University of Toledo, Toledo, OH, USA
ahmad.javaid@utoledo.edu

Abstract. Battery life and power consumption have been a challenging real-world problem for the internet of things (IoT). IoT applications in biomedical, agriculture, ecosystem monitoring, wildlife management, etc., need an accurate estimation of average battery life based on the environment and application. In this paper, we opt for an experimental approach and use various types of real-world environmental conditions such as the presence of interferences and high-intensity lights, to determine the actual power consumption of IoT nodes with a new set of off-the-shelf AA batteries for each scenario. We took readings in each of these environments such as an indoor Basketball Court, an Auditorium, and a room (our lab) and to verify results in outdoor conditions we chose parking lot as one of the testing environments. Further analysis and experimentation were performed to get detailed results. Results were obtained using widely used Zolertia Z1 hardware motes arranged in a specific and consistent pattern. We have compared our experimental results with simulated results in the Cooja simulator.

Keywords: Energy consumption · Battery life · Internet of Things

1 Introduction

In modern times, low powered IoT devices have evolved and gained popularity as well as attention amongst various developers and researchers. They form a critical part of many systems due to their high-performance capacities while using limited power. These nodes consist of low-powered microprocessors, sensors, communication chips and so on. All aspects of these systems, from designing the hardware to the protocol depend on the amount of power that is being consumed by such devices. The power consumption cannot be predicted as the amount of energy required varies with respect to various external factors such as the deployed application, the environment device functions in and so on. The current works on power consumption are mostly based on simulations and offer low reliability, and thus affecting the effective use of these devices in physical environments. The simulations run digitally and do not take into consideration the real

© ICST Institute for Computer Sciences, Social Informatics and Telecommunications Engineering 2017
M. Magno et al. (Eds.): S-Cube 2016, LNICST 205, pp. 137–148, 2017.
DOI: 10.1007/978-3-319-61563-9_12

world parameters such as high-intensity lights, temperature, humidity, the wind, etc. These parameters referred to as interferences, can cause a significant variation in the actual outcomes versus the simulations, which is shown in this work. This paper exploits experimental results in an actual environment with interference to present these unpredictable behavior.

The presented research was conducted using Zolertia Z1 hardware motes. These devices are compact and low powered which makes them easy to deploy and cost-effective. Natural or artificial lighting can prove to be a major source of interference towards the functioning of these low powered IoT devices. In an indoor environment, the energy consumption of a device varies with the lighting conditions which results in degradation of battery life of the device. These devices use two 1.5 V AA batteries. It is important to determine the battery-life when these devices are being used for some critical applications with this limited power source. Based on the domain of application, e.g., medical sensors, human life could be put at risk if this prediction or calculation is incorrect. The power consumption of these devices should be known before deployment. In this paper, we are considering experimental as well as simulated results. For this, we created a close-to-silent environment – an ideal environment devoid of any interference. Therefore, we could compare real-world readings with simulated results and gain some insights into better-predicting battery-life based on application and operational environment.

1.1   Related Work

Since the conception of Zolertia Z1, there has been much research on power analysis of Z1 motes because it is primarily a low power device. Power consumption is our priority, but measurement and estimation of power have also been an issue. In the past, researchers have implemented *powertrace*, a system for network level profiling for low power wireless network nodes. Powertrace tracks the estimated power consumption by employing energy capsules to trace the activities of transmission and reception of data packets. It has been experimentally proven that powertrace has an accuracy rating of 94% to the energy consumption of a device [1]. Power trace implements state tracking to estimate the power consumption of the local node and records the energy consumption in energy capsules that represent node-level activities such as packet reception or packet transmission. We have implemented the same system to analyze the power consumption of networks influenced by different environments to compare power consumption.

There are several works regarding energy consumption analysis, but most of them are through simulation. Very few have any real-world experimental data which shows how energy consumption varies according to change in lighting or other environmental conditions. Several researchers have monitored power consumption using powertrace in simulation. Moreover, the works discuss power consumption analysis for different applications using two motes in the simulation for both Z1 and Sky motes. The motive of these works was to provide total power consumption along with detailed results based on various modes such as T_x, R_x, idle power consumption and active power consumption [2–4]. Another work discusses an extensive accounting of network topologies in simulation, detailing the impact of topologies and the density of the network on power consumption. Having implemented both the random network and the grid network of topology in the simulation, this work uses 20, 30, 40, 45 nodes with changing distance of 20 m and 30 m between motes and varying R_x values of 20, 40, 60, 80, 100% for the grid topology [5]. Another simulation-based work calculated power consumption during an ongoing wormhole attack as well as when an IDS was running to prevent the attack [6].

One of the real-world work has deployed a pair of Zolertia Z1 motes and a pair of OpenMote in the testbed. One of the Z1 motes was connected to monsoon power monitor (which measures the energy consumption of the mote with microsecond precision), and the other mote, working as a proxy, was connected to a PC to collect data located a meter apart. The experiment is conducted for a total of 100 data packets with a packet interval of 1, 2 and 5 s for a total duration of 100, 200 and 500 s respectively [7]. There are some other comparative studies regarding energy consumption with parameters like single hop and multi-hop [8].

2 Experimental Setup

This paper concentrates on the real-world or physical experiments. While the simulation requires only the Contiki-Cooja environment, the physical experiment requires both the hardware and the Contiki OS code to be executed.

2.1 Hardware

The experimental setup is being employed on a low-power Zolertia Z1 mote equipped with an MSP430F2617 microcontroller. Z1 also features 8 Kb RAM and 92 Kb flash memory. In addition to the low-power microcontroller, the mote is equipped with a CC2420 transceiver [9], operating at 2.4 GHz, and IEEE 802.15.4, 6LowPAN and ZigBee protocols compliant. The additional features include a 3-Axis, ±2/4/8/16 g digital accelerometer (ADXL345) and a low-power digital temperature sensor (TMP102) with ±0.5 °C accuracy (in –25 °C–85 °C range). Since this device is designed to work in a range of 0.3 V to 3.6 V, it can be powered by two 1.5 V AA standard batteries. Figure 1(a) and (b) show the low-powered IoT device Zolertia Z1 and its actual board respectively. A new set of batteries was used for each experiment conducted in different environments such as the basketball court, auditorium, and lab. A testbed consisting of nine Zolertia Z1 nodes was used, out of which eight were running the broadcasting (BC) and one-to-one communication (unicasting, UC) applications. A ninth node was running alternatively the powertrace code to measure the energy consumption in joules (J). This was done to trace exactly how much power was consumed during each transmission. During the experiments, we started with eight nodes in 15 ft × 5 ft testbed of Z1 motes. After 15 min, we reduced the number of nodes to 6 and ran the BC and UC applications again. Subsequently, we reduced the number of nodes to 4 and then to 2 and repeated the same procedure. The data obtained from the experiments was recorded and compared. Proper drivers for Zolertia Z1 are available in TinyOS and Contiki as a part of the OS. It consists of MSP430 microprocessor, communication devices, sensors such as an accelerometer, and temperature sensor [10].

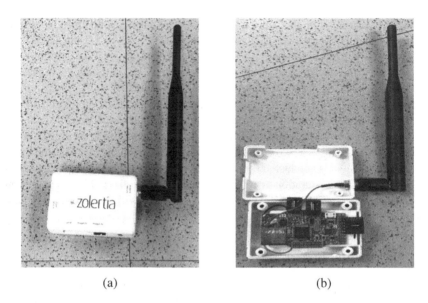

(a)   (b)

Fig. 1. (a) Zolertia Z1 low powered IoT device used for experiment, (b) Actual Zolertia Z1 board

2.2 Platform

Contiki OS is a very efficient open source OS for low-powered IoT devices because of its multi-tasking abilities despite the fact that most embedded networks and low powered IoT devices carry microcontrollers with small memory design. Due to the constrained size of its memory, Contiki OS is compact in its RAM usage and the size of the code. This can be seen from the fact that an average system with RPL routing based sleepy routers in IPv6 networking uses about 10 KB of RAM and 30 KB of ROM [11]. With major implementation in the field of wireless networks, Contiki OS has the advantage of providing both IPv4 and IPv6 communication [12, 13]. A running Contiki system consists of the kernel, libraries, the program loader, and a set of processes [14]. It can run on a variety of platforms like MSP430 which is employed in Zolertia Z1 and written in the C programming language.

A network with any topology can be created and checked for many different network parameters using Contiki. This can be done by running various example applications defined within Contiki, or by creating a custom library. For our use, we created a network topology of 15 ft × 5 ft grid and ran the same BC and UC applications for both the actual motes in the experimental setup and simulation. The testbed ensures that each set of neighboring nodes are at least 5 ft. apart, as illustrated in Figs. 2 and 3.

Fig. 2. Experimental setup in the indoor basketball court

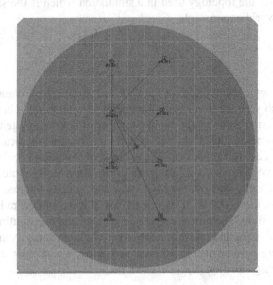

Fig. 3. Topology used in simulation

2.3 Operating Environment

Power consumption varies according to interference and change in environment. Changing this environment can allow observation of significant changes in power consumption. For analysis purpose, we chose a four different environments – (i) an indoor basketball court, (ii) an auditorium, (iii) our lab space, and (iv) an outdoor parking lot. For the basketball court and auditorium, we took readings with zolertia Z1 motes and observed power consumption with lights on and lights off. Moreover, for parking lot, we conducted an experiment with the same set of devices in varied temperature. To achieve this variation we have conducted the experiments at parking lot during day and night timings. Moreover, temperature ranges from 10 c to 20 c. For its justification, we made test bed of 15 ft × 5 ft. We observed significant changes in power consumption in a different environment as discussed in the results section of this paper. Figure 2 shows the setup used in the basketball court. For comparison, we used the same network topology in the Cooja simulation environment, as shown in Fig. 3.

2.4   Simulation

During this experiment, we used Cooja simulator for Contiki which is widely used for simulating network topology with many predefined libraries. This can be used to simulate networks with different examples such as broadcast and one to one communication. The Cooja simulator shows the physical layout of the network motes placed in accordance with the topology of the network [15–17]. Cooja simulator has the advantage of supporting the visualization of power consumption in the form of graphs for the entire network making it easier to understand the behavior of low powered IoT devices [1, 18]. Figure 3 shows the topology used in a simulation which is the same topology as used during real-world experiments.

3   Results

We measured energy consumption for the nodes in varying environmental conditions. We use Contiki powertrace to measure the energy consumption. The output from the powertrace application is the total time in a number of ticks the system spent transmitting, receiving and being idle. Ticks per second for a system is typically defined as the operating clock speed of it processor. The energy consumption is calculated using the typical operating voltage and current values of the Zolertia Z1 mote, as indicated by Table 1. When the radio was off, the MCU was idle; state is referred to as low power mode or low power mode (LPM). The time the MCU is on, and the radio is off, is being referred to as CPU time. The time the radio is receiving and transmitting with the MCU on is referred to as listen and transmit respectively. We ran some examples to see how energy consumption will change in different scenarios. We calculated energy with the help of the following equation [6]

$$Energy \text{ (mJ)} = \frac{(CPU * 0.5 + LPM * 0.0005 + Tx * 17.4 + Rx * 18.8) * 3}{32768} \qquad (1)$$

Where,
  CPU = Time for which mote was active
  LPM = Total time for which the mote was in low power mode
  T_x = Total transmission time
  R_x = Total listening time

Table 1. Zolertia Z1 mote operating conditions [10]

Typical conditions	Operating	Rating	Unit
MCU on	Radio Rx	18.8	mA
MCU on	Radio Tx	17.4	mA
MCU idle	Radio off	0.1	μA
MCU standby		0.5	μA
Voltage		3.6	V

Equation (1) is multiplied by three because we use a 3 V power supply. In this equation, all the parameters are according to the Zolertia Z1 specification and the denominator indicates the ticks per second value for Z1, i.e., 32768.

3.1 Broadcast

As we discussed earlier, we use 9 zolertia Z1 motes. A broadcast program of the eight-byte data packet was implemented on eight of these nine motes. In the ninth mote, we ran power trace program along with the original broadcast application, to record the actual energy consumption. Figure 4 shows the variation of energy consumption with respect to change in a number of nodes in the basketball court, auditorium and parking lot. We can compare energy consumption during a broadcast in the auditorium with and without lights also in the parking lot to verify experiment in an uncontrolled environment. If we observe this figure, we can see the significant variation in energy consumption during broadcasting with two nodes to eight nodes. With eight communicating in the network we can observe that energy consumption is almost 3.5 times more than two nodes communicating in a network.

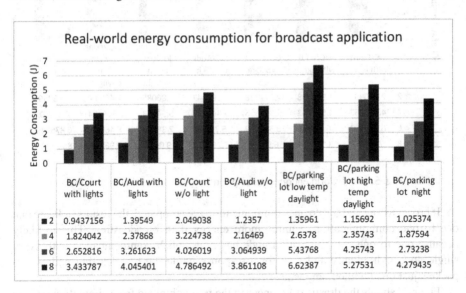

	BC/Court with lights	BC/Audi with lights	BC/Court w/o light	BC/Audi w/o light	BC/parking lot low temp daylight	BC/parking lot high temp daylight	BC/parking lot night
■2	0.9437156	1.39549	2.049038	1.2357	1.35961	1.15692	1.025374
■4	1.824042	2.37868	3.224738	2.16469	2.6378	2.35743	1.87594
■6	2.652816	3.261623	4.026019	3.064939	5.43768	4.25743	2.73238
■8	3.433787	4.045401	4.786492	3.861108	6.62387	5.27531	4.279435

Fig. 4. Real-world energy consumption for broadcast application

3.2 One to One Communication

In one to one or unicast communication, the same set of Zolertia Z1 motes were used with a brand new set of 1.5 V AA batteries. Powertrace was used in one of the nine motes and readings for the energy consumption were recorded. Figure 5 illustrates the comparison between one to one communications in the auditorium, basketball court, and parking lot. An exponential trend can be clearly observed with the increase in the number of nodes in a different environment from this figure. For both the auditorium and the court, the energy consumption with lights was less at the beginning, however, as the experiment progresses with time, significant changes could be noted with increased number of nodes. Also, a significant increase in energy consumption in the auditorium was noted compared to the indoor basketball court. This change could be attributed to greater interference due to high-intensity halogen lights in the court. Similarly, it can be observed with a change in the temperature energy consumption is also changes. That means during low-temperature energy consumption is more as compared to normal temperature as in dry atmosphere motes requires more energy to communicate with another node.

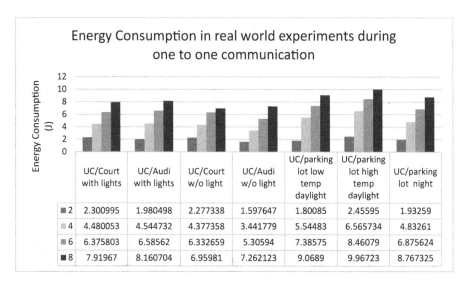

Fig. 5. Real-world energy consumption for one-to-one communication

If broadcasting and one to one communication are compared, the results indicate that one to one communication requires more energy than broadcasting. This is likely because one to one communication node has to establish communication with every single node individually and wait for a response while the broadcasting node sends packets just once without any wait.

Figure 6 shows the drastic differences in the trend obtained from simulation and the real-world experiments. An upward trend for broadcasting is observed but not as significant as one to one (unicast) communication. It should be noted that unicast trend indicates a rather decreasing trend for power consumption in the simulation while it was even worse than broadcasting application in the real-world. This clearly indicates that simulation-based results are highly unreliable due to the inaccurate or absence of model of the channel, path-loss, interference and other important parameters.

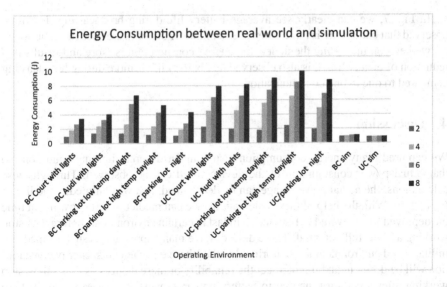

Fig. 6. Energy consumption comparison between various real-world scenarios and simulation results

3.3 Battery Life Estimation

After running the broadcast code for 30 min. in a network of 2/4/6/8 nodes while recording the power consumption of each node, we have formulated a graph as seen in Fig. 7 for the broadcast nodes in the physical environment. This figure illustrates a battery life estimate for all the experiments. The overall battery life (T) was calculated using the following equation:

$$E = I * T * V \tag{2}$$

E = Energy in Joules; I = Current drawn; T = Time; V = Voltage required

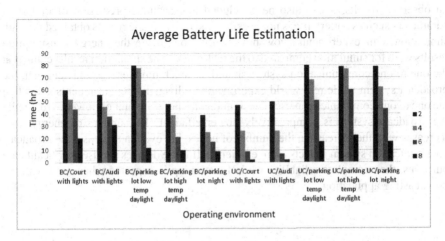

Fig. 7. Average battery life comparison in real-world environments.

In Fig. 7, we can clearly see average battery life during broadcasting. It can be observed that battery life is more when a lesser number of nodes are used in the network. As we keep on increasing the nodes, the energy consumption is more and results in a reduction of battery life. It is also observed that battery life is more during broadcasting compared to one to one communication.

4   Discussion

We captured many energy consumption results under different lighting conditions so that actual power consumption of the devices used can be observed. Through these calculations, the actual power usage can be determined, and we can predict the life of the battery. With the help of these calculations, we can predict exactly how much time the deployed low powered IoT devices will last in certain environments before they stop working at their full potential. These devices have many applications such as medical, military, and environmental monitoring. In all of these environments, energy consumption will be different and might affect the reliability of these devices as they might stop working after a certain time due to battery power exhaustion. For example, if these devices are used for healthcare monitoring, then the devices should have full functionality while the monitoring is underway. Similarly, for an agricultural farm, environmental factors such as humidity and temperature, play a major role in the quality of produce and timely detection of changes in these parameters will have a huge impact on crop production. The experiments in the open parking lot were aimed at specifically evaluating mote battery performance for such conditions/applications.

If an intruder attacks such an IoT network, its energy consumption would also increase, resulting in greater energy consumption and the potential for the device to run out of power. The power consumption of these IoT nodes has been observed in widely varied environments for optimum accuracy in results, thus generating data that is relevant to real world application designers. Any change in the environment affects battery life negatively, which results in unpredictable shutdowns due to loss of power. Based on observed results, it can also be concluded that accurate prediction of important parameters such as battery life is not possible due to unreliable results obtained through simulation. Our experiments show how wildly contrasting the energy consumption results were for simulation compared to the real-world. The simulation results claim that the one to one communication system should be much more energy efficient than the broadcast system while real-world experiments in diversified environments show that the one to one communication uses the significantly large amount of power to run while the broadcast system is comparatively power efficient. The amount of energy used increases with the increase in the number of nodes, but even in this case, the broadcast communication system reflects more efficiency. If these devices are used for healthcare purposes, then complete reliability while functioning is expected when used with the broadcasting application.

5   Conclusion

Considering the popularity of low powered IoT devices, it is important to understand the energy consumption of different applications in different environment. From the results, a significant change in energy consumption was observed, resulting in increased battery power consumption. These devices are popular for many applications, and such an analysis is important for them. These devices use limited power, so energy management is necessary and should be accurately predicted. In this paper, we conducted an analysis on energy consumption in different environments and observed that consumption varies continuously in various environment depending on the operating environment. To employ these low powered IoT devices for critical applications such as health monitoring and defense, a real-time energy consumption monitoring system should be in place which could alert a technician to take appropriate in case energy consumption levels are high. This would allow users to take appropriate action before system malfunction or critical damage.

References

1. Dunkels, A., Eriksson, J., Finne, N., Tsiftes, T.: Powertrace: network-level power profiling for low-power wireless networks (2011)
2. Velinov, A.M.A.: Running and testing applications for Contiki OS using Cooja simulator. In: International Conference on Information Technology and Development of Education – ITRO (2016)
3. Borgeson, J., Schauer, S., Diewald, H.: Benchmarking MCU power consumption for ultra-low-power applications. Texas Instruments, November 2012
4. Shnayder, V., Hempstead, M., Chen, B., Allen, G., Welsh, M.: BoSimulating the power consumption of large scale sensor network applications. In: SenSys 2nd International Conference on Embedded Networked Sensor Systems, pp. 188–200 (2004)
5. Qasem, M., Altawssi, H., Yassien, M.B., Al-Dubai, A.: Performance evaluation of RPL objective functions. In: IEEE International Conference on Computer and Information Technology; Ubiquitous Computing and Communications; Dependable, Autonomic and Secure Computing; Pervasive Intelligence and Computing (CIT/IUCC/DASC/PICOM) (2015)
6. Pongle, P., Chavan, G.: Real time intrusion and wormhole attack detection in Internet of Things (IoT). Int. J. Comput. Appl. **121**(9), July 2015
7. Looga, V., Ou, Z., Deng, Y., Jaaski, A.: Remote inference energy model for internet of things devices. In: 2015 IEEE 11th International Conference Wireless and Mobile Computing, Networking and Communications (WiMob), October 2015
8. Wang, Q., Hempstead, M., Yang, W.: A realistic power consumption model for wireless sensor network devices. In: 3rd Annual IEEE Communications Society on Sensor and Ad Hoc Communications and Networks, September 2006
9. Uwase, M., Bezunartea, M., Tiberghien, J., Dricot, J., Steenhaut, K.: ContikiMAC, some critical issues with the CC2420 radio. In: International Conference on Embedded Wireless Systems and Networks (2016)
10. Advancare: Zolertia Z1 Datasheet, March 2010. http://zolertia.sourceforge.net/wiki/images/e/e8/Z1_RevC_Datasheet.pdf. Accessed 16 Sept 2016

11. Contiki: Contiki: the open source OS for the internet of things. In: Contiki 2002. http://www.contiki-os.org/index.html. Accessed 18 Sept 2016
12. Tsiftes, N., Eriksson, J., Dunkels, A.: Low-power wireless IPv6 routing with ContikiRPL, April 2010
13. Tsvetkov, T.: RPL: IPv6 routing protocol for low power and lossy networks (2011)
14. Dunkels, A., Vall, B., Voigt, T.: Contiki - a lightweight and flexible operating system for tiny networked. In: 29th Annual IEEE International Conference on Local Computer Networks, December 2004
15. Sehgal, A.: Using the Contiki Cooja simulator, October 2013
16. Sehgal, A., Foster, I., Kesselman, C.: Using the Contiki Cooja simulator, 3 October 2013
17. Foster, I., Kesselman, C.: The Grid: Blueprint for a New Computing Infrastructure. Morgan Kaufman, San Francisco (1999)
18. Roussel, K., Song, Y., Zendra, O.: Using Cooja for WSN simulations: some new uses and limits. In: International Conference on Embedded Wireless Systems and Network - EWSN 2016, February 2016

Comparison of Power-Efficiency of Asthmatic Wheezing Wearable Sensor Architectures

Dinko Oletic[✉] and Vedran Bilas

Faculty of Electrical Engineering and Computing,
University of Zagreb, Unska 3, 10000 Zagreb, Croatia
{dinko.oletic,vedran.bilas}@fer.hr
http://www.fer.unizg.hr/liss

Abstract. Power-requirements of a wireless wearable sensor for quantification of asthmatic wheezing in respiratory sounds, a typical symptom of chronic asthma, are analysed. Two converse sensor architectures are compared. One featuring processing-intensive on-board respiratory sound classification, and the other performing communication-intensive signal streaming, employing compressive sensing (CS) encoding for data-rate reduction, with signal reconstruction and classification performed on the peer mobile device. It is shown that lower total sensor power, ranging from 216 to 357 µW, may be obtained on the sensor streaming the CS encoded signal, operating at the compression rate higher than 2x. Total power-budget of 328 to 428 µW is shown required in the architecture with on-board processing.

Keywords: m-health · Body sensor networks · Asthmatic wheeze detection · Digital signal processing · Compressed sensing · Power-analysis

1 Introduction

Asthma is one of the most widespread chronic respiratory disorders, requiring long-term treatment [1,2]. Quantification of its common symptom, occurrence of asthmatic wheezing in the respiratory sounds remains an open subject to research in the fields of pattern recognition [3–5], and biomedical sensor systems consisting of wearable sensors and smartphones (i.e. m-health) [6–9]. This paper builds upon previous research [10–15], and explores power-tradeoffs of asthmatic wheeze detection wireless wearable sensor architectures.

It is assumed that the sensor system consists of a body-worn sensor and a mobile device (i.e. smartphone). Sensor consists of the following subsystems: acoustic sensor, analog signal conditioning circuit, A/D converter, digital signal processing unit, and low-power radio for communication with smartphone [10]. Analysis covers three operating scenarios w.r.t. distribution of digitization, signal processing and communication among sensor system components.

In the first, (referent) operating scenario, sensor acquires the signal at Nyquist rate. Apart signal acquisition, no particular DSP processing tasks are

© ICST Institute for Computer Sciences, Social Informatics and Telecommunications Engineering 2017
M. Magno et al. (Eds.): S-Cube 2016, LNICST 205, pp. 149–162, 2017.
DOI: 10.1007/978-3-319-61563-9_13

performed on sensor. Raw signal is wirelessly streamed over to the smartphone, where respiratory sound classification is performed. Scenario is motivated by the idea of simplification of the sensor design, and using the smartphone as the main signal processing platform.

In order to lower quantity of data (i.e. power) streamed from sensor to smartphone, second scenario utilizes concept of compressed sensing (CS) [16–18] to mutually lower the data rate, whilst retaining the low complexity of the sensor. Sensor performs signal acquisition at the sub-Nyquist rate [12], simultaneously compressing it (CS encoding). Compressed signal is streamed over to the smartphone. There, an additional decoder subsystem block performs signal reconstruction [13,14]. Finally, classification is performed [15].

In third scenario, sensor performs on-board (on-patient) signal acquisition and respiratory sound classification [11,15] (at Nyquist-rate), and periodically reports the classification outcome to smartphone. Scenario enables for highest sensor autonomy (independence of the radio link quality and smartphone processing resources), and minimizes data traffic [10].

Paper is organized as follows: In Sect. 2 each of sensor's subsystems is analysed from the aspect of power efficiency. Based on this, total sensor power consumption is analysed in Sect. 3. Paper is concluded in Sect. 4.

2   Power Analysis of Sensor Subsystems

2.1   Acoustic Sensors and Analog Signal Conditioning

Sensor and analog signal conditioning circuit design complying with standardised guidelines for respiratory sounds acquisition [19,20] was analysed. Microphones and accelerometers were evaluated as sensors. Representative sensor technologies were evaluated: electret-condenser microphone (KEEG1542, Knowles), MEMS microphone with analog output (ADMP404, Analog Devices; ICS-40310, Invensense), MEMS microphone with digital output (ADM441, Analog Devices). Capacitive MEMS accelerometers were evaluated (ADXL337/345, Analog).

Table 1 shows that in comparison to electret-condenser microphones and accelerometers, analog MEMS microphones feature highest power-efficiency, enabling for power consumption as low as 16 µW (i.e. ICS-40310). However, they feature high output impedance. Classically used electret-condenser microphones exhibit worst power-efficiency. Accelerometers offer comparable consumption to microphones, but may feature lower bandwidth and sensitivity. Advantage of digital systems-on-chips (SoC), such as ADMP441 or ADXL355 is integration of a complete signal chain, consisting of sensor, analog conditioning, ADC, and standard encoding of digitized output signal (I^2S or SPI).

Analog signal conditioning circuit for respiratory sound acquisition accommodates several functionalities: (1) signal amplification, as the typical sensor's output signal magnitudes reside in range of 1 to 10 mV (see typical sensitivities in Table 1). Amplifier's input is required to handle sensors output impedance typically in order of kΩ. (2) band-pass filtering with lower corner frequency around 100 Hz to filter-out heart sounds, and upper corner frequency adjusted to sampling frequency for anti-aliasing. Assuming a microphone model chosen such to filter-out the low-frequencies by its frequency-characteristics, and that anti-aliasing is realised by passive RC filter, power consumption of an conditioning circuit based on a single instrumentation amplifier, such as INA333, was estimated at approx. 85 µW by Spice simulation.

Table 1. Comparison of acoustic sensors' power consumptions.

Technology	Component	Sensitivity	Imped	Power
MEMS mic., dig. (I^{2}S)	ADMP441	−26 dBFS	-	2520 µW @ 1.8 V
Electret cond. mic.	KEEG1542	−42 dB	2.2 kΩ	1000 µW @ 2.0 V
Analog accel.	ADXL337	300 mV/g	32 kΩ	900 µW @ 3.0 V
MEMS mic., analog	ADMP404	−38 dBV	200 Ω	375 µW @ 1.5 V
Accel., digital (SPI)	ADXL345	3.9 mg/LSB	-	350 µW @ 2.5 V
MEMS mic., analog	ICS-40310	−37 dBV	4.5 kΩ	16 µW @ 1.0 V

2.2 Signal Digitization

Two cases of signal digitization were analysed. First is Nyquist-rate signal sampling at 2 to 8 kHz [11] for scenarios of on-board processing or raw signal streaming), and second is compressive sampling (CS) at temporally non-uniform time-instants, as proposed in [12,14]. In case of CS, ADCs were tested at sub-Nyquist sampling rate corresponding to signal compression ratios of 2x to 8x (min. 250 Hz). Power efficiency tradeoffs of 12, 16, and 24 bit successive approximation (SAR) and sigma-delta analog to digital converters (ADCs) were compared. Components were chosen to support on-demand operating (triggered by signal processor), and entering power-saving state upon completing the conversion.

Table 2. Parameters of the tested ADCs

Technology	Component	ENOB	Nominal sample-rate	Average power @ 1 kSPS
12-bit SAR	ADS7924	11	10 kS/s	10 µW
16-bit SAR	AD7684	14	100 kS/s	15 µW
12-bit sigma-delta	ADS1014	12	3.3 kS/s	92 µW
16-bit sigma-delta	ADS1114	16	0.860 kS/s	368 µW
24-bit sigma-delta	ADS1251	19	20 kS/s	1.95 mW

A list of representative components with their respective performance is listed in Table 2. From power-up time, number of erroneous conversion samples, and conversion time, total active time was estimated for each component. From the total active times, power consumptions at the nominal sampling rate, and the sleep powers, average powers of the active/sleep duty-cycle were extrapolated, for the whole analysed range of sampling frequencies from 250 Hz to 8 kHz.

Figure 1 confirms that the lowest power is obtained for ADC-s featuring a combination of lowest supply voltage, active and sleep current, and supporting high throughput. Specifically, for the required range of sample rates, SAR models show clear advantage in average power over sigma-delta. With the 24-bit sigma-delta, 1 mW suffices for the average sample rate of merely 500 Hz. Thus, 16-bit SAR is considered optimal for respiratory sound digitization, consuming in range of 6 to 123 µW for the range of sample rates of 250 Hz to 8 kHz. In comparison to 12-bit SARs, consumption of the 16-bit SAR is about 50% higher.

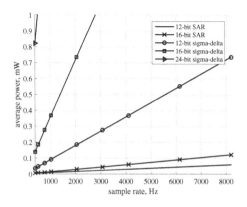

Fig. 1. Comparison of average power consumption of 12, 16 and 24-bit SAR and sigma delta ADCs in duty-cycle mode w.r.t sample rates of 250 Hz to 8 kHz.

2.3   Signal Processing

Processing Cores for Respiratory Sound Classification. Problem of asthmatic wheeze detection comes down to identification and spectro-temporal localization of unknown, temporally-changing instantaneous frequencies of individual frequency lines of asthmatic wheezing. Algorithms recently proposed for DSP implementation include either fast, heuristic algorithm [11] (i.e. referent), or more robust HMM-based [15] algorithms. Power-cost of their execution on commercial processing cores is analysed here. As a general rule, processing cores were selected to feature lowest active state power at highest operating frequency, in combination with low sleep state power, yielding potentially lowest average power [21]. Table 3 summarizes a list of the tested cores.

Three categories were analysed. First were the proprietary audio DSP cores, taking advantage of architectural accelerators for DSP functions, such as parallel multiply-and-accumulate units, barrel-shifters for floating-point operations, vector multiply, hardware FFT coprocessors, specific data transport I/O units such as I^2S. Also they are typically supported with extensive library of software functions for audio processing. 16-bit fixed-point lowest-power DSP cores were evaluated for on-board signal processing: TMS320C5535 (Texas Instruments) and ADSP2188N (Analog Devices). They were compared to a legacy 16-bit 56xxx core MC56F8006 (Freescale Semiconductors), and higher powered 32-bit ColdFire core MCF51MM128 (Freescale Semiconductors).

Table 3. Parameters of the tested digital signal processors.

Processing core	Component	Freq., MHz	µW/MHz	Sleep, µW
audio DSP, 32-bit ColdFire	MCF51MM128	50	1740	84.0
audio DSP, 16-bit 56800E	MC56F8006	32	4282	521.4
audio DSP, 16-bit ADSP-21xx	ADSP2188N	80	562	180.0
audio DSP, 16-bit C55xx	TMS320C5535	100	220	220.0
high-perf. MCU, 32-bit ARM Cortex-M3	STM32L151C8	32	540	25.0
signal acq. MCU, 16-bit ARM 7 TDMI	ADUC7060	10	775	137.5
low-power MCU, 32-bit ARM Cortex-M0	LPC1102	50	462	6.6
low-power FRAM MCU, 16-bit MSP430	MSP430FR572x	24	275	19.2
Bluetooth SoC, 8-bit 8051	CC2541	32	628	2.7
Bluetooth SoC, 16-bit ARM Cortex-M0	nRF51422	32	495	6.9
Bluetooth SoC, 32-bit ARM Cortex-M4	BGM113	38.4	307	2.7
Bluetooth SoC, 32-bit ARM Cortex-M3	CC2640	48	110	4.9
Bluetooth SoC, 32-bit ARM Cortex-M4	nRF52832	64	100	1.7

Second category were general purpose MCU-s. High performance 32-bit ARM Cortex-M3 (STM32L151C8, ST Microelectronics) was compared to lower-powered ARM Cortex-M0 (LPC1102, Linear Technologies). 32-bit ARM cores were evaluated against proprietary 16-bit MSP430 core clocked at 2x lower frequency w.r.t. ARM Cortex-M0, but executing code from ultra-low power ferroelectric (FRAM) program memory (MSP430FR572x, Texas Instruments). Also, a dedicated signal acquisition controller based on older, 16-bit ARM 7 core coupled with high precision ADC, (ADUC7060, Analog Devices) was included.

Third category were processing cores embedded in system-on chip (SoC) Bluetooth 4 communication modules. Latest generation SoC featuring 32-bit

ARM Cortex-M3 (CC2640, Texas Instruments) is compared to two different ARM Cortex-M4 cores (nRF52832, Nordic Semiconductors; BGM113, Silicon Labs). They were compared to previous-generation SoCs featuring 16-bit ARM Cortex M0 (nRF51422, Nordic Semiconductors), and 8-bit 8051 core (CC2541, Texas Instruments).

Execution times of two analysed algorithms were derived from their respective analytical execution models given in [11,15]. Models show that algorithms' execution time is dominantly dependent on: (1) frequency resolution (number of observed frequency states M), and (2) number of frequency lines L. Motivated by the dependence of execution time on signal content, a test-environment was constructed to asses the dependency of average processing power to the symptoms severity, simulating the realistic operating conditions. Symptoms severity was modelled by: (1) percentage of respiratory cycle obstructed by wheezing (wheeze rate [2]), and (2) symptom occurrence frequency.

Execution time of both algorithms was calculated on each processing core for each combination of wheeze rate, symptom rate, number of processed frequency states (M). Cores' operating frequency, register width w.r.t. assumed 16-bit data width, and cost of multiplication w.r.t. addition were taken into consideration. Knowing the intervals between consecutive processing, processing duty-cycle (portion of active-time) was calculated from execution time. Finally, average processing power was calculated, using the active and sleep power. Sleep power was based on power-state where all required periphery for short wakeup, periodic signal sampling is operative, and the memory content is retained.

Example results, showing increase of average power proportional to symptoms rate and wheeze rate, for HMM-based algorithm are shown in Fig. 2, contrasting algorithm execution on two most representative cores: 100 MHz 16-bit audio processing DSP (C5535), and 48 MHz 32-bit general purpose ARM Cortex-M3 core within Bluetooth 4 SoC (CC2640). After normalization of clock frequencies, Cortex-M3 turns out 25% more efficient.

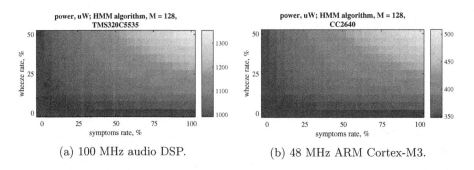

(a) 100 MHz audio DSP.   (b) 48 MHz ARM Cortex-M3.

Fig. 2. Power requirements on a 16-bit audio DSP and general purpose MCU.

Overall results are shown in Fig. 3. In Fig. 3a cores are sorted by worst-case power required for processing of wheezing w.r.t. power for processing of

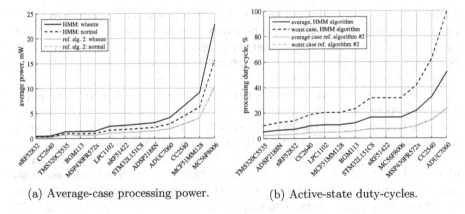

(a) Average-case processing power.   (b) Active-state duty-cycles.

Fig. 3. Ranking of processing cores by resources for wheeze classification.

normal respiratory sound, by both algorithms. It can be seen that for HMM-based algorithm, processing of wheezing may require approx. up to 45% more power than processing of normal respiratory sounds. On the other hand, referent algorithm shows negligible difference.

Best performance are obtained for ARM Cortex-M4 and M3 cores in Bluetooth 4 SoCs (nRF52832 and CC2640). Best overall results are obtained on a 64 MHz Cortex-M4 (nRF52832), ranging from 308 to 452 µW. Dedicated low-power audio C55xx DSP (TMS320C5535) requires approximately 2.7 times more average power. Worst efficiency is obtained with ADUC7060 signal acquisition controller, high-performance 32-bit ColdFire audio DSP core (MCF51-MM128), and the legacy 16-bit 568xx DSP core (MC56F8006). Also, legacy Bluetooth SoC module featuring 8051 core (CC2541) proves suboptimal due to 8-bit architecture, low clock-frequency etc.

Real-time processing constraints are analysed by examining average and worst-case processing duty-cycles, compared in Fig. 3b. Results show that least resources are spent by dedicated audio DSPs TMS320C5535 (worst-case 10% of processing time) and ADSP2188N. It is shown that due to low max. Clock-frequency (only 10 MHz), ADUC7060 signal-acquisition controller hardly meets worst-case real-time requirements when running HMM-based classification algorithm. Also, 8051 and MSP430 spend high portions of their processing time, 60% and 40%, respectively.

Processing Cores for CS Encoding. In the operating scenario of compressed signal streaming, power requirements of the CS signal encoder implementing sub-Nyquist sampling of analog input signal, at psudo-random, non-uniformly spaced sampling instants [12,14], are evaluated. As ADC power was covered in Sect. 2.2, analysis focuses on power spent on processing tasks implementing the LFSR pseudorandom number generator and the sampling period scheduler blocks in MCU software, and operation of the MCU's timer peripheral unit.

CS-encoding may be broken down to following tasks: (1) generation of LFSR pseudo-random output, (2) sampling-instant scheduling (3) timer setup of the timer, (4) triggering the ADC conversion. Cost of MCU implementation within FreeRTOS was empirically verified on prototype implementation on MSP430 to approx. 150 instructions per single CS-encoded sample.

Total cost of CS encoding was simulated for a range of CS sub-Nyquist sample rates corresponding to compression ratios of 2, 4, 5.33, and 8 w.r.t. Nyquist sampling frequency of 2 kHz. In addition to MSP430, power-cost of CS encoding was simulated on several additional MCU cores: on ADUC7060 signal acquisition controller, and on MCUs within Bluetooth 4 SoCs nRF52832, CC2640, BGM113, nRF51422 and CC2540. Results in Fig. 4 show that most efficient implementation may be achieved on Bluetooth 4 SoC ARM Cortex cores. On nRF52832 power for CS encoding ranges from 17 to 63 µW, while on CC2640 costs from 22 to 73 µW. It is shown that CS encoding on nRF52832 in worst simulated case spends less than 1% of processing time.

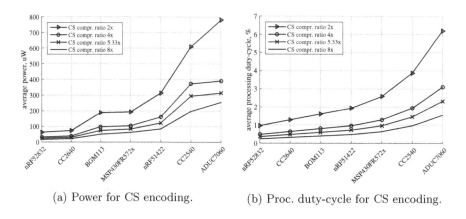

(a) Power for CS encoding.   (b) Proc. duty-cycle for CS encoding.

Fig. 4. Ranking of processing cores by resources for CS encoding.

2.4   Bluetooth Communication

Bluetooth 4.x (i.e. Smart, Low Energy) radio technology is evaluated for wireless data transfer, as it enables for interoperability with smarphones and medical certification [6], while retaining low-power operation. Highest level of integration is provided with system-on-chip (SoC) modules, packaging digital radio, radio controller implementing Bluetooth stack, an application processor, and a variety of standardized peripheral interfaces.

State-of-the-art Bluetooth 4 SoCs are analysed from stand point of power consumption: CC2640, CC2541 (Texas Instruments), BGM113 (Silicon Labs) and nRF52832 (Nordic Semiconductors). Table 4 compares their average power in most characteristic operating states: radio transmission (TX), radio listening (receiving, RX) and sleep. Power reduction in TX and RX of order of magnitude of 2 to 3 times can be observed when comparing previous and actual generations of Bluetooth 4 SoCs (CC2541 w.r.t. CC2640, nRF52832, and BGM113). Increase of processing power enables for implementation of respiratory sound classification algorithms on-board SoC's application processor.

Bluetooth 4 communication protocol is designed to foster low average power by featuring intermittent, short active time (TX, RX) of the radio, in combination with long sleep time in between connection intervals. Data packets are exchanged only at predefined periodical *connection intervals*, during so-called *connection events*. Upon completion of the connection event, radio is put to sleep until the next one [22]. Duration of connection event is minimized by high throughput (typically 2 Mbit over-the-air). Typical waveform of the CC2640 radio's power-supply current measured during the connection event, segmented into a sequence of common power-states is shown in Fig. 5a (see labels 1 to 6).

Table 4. Parameters of the tested Bluetooth 4 SoC modules.

Component	Application processor	TX, mW	RX, mW	Sleep, µW
CC2541	8-bit 8051	36.4	35.8	2.0
BGM113	32-bit ARM Cortex-M4	16.3	16.1	2.6
nRF52832	32-bit ARM Cortex-M4	13.1	12.0	2.8
CC2640	32-bit ARM Cortex-M3	11.3	10.9	1.9

Due to number of parameters influencing durations of each power-state, we focused our power analysis on CC2640, on account of availability of extensive Bletooth power estimation guidelines, tools, and data [22]. Analysis assumes following parameteres and limitations of CC2640. Power is measured at supply voltage of 1.8 V. Output power of transmitter is set to 0 dBm as communication between sensor and smartphone is taking place at the very short range (i.e. <10 m). Maximal payload size during single connection event is limited by Bluetooth software stack to 256 bytes. Time between successive connection intervals may range from minimally 7.5 ms to maximally 4.0 s.

With given constraints, average power was calculated for each of three operating scenarios: (1) streaming of uncompressed data, digitized at Nyquist rate. Cases of sampling (streaming) rates of 8 kHz and 2 kHz are singled out. 8 kHz case corresponds to case where the referent crest-tracking algorithm [11] is employed for classification on smartphone. 2 kHz case corresponds to classification by HMM-based algorithm [15]. (2) in scenario of CS compressed signal streaming, 4 compression ratios w.r.t Nyquist frequency of 2 kHz were analysed: 2, 4, 5.33 and 8x. Payload size is calculated w.r.t. original signal block size of $N = 256$ and 75% overlap. Also, each TX payload size is increased by 2 additional bytes needed for pseudorandom seed. (3) scenario of respiratory sound classification on-board sensor. Here, binary block-wise classification outcome is encoded in periodically sent report messages. Connection period and payload size depend on classification algorithm (sampling frequency, signal block size), and payload content: whether the stream of raw binary classification outcomes corresponding to each signal blocks is sent, or if wheeze-rate is calculated for a predefined temporal window. In all scenarios, 2-byte RX acknowledge message is assumed.

Relative contributions of the payload size and connection interval to average power were compared, by accumulating (buffering, storing) the TX data on sensor for multiple connection intervals spanning up to the maximal payload size, and then transmitting it in bulk. Table 5 summarizes tested scenarios, nominal payload sizes, and the span of possible connection intervals supporting the transmission given the payload size limitations (i.e. 256 bytes on CC2640).

Table 5. A list of tested communication scenarios, with best-case average power.

scenario, case	min. payload TX/RX, bytes	conn. intvl. span, ms	min. avrg. power, µW
Nyquist-rate streaming, f_s 8 kHz	256/2	16–32	914
Nyquist-rate streaming, f_s 2 kHz	128/2	31.25–62.5	373
CS streaming, compr. 2x	$(64 + 2)/2$	31.25–125	168
CS streaming, compr. 4x	$(32 + 2)/2$	31.25–250	81
CS streaming, compr. 5.33x	$(24 + 2)/2$	31.25–250	79
CS streaming, compr. 8x	$(16 + 2)/2$	31.25–250	77
class. result reporting	2/2	125–4000	8

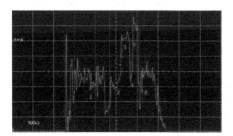

(a) Example waveform of current measured during a single Bletooth 4 connection event: 1 - RTOS wake-up, radio setup; 2 - radio on, transition to RX; 3 - radio listening (RX); 4 - transition from RX to TX; 5 - radio transmission (TX); 6 - processing the received packets, going to sleep [22].

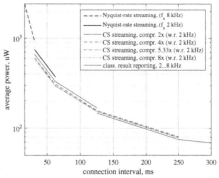

(b) Average power spent on Bluetooth 4 communication w.r.t. time between successive connection events.

Fig. 5. Power requirements of Bluetooth 4 communication.

Spans of average powers required for communication in each operating scenario w.r.t. time between successive Bluetooth connection events are shown in Fig. 5b.

It is shown that due to very short active times (i.e. high data rate), sleep power spent in-between connection intervals dominantly influences average communication power, much more than the change of payload size. This causes the average power to exponentially fall with increasing connection interval. Thus, it is proposed to maximally prolong (sleep) time between connection intervals by accumulating data, up to maximal transmission packet payload size.

Nyquist-rate data streaming proves most costly, costing 914 µW at 8 kHz (see Table 5). Drastic decrease in case of Nyquist-rate streaming at 2 kHz is primarily due to increase of connection intervals. Identical mechanism is the reason for decrease from 168 to 81 uW when step-up from CS compression ratio of 2x to 4x. On the other hand, minimal difference in average power is observed in the cases of identical connection intervals, where only payload size is increased (e.g. at the CS compression ratios 4x, 5.33x, and 8x). In scenario of on-board classification, minimal average power of only 8 µW is achieved at the maximal connection interval of 4 s.

3   Total Power Consumption

Here, total power of asthmatic wheeze sensor is analysed for each of three operating scenarios from Sect. 1. To enable for comparable performance in all operating scenarios, analysis is based on a sensor architecturally constituting of common subsystem components. As a sensor, analog MEMS microphone (such as ICS-40310) in combination with analog front-end from Sect. 2.1 is proposed. 16-bit SAR ADC (e.g. AD7684) is taken for digitalization. Processing and communication is implemented on the Bluetooth 4 SoC featuring the ARM Cortex-M4 processing core, proven optimal for both on-board classification and CS encoding tasks. In CS scenario, power-analysis is focused on compression ratios of 2x to 5.33x. Analysis is based on the representative CC2640 SoC.

Total powers are compared in Fig. 6. Being constantly powered and architecturally identical, the sensor and the analog conditioning circuit contribute equally to total power by 101 µW in all scenarios. Power contributions of remaining subsystems are scenario-dependent.

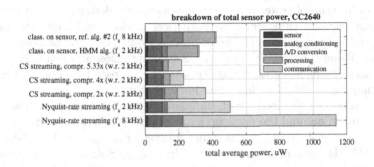

Fig. 6. Breakdown of total power per subsystems for different scenarios.

In the scenario of on-board classification, lower total power is obtained for the case of HMM-based algorithm operating on signal sampled at 2 kHz. Total power averaged 320 µW, with a major share of 56% being taken by classification algorithm. Classification using the referent crest-tracking algorithm results in 31% higher power (i.e. 420 µW).

In scenario of streaming of CS-encoded signal, total power scales down expectedly with increasing compression ratio. At the lowest compression ratios of 4x and 5.33x, it yields 228 and 216 µW, respectively. Majority of power is spent on communication. However, significant processing share related to CS encoding occurring at low compression ratios (e.g. 76 µW for compr. ratio of 2x) points to inefficiency of MCU software implementation of CS encoding. This could be improved by implementing CS encoder in hardware.

Scenario of uncompressed signal streaming virtually excludes any processing, and largest portion of power is spent on communication, proportional to the sample-rate. In best case (at 2 kHz, assuming classification using HMM-based algorithm on smartphone), power totalled 505 µW. At 8 kHz it doubled to 1138 µW. Thus, streaming of uncompressed signal proves to be the worst solution.

4   Conclusion

Architecture of the sensor for detection of asthmatic wheezing was analysed from the perspective of energy efficiency. Analysis has shown that analog MEMS microphones feature best power-efficiency, and with the proposed analog signal conditioning circuit total about 100 µW. For signal digitization, 16-bit successive approximation (SAR) ADC architecture proved optimal. Power analysis of wireless packet transfer via Bluetooth 4 has confirmed that power savings are more affected by connection intervals, than by payload size.

Lowest total power, ranging from 216 to 357 µW, may be obtained on the sensor performing CS encoding, operating at the compression rate higher than approx. 2x. By requiring less processing power, it outperforms best-case on-board classification 1.8 times. Also, by reducing the communication cost, it yields 2.2 times lower total power w.r.t. uncompressed signal streaming. This confirms usability of practically implemented CS encoding in systems where off-loading the sensor in terms of power consumption is a primary design criteria. CS offloads the communication subsystems on both peer devices, and shifts the most of the acquisition and processing power-burden from sensor to the processing on the smartphone (i.e. into the cost of CS reconstruction and respiratory sound classification). Efficiency of the MCU-based LFSR pseudorandom CS encoder design may be increased by hardware implementation.

In contrast, sensor design with on-board processing minimizes power spent on communication, and the bottleneck are respiratory sound classification algorithms. Power analysis of the processing subsystem has shown that 32-bit ARM Cortex M3/M4 cores embedded within Bluetooth 4 SoC modules feature optimal trade-off between performance and power consumption. Total power of 328 to 428 µW is observed.

References

1. Masoli, M., Fabian, D., Holt, S., Beasley, R.: Global Burden of Asthma. Medical Research Institute of New Zealand, Wellington (2010)
2. Boner, A.L., Piacentini, G.L., Peroni, D.G., Irving, C.S., Goldstein, D., Gavriely, N., Godfrey, S.: Children with nocturnal asthma wheeze intermittently during sleep. J. Asthma **47**(3), 290–294 (2010)
3. Hadjileontiadis, L.J.: Lung Sounds: An Advanced Signal Processing Perspective. Synthesis Lectures on Biomedical Engineering, vol. 9. Morgan & Claypool (2008)
4. Bahoura, M.: Pattern recognition methods applied to respiratory sounds classification into normal and wheeze classes. Comput. Biol. Med. **39**(9), 824–843 (2009)
5. Lozano, M., Fiz, J.A., Jané, R.: Automatic differentiation of normal and continuous adventitious respiratory sounds using ensemble empirical mode decomposition and instantaneous frequency. IEEE J. Biomed. Health Inform. **20**(2), 486–497 (2016)
6. Chen, M., Gonzalez, S., Vasilakos, A., Cao, H., Leung, V.C.: Body area networks: a survey. Mob. Netw. Appl. **16**, 171–193 (2011)
7. Lin, B.-S., Yen, T.-S.: An FGPA-based rapid wheezing detection system. Int. J, Environ. Res. Pub. Health **11**(2), 1573–1593 (2014)
8. Reyes, B.A., Reljin, N., Chon, K.H.: Tracheal sounds acquisition using smartphones. Sensors **14**(8), 13830–13850 (2014)
9. Boujelben, O., Bahoura, M.: FPGA implementation of an automatic wheezes detector based on MFCC and SVM. In: 2016 2nd International Conference on Advanced Technologies for Signal and Image Processing (ATSIP), pp. 647–650. IEEE (2016)
10. Oletic, D., Bilas, V.: Wireless sensor node for respiratory sounds monitoring. In: Anton, F. (ed.) IEEE I2MTC 2012, pp. 28–32. IEEE (2012)
11. Oletic, D., Arsenali, B., Bilas, V.: Low-power wearable respiratory sound sensing. Sensors **14**(4), 6535–6566 (2014)
12. Oletic, D., Skrapec, M., Bilas, V.: Prototype of respiratory sounds monitoring system based on compressive sampling. In: Zhang, Y.-T. (ed.) The International Conference on Health Informatics. IP, vol. 42, pp. 92–95. Springer, Cham (2014). doi:10.1007/978-3-319-03005-0_24
13. Oletic, D., Skrapec, M., Bilas, V.: Monitoring respiratory sounds: compressed sensing reconstruction via OMP on Android smartphone. In: Godara, B., Nikita, K.S. (eds.) MobiHealth 2012. LNICSSITE, vol. 61, pp. 114–121. Springer, Heidelberg (2013). doi:10.1007/978-3-642-37893-5_13
14. Oletic, D., Bilas, V.: Energy-efficient respiratory sounds sensing for personal mobile asthma monitoring. IEEE Sens. J. **16**(23), 1 (2016)
15. Oletic, D., Skrapec, M., Bilas, V.: Hidden Markov model in spectro-temporal tracking of asthmatic wheezing in respiratory sounds. In: Lacković, I., Vasic, D. (eds.) 6th European Conference of the International Federation for Medical and Biological Engineering. IP, vol. 45, pp. 5–8. Springer, Cham (2015). doi:10.1007/978-3-319-11128-5_2
16. Candès, E.J., Wakin, M.B.: An introduction to compressive sampling. Sig. Process. Mag. **25**(2), 21–30 (2008). IEEE
17. Kanoun, K., Mamaghanian, H., Khaled, N., Atienza, D.: A real-time compressed sensing-based personal electrocardiogram monitoring system. In: Design, Automation Test in Europe Conference Exhibition (DATE), pp. 1–6, March 2011
18. Bellasi, D.E., Benini, L.: Energy-efficiency analysis of analog and digital compressive sensing in wireless sensors. IEEE Trans. Circ. Syst. I: Regul. Pap. **62**(11), 2718–2729 (2015)

19. European respiratory review, 10 2000
20. Moussavi, Z.: Fundamentals of respiratory sounds and analysis. Synth. Lect. Biomed. Eng. **1**(1), 1–68 (2006)
21. Benini, L., de Micheli, G.: System-level power optimization: techniques and tools. ACM Trans. Des. Autom. Electron. Syst. **5**, 115–192 (2000)
22. Texas Instruments. Application report swra478a: measuring bluetooth smart power. Technical report, January 2016

Miniaturised Flame Ionisation Detector for Explosion Protection in Civil Sewerage Networks

Jan Förster[1(✉)], Winfred Kuipers[2], Christian Koch[1], Christian Lenz[3], Steffen Ziesche[3], and Dominik Jurkow[4]

[1] Krohne Innovation GmbH, Ludwig-Krohne-Str. 5, 47058 Duisburg, Germany
j.foerster@krohne.com
[2] Krohne Messtechnik GmbH, Ludwig-Krohne-Str. 5,
47058 Duisburg, Germany
[3] Fraunhofer Institue IKTS, Winterbergstr. 28, 01277 Dresden, Germany
[4] VIA Electronics, Robert-Friese Str. 3, 07629 Hermsdorf, Germany

Abstract. This work presents a new approach to enhance the civil safety by monitoring the civil sewerage networks to prevent formation of explosive atmospheres and thus enabling early initialisation of counter measures. For this approach a new system with a miniaturised flame ionisation detector (FID) as embedded sensor has been developed. The micro FID embeds the fluidic components, the micro burner, the electrical structures for ignition and ion current measurement, and resistive temperature measurement elements in one monolithic ceramic component. Characterisation of the micro FID revealed good sensor performance with high sensitivity and reduced gas consumption compared to conventional FIDs. Thus, this micro FID is an excellent choice for an embedded sensor in the context of monitoring the civil sewerage.

Keywords: Monitoring of civil infrastructure · Civil safety · Embedded sensor · Flame ionisation detector · Ceramic multilayer technology

1 Introduction

Civil sewerage networks provide a higher explosion risk for the general public than commonly assumed. Accidentally spilled fuels, traffic accidents, or even wilfully inserted flammable fluids might easily lead to an explosive atmosphere in the sewerage networks. In addition, slow running or residential waste water can form atmospheres with a high concentration of fermentation gases, which also leads to an explosive atmosphere in the sewerage networks. Explosions in the sewerage networks are especially dangerous because they normally result in massive destruction of the infrastructure. Thus, they have a high potential risk of injuring the general public. Explosions in the sewerage networks due to flammable fluids as well as due to fermentation gases have already repeatedly led to massive infrastructure damage and injuries of affected persons [1, 2]. Therefore, it is necessary to minimise the explosion risk in the sewerage networks.

© ICST Institute for Computer Sciences, Social Informatics and Telecommunications Engineering 2017
M. Magno et al. (Eds.): S-Cube 2016, LNICST 205, pp. 163–174, 2017.
DOI: 10.1007/978-3-319-61563-9_14

A minimisation of the explosion risk can only be achieved by continuous monitoring of the atmosphere in the sewerage, which allows detecting the potential formation of an explosive atmosphere at a very early stage. Thus, countermeasures can be initiated in time to prevent the formation of explosive atmospheres. Estimations of the potential explosion risk show that risk mitigation by continuous monitoring can reduce the explosion risk for critical locations from a high risk for the public to moderate or small risk. Unfortunately, devices for continuous monitoring of the sewerage do not exist yet. Nowadays, the atmosphere of the sewerage is only measured intermittently during maintenance work. Therefore, this work aims to build a system with embedded sensing which allows the continuous monitoring of the civil sewerage networks.

In order to be capable of detecting a potential formation of an explosive atmosphere at an early stage, the system needs a very sensitive sensing element. For this sensing element a variety of measurement principles exist (e.g. IR absorption sensor, catalytic heat tone sensor, electrochemical sensor, flame ionisation detector). Most of these measurement principles do not provide a sufficient sensitivity or selectivity to allow a reliable early detection of the formation of an explosive atmosphere. In addition, many of these measurement principles are not applicable to the harsh environmental conditions of the sewerage. However, the flame ionisation detector (FID) has a very high sensitivity and selectivity towards hydrocarbons and is therefore an adequate measurement principle in this context. Furthermore, the FID is quite insensitive to the environmental conditions in the sewerage network. These properties make the FID the ideal measurement principle for a system with embedded sensing to monitor the sewerage.

2   FID Theory and System Overview

In order to better understand the functionality of the system a short introduction of the working principle of an FID is given before the embedded sensing is explained.

2.1   Working Principle of an FID

The working principle of an FID is based on the ionisation of organic material in a hydrogen flame and the detection of the resulting ion current in an electric field [3]. Figure 1 shows a schematic drawing of a conventional FID. In an FID, hydrogen and air are inserted by nozzles into a burning chamber where the hydrogen is ignited. Normally, FIDs have a very high gas consumption of at least 30 ml/min hydrogen and 300 ml/min air [4]. Sample gas containing organic material to be analysed is added to the hydrogen. The organic material is ionised in the hydrogen flame. An electric field applied to the hydrogen flame extracts these ions. As a result, these ions generate a small current which is direct proportional to the amount of hydrocarbons in the organic material.

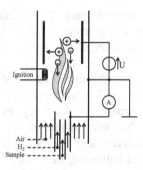

Fig. 1. Schematic drawing of a conventional FID

2.2   The Micro FID as Embedded Sensor

The overall system consists of the embedded sensing device and some peripherals for controlling. The embedded sensing device of the system consists of the FID with all its necessary elements. The aforementioned high gas consumption of conventional FIDs is not applicable to the context of monitoring the sewerage where reduced gas consumption is essential to allow long intervals between maintenance of the system. Here, miniaturised FIDs might offer adequate solutions with reduced gas consumption and appropriate sensor properties [5–7]. In addition, miniaturised FIDs allow the use of pure oxygen as a combustion gas instead of air, which leads to a further reduction of gas consumption [7]. However, these miniaturised FIDs suffer from reduced long term stability due to the non-monolithic integration in silicon-based microsystems. Therefore, our novel approach embeds the full FID system with its electrical and fluidic functionality in a monolithic ceramic component. This approach does not only combine the reduced gas consumption and good sensor performance of miniaturised FIDs and the excellent long term stability of a monolithic ceramic body, but also adds the benefit of cost-effective batch fabrication [8].

Figure 2a shows a schematic drawing of the micro FID. As shown, this ceramic component embeds electrical and fluidic components in a monolithic ceramic body. It consists of a micro burner in counter-current configuration for the hydrogen flame,

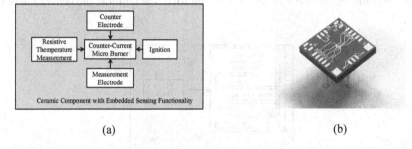

(a)   (b)

Fig. 2. Schematic drawing of the micro FID (a) and a photograph of the constructed micro FID (b)

ignition elements to start the hydrogen flame, counter and measurement electrodes to extract the generated ions, and several resistive thermometers to monitor the burning process. In order to analyse the effect of the micro burner on the sensor properties different nozzle sizes have been implemented.

Figure 2b shows a photograph of the micro FID with its electrical connections above and its fluidic interfaces underneath. The whole micro FID with all necessary internal components realised has outer dimensions of just 1.5 cm × 1.5 cm × 0.25 cm. It was manufactured in a monolithic low temperature cofired ceramic (LTCC) body using multilayer technology [8]. This technology allows the 3D-integration of electrical and fluidic elements by stacking and laminating of multiple structured LTCC green tapes followed by a co-firing process.

As mentioned before, some additional peripherals complete the system. These peripherals consist of components for the control of the gas flows, components for the power supply, and components to acquire the data of the embedded sensing device.

3   Characterisation of the Micro FID

The micro FID is the most important part of the described system. Thus, characterisation of its properties to analyse its functionality is crucial. Therefore, comprehensive measurements to determine gas consumption, sensitivity, noise, and detection limits of the micro FID have been performed with a fundamental measurement setup. This measurement setup can be transformed into a fully functional demonstration device by just a few further developments.

3.1   Measurement Setup

As shown in Fig. 3 the laboratory measurement setup consists of components to control the gas flows, the sample gas composition, and the electrical supplies. In order to achieve precise gas flows at low gas flow rates flow controllers are used to set the gas flows of the combustion gases. In addition, gas cylinders with nitrogen and a mixture of 1% methane (CH_4) in nitrogen are installed to provide sample gases. With the help of mass flow controllers and valves these two gases can be combined in any composition which enables detailed sensitivity measurements with this setup. The already existing peripheral components of the system for the control of the ignition, the generation of the

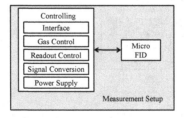

Fig. 3. Schematic drawing of the measurement setup

polarisation voltage and the ion current measurement are used in this measurement setup. Thus, just the timing control of the measurements and the handling of the measurement data have been realized in a Matlab™ programme on the measurement PC.

3.2   Determination of Minimum Gas Consumption

The first step of the characterisation was to determine the minimum gas consumption. As the hydrogen flame inside the micro FID cannot be visually inspected, the easiest way to monitor whether the flame is burning or not is measuring the surface temperature. If the hydrogen flame is burning, the surface temperature rises significantly within a few seconds.

Figure 4 shows the spatial distribution of the temperature at the surface of the micro FID for gas flows of 24 ml/min hydrogen and 12 ml/min oxygen. For a better orientation, the micro burner inside the micro FID is illustrated by a dotted line. As can be seen in the thermal image in Fig. 4, the hottest point of the surface is in the centre. At this point, the two combustion gases coming out of the nozzles mix and form the hydrogen flame. Furthermore, Fig. 4 shows that the temperature distribution follows the geometry of the micro burner because the temperature at the outlets is higher than the temperature at the nozzle inlets. Generally, from Fig. 4 it can be said, that the surface temperature decreases with rising distance from the center. Therefore, for the determination of the minimum gas flows, only the temperature at the centre of the surface has been taken into account.

Figure 5 illustrates the measured surface temperature at different gas flow rates of hydrogen and oxygen (always half of the hydrogen flow) for four different sizes of the micro burner nozzles. To enhance the readability of the graph, only results for a burning hydrogen flame are plotted in Fig. 5. As can be seen in that figure, the surface temperature rises with increasing gas flow rates. Furthermore, it can be seen that the micro burner with the biggest nozzle size needs at least gas flows of about 16 ml/min hydrogen and 8 ml/min oxygen to keep the hydrogen flame stable. At lower gas flow rates the hydrogen flame extinguishes. For smaller nozzle sizes the gas flows can be further reduced. The micro burner with half the nozzle size needs at least only approximately 10 ml/min hydrogen and 5 ml/min oxygen to keep the hydrogen flame

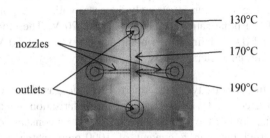

Fig. 4. Overlap of photograph of the micro FID surface and thermal image in false colour representation showing the spatial distribution of the surface temperature

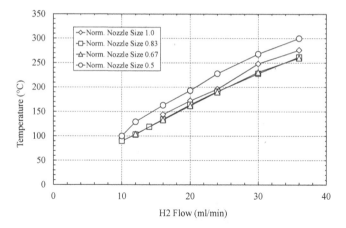

Fig. 5. Surface temperature at the centre of the micro FID vs. hydrogen gas flow for four different nozzle sizes and stoichiometric oxygen gas flow

alive. On the one hand, these minimum gas flow rates are below the necessary gas consumption of a conventional FID. On the other hand, even lower minimum gas flow rates for other micro FIDs have been reported in literature [9]. However, in the context of our application these gas flow rates were small enough to continue with the characterisation.

3.3 Sensitivity

The first step for the characterisation of the sensitivity of the micro FID is the determination of an adequate operating point, i.e., finding the best relation between polarisation voltage and current. Therefore, the gas flows of hydrogen and oxygen as well as the flow of the sample gas are set to a constant value while the polarisation voltage is swept from -100 V to $+100$ V. The result of such a measurement is shown in Fig. 6a. For that measurement the gas flows for hydrogen and oxygen have been set to 20 ml/min and 10 ml/min respectively. The sample gas composition consisted of 9000 ppm methane in nitrogen and its flow was 10 ml/min. As can been seen in Fig. 6a, the current as a function of the polarisation voltage is almost symmetric. For low polarisation voltages the current strongly increases with rising polarisation voltage until it saturates for a polarisation voltages of about 20 V. Therefore, the operating point of the micro FID is defined at a polarisation voltage of 20 V. All following measurements for the characterisation of the sensitivity have been performed at this operating point.

To determine the sensitivity of the micro FID, the gas flows of hydrogen and oxygen are set to a constant value again and the polarisation voltage is set to the operating point. The flow of the sample gas is also set to a constant value, whereas its composition is varied between a content of 1000 ppm methane in nitrogen and 9000 ppm methane in nitrogen. The result for such a measurement with a hydrogen flow of 20 ml/min, an oxygen flow of 10 ml/min, and a sample flow of 10 ml/min is

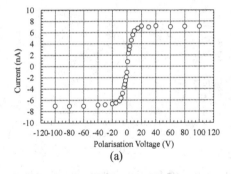

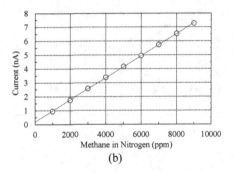

(a)   (b)

Fig. 6. Measured current for a constant sample gas composition as a function of the applied polarisation voltage (a) and measured current for a constant polarisation voltage as a function of the sample gas composition (b)

shown in Fig. 6b. As can be seen in this figure, the current linearly increases with growing methane content in the sample gas. This behaviour is as expected from an FID.

The sensitivity of the micro FID can be extracted from Fig. 6b. Its value corresponds to the slope of the current as a function of the sample gas composition. Here, the relative sensitivity is approximately 0.79 pA per 1 ppm methane in nitrogen. The relative sensitivity is a direct measure of how much current is to be expected at a certain content of organic material in the analysed sample. In the context of monitoring the civil sewerage this parameter is of high importance because it determines the possible detection resolution of the embedded sensing of the system.

However, the relative sensitivity does not give any information on how effective the FID works. To determine the effectiveness of the FID the absolute amount of organic material in the analysed sample must be taken into account. Thus, this kind of sensitivity shows how much charge carriers of an organic sample are ionised. As this value corresponds to the absolute amount of organic material, it is referred to as absolute sensitivity. Even if this value is not as crucial in the context of monitoring the civil sewerage as the relative sensitivity, it is the main parameter FIDs are compared by. For the given scenario in Fig. 6b the absolute sensitivity is approximately 8.86 mC/gC, which is lower than the values of up to 15 mC/gC reported for conventional or micro FIDs [3, 10].

Both, the relative sensitivity value and the absolute sensitivity value are valid for one specific set of gas flows only. If any of the gas flows change, the sensitivity value will change too. Therefore, the relative and the absolute sensitivity of the micro FID have been determined for multiple sample gas flows as well as for several combustion gas flows. The sample flow has been varied from 1 ml/min to 16 ml/min. The hydrogen flow has been set to 12 ml/min, 16 ml/min, 20 ml/min, and 24 ml/min and the oxygen flow was always set to half of the hydrogen flow.

The results for constant hydrogen and oxygen flows of 24 ml/min and 12 ml/min respectively are shown in Fig. 7. As can be seen from Fig. 7a, the relative sensitivity increases with growing sample flow until it levels out or even decreases again with further growing sample flows. The sample flow which corresponds to the highest

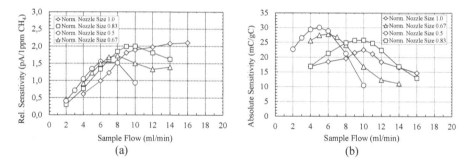

Fig. 7. Relative sensitivity (a) and absolute sensitivity (b) as a function of the sample flow for a constant hydrogen and oxygen flow of 24 ml/min and 12 ml/min respectively

relative sensitivity of a micro FID shifts from 6 ml/min to 14 ml/min with increasing FID nozzle size. In addition, a higher maximum value can be reached with increasing nozzle size. Figure 7b shows that the absolute sensitivity of the micro FIDs first increases with growing sample gas flows and then decreases again with further growing sample gas flows. Just like for the relative sensitivity, the maximum values of the absolute sensitivity shift to higher sample flow rates with increasing nozzle size. In contrast to the relative sensitivity, the maximum value of the absolute sensitivity is accomplished by the micro FID with the smallest nozzle. The absolute sensitivity of approximately 29.9 mC/gC is twice as high as the values reported in literature [3, 10]. This indicates an outstandingly good effectiveness of the developed micro FID.

The maximum values of the relative and the absolute sensitivity for the other sets of hydrogen and oxygen flows are summarised in Tables 1 and 2. The sample gas flows for the results shown in these tables correspond to the sample gas flows for the maximum values in Fig. 7a and b. The results from these two tables show that both, the relative and the absolute sensitivity, decrease with reduced hydrogen and oxygen flows. However, the overall dependency of the relative and absolute sensitivity on the sample flow as described before still occurs at reduced hydrogen and oxygen flows. Thus, a trade-off between gas consumption and sensitivity has to be found to match the requirements for the embedded sensor in the context of monitoring the civil sewerage.

Table 1. Maximum values of the relative sensitivity for given hydrogen and oxygen flows

Hydrogen and oxygen Flow (ml/min)	Relative sensitivity (pA/1 ppm methane)			
Norm. nozzel size	1.0	0.83	0.67	0.5
12/06	–	–	–	0.43
16/08	–	1.06	0.91	0.76
20/10	1.49	1.54	1.34	1.13
24/12	2.10	2.00	1.72	1.55

Table 2. Maximum values of the absolute sensitivity for given hydrogen and oxygen flows

Hydrogen and oxygen flow (ml/min)	Absolute sensitivity (mC/gC)			
Norm. nozzel size	1.0	0.83	0.67	0.5
12/06	–	–	–	10.7
16/08	–	15.4	16.2	16.8
20/10	16.4	20.9	22.2	23.5
24/12	22.4	25.7	27.7	29.9

3.4   Noise, Leakage Current and Detection Limit

In theory, the embedded sensor could yield a very low detection limit with the reported values of the relative sensitivity. The detection limit represents the smallest concentration of hydrocarbon in the sample gas which can be detected reliably. However, the detection limit is restricted by the noise of the micro FID [8].

In general, the noise of a micro FID originates in fluctuations of the hydrogen flame as well as in a leakage current [9]. If there is a leakage current present, its noise will contribute to the overall noise of the micro FID. The higher the leakage current is the more noise it will contribute to the overall noise. Therefore, measurements to determine leakage current and noise were of high interest.

Figure 6b shows that the dotted line representing the relative sensitivity does not meet the point of origin but has a small offset. This offset is due to leakage current, i.e. there is always a small current present in the micro FID even if there is no organic material in the sample. Thus, there is leakage current present in the micro FID which might contribute to the overall noise.

In order to determine the leakage current of the micro FIDs, the flows of hydrogen and oxygen are set to specific values while the sample composition is constantly set to pure nitrogen. The polarisation voltage is then swept from -100 V to $+100$ V. The result of such a measurement for hydrogen and oxygen flows of 20 ml/min and 10 ml/min respectively is shown in Fig. 8a. The graph shows a clear ohmic behaviour, which corresponds to a system resistance of approximately 24 GΩ.

The conductance of the ceramic material changes with temperature [8]. Therefore, the leakage current has been measured at several combustion gas flows to observe the influence of the combustion temperature on the insulation resistance. The results of these measurements are shown in Fig. 8b. The graph shows two different temperature regimes. For temperatures above 170 °C the insulation resistance decreases with rising temperature. This behaviour is in accordance to the physical understanding of an insulator. For temperatures less than 170 °C the insulation resistance decreases with falling temperature and even drops by several orders of magnitudes at a temperature around 100 °C. This behaviour is quite in contrast to the physical understanding of an insulator. However, it can be explained by the function of an FID. The product of the combustion of hydrogen and air is water vapour. This water vapour has a high vapour pressure. Thus, it starts to condense at temperatures just below 100 °C. As the hottest point of the micro FID is just above 100 °C, several parts of the micro FID are cooler

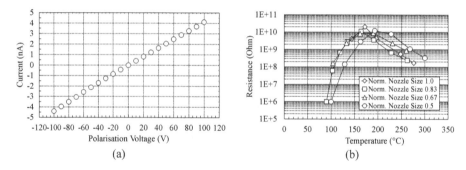

Fig. 8. Leakage current as a function of the polarisation voltage for hydrogen and oxygen flows of 20 ml/min and 10 ml/min respectively (a) and derived isolation resistance of the micro FIDs as a function of the surface temperature (b)

than 100 °C and thus, condensation of the water vapour occurs. The condensation film between the polarisation electrodes reduces the insulation resistance. Not only causes the condensation a high leakage current but it might also lead to fluidic disturbances. As a consequence, to obtain a working micro FID with low gas consumption measures against the condensation are obligatory.

As the operation of the micro FID with noticeable condensation effects does not represent realistic operating conditions at all, only measurements without any noticeable condensation effects are taken into account for the noise estimation. The noise was estimated using the standard deviation σ. It is defined as ±3σ [9]. Therefore, the standard deviation of the signal during time periods of 100 s was calculated. As the signal to noise ratio is most crucial at very low signal levels, the noise estimations have been performed without any methane content in the sample gas. The results are shown in Fig. 9a. This graph shows that the noise increases from a few picoamperes to values above 30 pA with increasing hydrogen flow. As the temperature and thus the leakage current also rises with increasing hydrogen flow, it is most probable that there is a dependency of the noise on the leakage current. This dependency is shown in Fig. 9b. Here, it can be seen, that the noise increases with increasing leakage current. As the

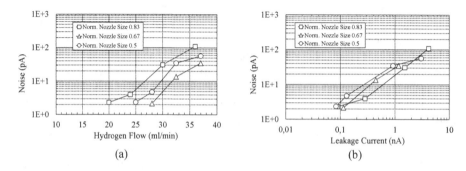

Fig. 9. Noise (±3σ) of three different nozzle sizes as a function of the hydrogen flow (a) and as a function of the leakage current (b)

curves for different nozzle sizes overlap quite well, the noise presumably depends most strongly on the leakage current. Thus, reducing the leakage current by additional guard electrode structures should lead to a noticeable noise minimisation.

With these estimated noise values and the measured relative sensitivity values the detection limit of the micro FID can be calculated. It is defined as two times the noise divided by the relative sensitivity [9]. For the smallest noise value of 2.2 pA at an hydrogen flow of 20 ml/min and the corresponding relative sensitivity value of 1.73 pA/ppm the detection limit of the micro FID is approximately 2.5 ppm, i.e., a methane concentration of 2.5 ppm in the sample gas can be detected by our embedded sensor. For the lowest noise values of the micro FIDs with the other nozzle sizes comparable detection limits between 3 ppm and 4 ppm have been achieved.

In the context of monitoring the sewerage system these detection limits are more than adequate. Furthermore, the noise of our micro FID and its detection limit are in good accordance to the values of other micro FIDs reported in literature [9]. However, these values are not as good as the values of conventional FIDs [3, 4, 9].

4 Conclusion

A novel approach to enhance the civil safety by monitoring the sewerage networks for formation of explosive atmospheres with the help of a system using a miniaturised FID as an embedded sensor was presented. The micro FID was successfully produced using LTCC ceramic multilayer technology. The characterisation of the micro FID revealed a good overall performance. The gas consumption could be reduced to a hydrogen flow of 12 ml/min and an oxygen flow of 6 ml/min which is less than half of the hydrogen flow in conventional FIDs. Further reduction of the gas consumption might be achieved by improving the size of the ceramic body as well as by pre-heating the micro FID. The measured absolute sensitivity of 29.9 mC/gC testifies an excellent effectiveness of the micro FID. Thus, it can be used to detect small quantities of organic material in the sample gas. However, the noise level of several picoamperes limits the detection capability of the micro FID to approximately 2.5 ppm in the best case. Therefore, further improvement must deal with reducing the noise by introducing a guard electrode structure and thus minimising the leakage current.

Acknowledgments. This work is part of the project "FIDEX – Autonomer Mikroflammen-ionisations-detektor für den Explosionsschutz in zivilen Kanalisationsnetzen" and is financially supported by the German *Bundesministerium für Bildung und Forschung BMBF* (#13N13271).

References

1. Flammeninferno nach Explosion von Bahn-Zisternenwagen. Neue Züricher Zeitung (2009)
2. Explosion in der Kanalisation. Stuttgarter Zeitung (2016)
3. Hill, H.H., McMinn, D.G.: Detectors for capillary chromatography. J. Chem. Anal., 7–21 (1992)

4. Amirav, A., Tzanani, N.: Electrolyzer-powered flame ionization detector. Anal. Chem. **69**, 1248–1255 (1997)
5. Zimmermann, S., Wischhusen, S., Müller, J.: Micro flame ionization detector and micro flame spectrometer. J. Sens. Actuators B **63**, 159–166 (2000)
6. Kuipers, W.J., Müller, J.: A planar micro-flame ionization detector with an integrated guard electrode. J. Micromech. Microeng. **18** (2008)
7. Kuipers, J., Müller, J.: Characterization of a microelectromechanical systems-based counter-current flame ionization detector. J. Chromatogr. A **1218**, 1891–1898 (2011)
8. Lenz, C., Neubert, H., Ziesche, S., Förster, J., Koch, C., Kuipers, W., Deilmann, M., Jurkow, D.: Development and characterization of a miniaturized flame ionization detector in ceramic multilayer technology for field applications. In: Proceedings of Eurosensors (2016)
9. Kuipers, W.J.: Design, Fabrication and Characterization of a MEMS-Based Counter-Current Flame Ionization Detector. Doktor Hut Verlag, München (2011)
10. Grob, R.L.: Modern practice of gas chromatography, 3rd edn. Wiley, New York (1995)

Relative Translation and Rotation Calibration Between Optical Target and Inertial Measurement Unit

Manthan Pancholi[1]($\boxtimes$), Svilen Dimitrov[1], Norbert Schmitz[1],
Sebastian Lampe[2], and Didier Stricker[1]

[1] German Research Center for Artificial Intelligence,
Trippstadter Strasse 122, 67663 Kaiserslautern, Germany
{manthan.pancholi,svilen.dimitrov,norbert.schmitz,
didier.stricker}@dfki.de
[2] Volkswagen Group Research, 38436 Wolfsburg, Germany
http://av.dfki.de/

Abstract. Cameras and Inertial Measurement Units are widely used for motion tracking and general activity recognition. Sensor fusion techniques, which employ both Vision- and IMU-based tracking, rely on their precise synchronization in time and relative pose calibration. In this work, we propose a novel technique for solving both time and relative pose calibration between an optical target (OT) and an inertial measurement unit (IMU). The optical tracking system gathers $6DoF$ position and rotation data of the OT and the proposed approach uses them to simulate accelerometer and gyroscope readings to compare them against real ones recorded from the IMU. Convergence into the desired result of relative pose calibration is achieved using the adaptive genetic algorithm.

Keywords: Relative pose calibration · Inertial measurement unit · Tracking calibration · Genetic algorithm

1 Introduction

This paper briefly introduces the reader to the needs in the field of pose tracking for augmented reality applications. Then it summarizes its main contribution of relative pose and time calibration between an OT and an IMU. A survey of the related work is presented before explaining the theoretical part of the developed calibration approach. The largest portion of the paper is the actual implementation, followed by convergence results of the rotation and translation, as well as the time synchronization.

1.1 Motivation

$6DoF$ pose estimation is important in the field of activity recognition, motion recognition, and robotics. Most techniques use visual-based tracking, which suffer

© ICST Institute for Computer Sciences, Social Informatics and Telecommunications Engineering 2017
M. Magno et al. (Eds.): S-Cube 2016, LNICST 205, pp. 175–186, 2017.
DOI: 10.1007/978-3-319-61563-9_15

from bad lighting conditions. Other techniques employ IMUs, which suffer from magnetometer distortions and integration drift. Recently, sensor fusion techniques which combine both types of sensors to gain precise tracking, are trending in research. To improve their recognition accuracy they rely on relative pose calibration between the sensors and synchronization in time.

1.2   Contribution

In this work, we propose a novel technique for estimating the three-dimensional translation and three-dimensional rotation offset between an OT and an IMU, as well as synchronization of their readings in time. It first gathers simultaneous data from tracked OT with $6DoF$ pose, and accelerometer and gyroscope readings from IMU over a short period of time. Then it generates simulated accelerometer and gyroscope readings based on the real measurement from the optical tracking system. These simulated readings are compared against the real IMU readings in a genetic algorithm to find out the best fitting $6DoF$ translational and rotational offset between them. Then it repeats the genetic algorithm with shifted readings in order to minimize their time delay. Hardware-wise, besides the optical tracking system and the IMU itself we do not rely on any other external hardware like a turntable or other complex apparatus.

1.3   Related Work

With the research in vision- and inertial-based tracking and their simultaneous usage emerges the need of their calibration as a combination. J. Alves and J. Lobo published first results in this field by aligning the rotation between a camera and an IMU using vertical vision features and the vertical gravity vector measured by an accelerometer [1]. They later refined their work by including the translation calibration using a simple passive turntable and static images [6]. A year later Mirzaei and Roumeliotis proposed a Kalman filter-based algorithm for IMU-camera calibration, where they removed the calibration constraints of a special setup [8]. The follow-up research continued refining those results by using different Kalman filter adaptations and hardware [4,5,10]. In filtering framework approach, estimation of the pose of IMU is required, which is generally non-trivial to achieve and requires complex modeling. Yet all of the mentioned research considers a relative pose calibration between a camera and an IMU, while in our case we are interested in the relative pose calibration between an OT and an IMU using the adaptive genetic algorithm in corporate with simulating the IMU readings. In this sense, our research direction is also similar to the estimation of the relative 6DoF pose. To our knowledge, the relative pose calibration by simulating IMU readings is not researched yet.

2   Relative Pose Calibration Approach

In this section, the calibration procedure is formulated to determine $6DoF$ relative pose between the OT and the IMU. We start by introducing three separate reference frames which have been considered.

- *Global frame G:* The pose of the OT is represented with respect to this coordinate frame which is fixed in the environment.
- *Optical frame O:* The OT represents this frame.
- *IMU frame I:* The IMU represents this frame and all the inertial measurements are expressed in this coordinate frame.

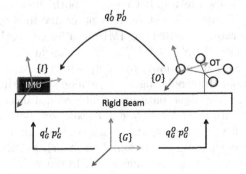

Fig. 1. Global (G), Optical (O) and IMU (I) reference frames (x-axis red, y-axis green, z-axis blue). The unknown transformation from the OT frame to the IMU reference frame can be expressed by unit quaternion q_O^I (rotation from O to reference frame I) and translation vector P_O^I (3D position of the IMU with respect to frame O). Similarly, the known pose of the OT is expressed by q_G^O (rotation from G to O) and P_G^O (3D position of the OT with respect to frame G). (Color figure online)

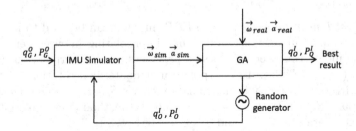

Fig. 2. Calibration algorithm flow diagram

Our approach consists of two major schemes, namely *IMU Simulator* and *Genetic Algorithm (GA)*. Figure 2 illustrates overview of our calibration algorithm. The IMU Simulator uses the recorded tracking data (q_G^O, P_G^O) of the OT and the unknown offsets (q_O^I, P_O^I) randomly generated by the GA to simulate corresponding IMU readings, represented as simulated angular velocity $\vec{\omega}^I_{sim}$ and acceleration $\vec{a}^I_{sim}$ in the IMU reference frame. As a next step, simulated data is compared with the real data captured from the IMU to calculate the fitness values as explained later in Subsect. 2.2. Depending on the fitness values, GA generates new offsets in each iteration until the best individual (q_O^I, P_O^I) is found. To demonstrate the ability of our proposed approach, methodology has been discussed in the following sections.

2.1 Inertial Sensor System Simulation

Using optical tracking system, we can perceive "tracking" as measurement of the position and orientation (q_G^O, P_G^O) of the OT with multiple markers. Inertial sensor system simulation uses these measurements to simulate IMU readings in terms of angular velocity and acceleration. The IMU and the OT are fixed on a single rigid body as shown in Fig. 1. Generally, both these system data arrives at different frequency rates. Therefore, it is necessary to compute the pose of the OT at the same rate as the arriving IMU data for comparison. To solve this problem we interpolate the q_G^O and P_G^O at the timestamps t^{IMU} of real IMU. There are several methods available to interpolate the 3D positions and unit quaternion orientations. Interpolating in quaternion space using unit quaternion representation ensures a unique path under all circumstances. For the position interpolation we are using *Cubic Spline Interpolation* method with a "not-a-knot" condition, which means that, at the first and last interior break, even the third derivative is continuous (up to round-off error). So, there are no breaks at any knots. Continuity of this method is C^2. In our case we have known P_G^O positions (knots) corresponding to optical timestamps $t^{optical}$. So, for the given data points $(t_1^{optical}, P_{G,1}^O), ..., (t_n^{optical}, P_{G,n}^O)$, $S(t^{optical})$ is a cubic interpolating spline function for this data if [7],

$$S(t_i^{optical}) = P_{G,i}^O, i = 1, ..., n. \tag{1}$$

Applying "not-a-knot" condition, which is:

$$\dddot{S}_1(t_2^{optical}) = \dddot{S}_2(t_2^{optical}), \dddot{S}_{n-2}(t_{n-1}^{optical}) = \dddot{S}_{n-1}(t_{n-1}^{optical}), \tag{2}$$

Spherical Linear Interpolation (SLERP) method can be used to interpolate between two unit quaternions. But, while interpolating between series of the unit quaternions, this method doesn't provide smooth interpolation curve at the nodes (q_G^O at $t^{optical}$). To interpolate unit quaternion rotations of the OT at t^{IMU} with C^2 continuity in interpolation curve, *Spherical Spline Quaternion Interpolation (SQUAD)* [2] is used. The *SQUAD* method does cubic interpolation between data points $q_{G,i}^O$ and $q_{G,i+1}^O$ using Eqs. 3 to 7.

$$Slerp(q_{G,i}^O, q_{G,i+1}^O, T) = q_{G,i}^O \frac{sin((1-T)\theta)}{sin(\theta)} + q_{G,i+1}^O \frac{sin(T\theta)}{sin(\theta)} \tag{3}$$

$$cos(\theta) = q_{G,i}^O \cdot q_{G,i+1}^O \tag{4}$$

Where $T \in [0, 1]$ depending on the value of t^{IMU} lying between two consecutive $t_i^{optical}$ and $t_{i+1}^{optical}$ where we want to interpolate the quaternion,

$$T = \frac{t^{IMU} - t_i^{optical}}{t_{i+1}^{optical} - t_i^{optical}}, \tag{5}$$

$$Squad(q_{G,i}^O, q_{G,i+1}^O, s_i, s_{i+1}, T)$$
$$= Slerp(Slerp(q_{G,i}^O, q_{G,i+1}^O, T), Slerp(s_i, s_{i+1}, T), 2T(1-T)), \tag{6}$$

The point s_i and s_{i+1} are called inner quadrangle points which guarantee continuity across segments. For the data set of unit quaternions $(q_{G,1}^O, q_{G,2}^O, ..., q_{G,n}^O)$, $s_1 = q_{G,1}^O$ and $s_n = q_{G,n}^O$.

$$s_i = q_{G,i}^O \exp(-\frac{\log((q_{G,i}^O)^{-1} * q_{G,i+1}^O) + \log((q_{G,i}^O)^{-1} * q_{G,i-1}^O)}{4}) \qquad (7)$$

After applying interpolation procedures, the IMU pose with respect to the global frame is calculated using Eqs. 8 and 9, by considering unknown relative pose (q_O^I, P_O^I) and known pose (q_G^O, P_G^O) at t^{IMU} timestamps.

$$q_G^I = q_G^O q_O^I, \qquad (8)$$

$$P_G^I = P_G^O + q_G^O P_O^I conj(q_G^O), \qquad (9)$$

The reason behind interpolating the pose corresponding to timestamps t^{IMU} is to calculate simulated instantaneous inertial measurement readings to compare with real readings acquired from the IMU at timestamps t^{IMU}. The simulated angular velocity $\vec{\omega}^I_{sim}$ in the IMU frame is calculated by taking the derivative of quaternion $\frac{dq}{dt}$ as expressed in Eq. 10.

$$\vec{\omega}^I_{sim} = 2conj(q_G^I)\dot{q}_G^I, \qquad (10)$$

An accelerometer measures the external specific force acting on the IMU sensor. The specific force consists of both, the sensor's acceleration and the Earth's gravity. Also, the IMU measures gravitational acceleration in the opposite direction of gravitational force. In our case gravity is acting towards the negative Z-axis direction of global reference frame (G). So, the gravitational acceleration vector $\vec{a}^G_g$ consists positive acceleration g in Z-axis direction (Eq. 11).

$$\vec{a}^G_g = (0, 0, 9.81)ms^{-2}, \qquad (11)$$

Acceleration in G frame $\vec{a}^G_{I,i}$ is calculated by adding $\vec{a}^G_g$ to the net linear acceleration from the change in positions P_G^I at each time instances t^{IMU} according to Eq. 12. But, to compare with real IMU accelerometer readings, $\vec{a}^G_{I,i}$ needs to be expressed in the IMU reference frame by rotating it according to q_G^I as in Eq. 13.

$$\vec{a}^G_{I,i} = \frac{v_i^G - v_{i-1}^G}{t_i^{IMU} - t_{i-1}^{IMU}} + \vec{a}^G_g, \qquad (12)$$

$$\vec{a}^I_{sim,i} = conj(q_{G,i}^I)\vec{a}^G_{I,i}q_{G,i}^I, \qquad (13)$$

Where, v_i^G is the velocity at i^{th} time instance t_i^{IMU}. Calculated $\vec{\omega}^I_{sim}$ and $\vec{a}^I_{sim}$ will be compared with the real IMU data $(\vec{\omega}^I_{real}, \vec{a}^I_{real})$ in *Genetic Algorithm* technique to solve the calibration problem.

2.2   Genetic Algorithm

In this work, we propose the usage of an Adaptive Genetic Algorithm [3] to find the rotational and positional offsets between the OT and the IMU. It maintains a population of n possible solutions with associated fitness values. Parents, in this case rotations or translations, are sorted to produce new population based on their fitness value, being the mean value of the difference between the simulated values ($\overrightarrow{\omega}^I_{sim}$, $\overrightarrow{a}^I_{sim}$) and the real values ($\overrightarrow{\omega}^I_{real}$, $\overrightarrow{a}^I_{real}$), explained later in this section. New generations of solutions are produced near the top previous solutions using uniform distribution, which contain on average more good genes than previous generation. Once the population has converged and is not producing new populations noticeably different from those in previous generations, the algorithm itself is said to have converged to a set of solutions to the problem at hand. This concept should be applied two times, first to get rotation offset q^I_O while keeping translation offset $P^I_O = 0$ followed by the second step, which involves fixing the rotation offset obtained in the first part and searching for the best translation offset P^I_O. Note that the above is possible since we can use a gyroscope simulation readings for comparison, which should not be affected by the translation. In this case, fitness values F_{gyro} are calculated according to the Eq. 14.

$$F_{gyro} = \frac{\sum_{i=1}^{N} |\overrightarrow{\omega}^I_{sim,i} - \overrightarrow{\omega}^I_{real,i}|}{N}, \tag{14}$$

For the translational offset approximation, the accelerometer readings are used to calculate fitness values F_{acclr}. Where N is a number of samples.

$$F_{acclr} = \frac{\sum_{i=1}^{N} |\overrightarrow{a}^I_{sim,i} - \overrightarrow{a}^I_{real,i}|}{N}, \tag{15}$$

3   Experiment

3.1   Hardware

To justify the accuracy of our calibration algorithm we carried out several experiments with hardware including, *ART* optical tracking system and the *EPSON* IMU. *ART* provides 6DoF pose (q^O_G, P^O_G) of the optical target with four markers, these measurements are retrieved through *DTrack2 SDK* at 60 Hz frequency. The IMU is a M-G350-PD11 model manufactured by *EPSON*, which provides angular velocity $\overrightarrow{\omega}^I_{real}$ and acceleration data $\overrightarrow{a}^I_{real}$ at 125 Hz. Both of these are mounted on a 45 cm long rigid beam (see Fig. 3), the IMU on one end and the OT on the other end with freedom to vary the distance in between them.

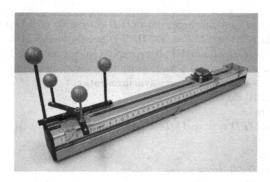

Fig. 3. 45 cm long rigid beam mounted with OT and IMU

3.2   Data Acquisition

At the start of each experimental trial we perform free non-specified movement around each axis of the beam for approximately 30 s, and gather the data from OT and the IMU system. There is no constraint on how one should move the beam during experiment. $6DoF$ pose is interpolated from 60 Hz to 125 Hz as explained in Sect. 2.1 to get $\overrightarrow{\omega}^I_{sim}$ and $\overrightarrow{a}^I_{sim}$. Random generation of q^I_O and P^I_O is explained in Sect. 3.3.

3.3   Genetic Algorithm Implementation and Parameters

Algorithm 1 illustrates a pseudo-code of the implementation of the genetic algorithm:

Initial Run: Using uniform distribution, here we generate 10000 random seeds (q^I_O, P^I_O), out of which 1000 best are selected for our adaptation iterations. We place no limit on the rotation direction, while for the translation all the three axes are limited to be in the range of $[-1, 1]$ meters. In order to evaluate our resulted genes (q^I_O, P^I_O) we compute corresponding simulated gyroscope and acceleration readings for comparison with the real ones by calculating the average over the values of the vector difference between simulated and real vectors (Eqs. 13 and 14).

Since the double differentiation of discrete positions generates artifacts, window based sliding average smoothing over the simulated acceleration readings is required before comparing them with the real ones [9]. We considered a window size of 7 discrete values.

Input: 60 Hz 6DoF optical target data OTD consisting of 3-D position $OTPos$
and 3-D rotation $OTRot$, 125 Hz 3-D accelerometer $AReal$ and 3-D
gyroscope $GReal$ inertial measurement unit data $IMUD$

Output: 6-DoF translational v and rotational r offset between the OT and the
IMU as well as their time synchronization t

for $s \leftarrow -10$ **to** 10 **do**

    shift OTD by s

    synchronize OTD rate to $IMUD$ rate with Spline and SQUAD

    $v_s \leftarrow (0,0,0)$

    for $i \leftarrow 0$ **to** 9999 **do**

        $rq_i \leftarrow$ random quaternion

        $GSim \leftarrow$ simulated values according to rq and v_s

        $qdist_i \leftarrow avg(|GSim - GReal|)$

    $sort(rq$ by $qdist)$

    $maxangle \leftarrow 60$

    for $repeat \leftarrow 0$ **to** 9 **do**

        for $i \leftarrow 0$ **to** 249 **do**

            for $axis \leftarrow 0$ **to** 2 **do**

                $maxangle \leftarrow maxangle * (repeat - 1)/repeat$

                $rangle \leftarrow$ random angle between $\pm maxangle$

                $rq[250 + i * axis] \leftarrow rq_i$ rotated over $axis$ by $rangle$

                $GSim \leftarrow$ simulated angular velocities according to rq

                $qdist_i \leftarrow avg(|GSim - GReal|)$

        $sort(rq$ by $qdist)$

    $r_s \leftarrow rq_0$

    $maxdist \leftarrow \pm 1$

    for $i \leftarrow 0$ **to** 9999 **do**

        $rv_i \leftarrow$ random vector; $ASim \leftarrow$ simulated values according to rv and q_s

        $vdist_i \leftarrow avg(|ASim - AReal|)$

    $sort(rv$ by $vdist)$

    $maxdist \leftarrow 0.1$

    for $repeat \leftarrow 0$ **to** 9 **do**

        for $i \leftarrow 0$ **to** 249 **do**

            for $axis \leftarrow 0$ **to** 2 **do**

                $maxdist \leftarrow maxdist * (repeat - 1)/repeat$

                $vtrans \leftarrow$ random vector between $\pm maxdist$

                $rv[250 + i * axis] \leftarrow rv_i$ translated over $axis$ by $vtrans$

                $ASim \leftarrow$ simulated accelerations according to rv

                $smooth(ASim)$

                $vdist_i \leftarrow avg(|ASim - AReal|)$

        $sort(rv$ by $vdist)$

    $v_s \leftarrow rv_0$

$t \leftarrow s[min(v_s + q_s)]$

return t, v_s, r_s

Algorithm 1. CALIBRATE-OT-IMU synchronizes and calibrates the relative translation and orientation between optical target and inertial measurement unit

Adaptation Iterations: We converge to the desired rotation or translation by filtering out the best 250 results out of 1000. Then for each axis we rotate or displace by a given factor f, depending on the iteration progress. The factor is being reduced according to the formula in Eq. 16.

$$f = \frac{iterations - 1}{iterations} \tag{16}$$

The initial rotation range is set in the range $\pm 60°$, while the translation range is set to ± 10 cm. 10 iterations are performed, which means that on the second iteration the rotational range will be $\pm 54°$ and the translation range will be ± 9 cm. We choose again a random value in the range using uniform distribution. This way, 250 best population from the previous iteration are stored and 750 new population around them are generated in each iteration.

Time Shifting: We store the best result and its fitness value after each run of the genetic algorithm. Then, the tracked IMU real data is shifted over the time line followed by rerunning the algorithm to see for which time shift the best result is achieved. We do this, because our initial synchronization suffers from hardware constraints like IMU data latencies.

4   Results

The effectiveness of the proposed approach is measured in terms of how it converges to the desired results in terms of rotation offset, translation offset, and time synchronization. The translation reference estimate (T) for this experiment is obtained by measuring the distance of the IMU reference frame I origin from the optical target frame O origin based on the information provided in the data sheets of ART[1] and $EPSON$ IMU[2]. During the experiments, the translation offset from O to I is $T = (0.40, 0.025, -0.07)$ m and the rotation offset was set to be zero using calibration technique provided in ART tracking system. By plotting the data captured from both sensor systems, time delay was measured to be between 32 and 40 ms. An exact time delay during the experiment couldn't be measured due to sampling rate disturbances in both DTrack and Epson recording soft- and hardware. We performed several experiments with this ground truth and ran the algorithm multiple times to measure its different outputs. From those the computed translations had an average 3D difference of $(0.0032837, 0.0059151, -0.00427)$ m, and the quaternion rotation had component wise an average difference of $(0.000656, -0.00515105, -0.00317474, 0.0357037)$. Sections 4.1, 4.2 and 4.3 show our genetic algorithm convergence to its best chosen rotation offset, translation offset, and time offset in the experiment with the mentioned reference estimates.

---

[1] ART System User Manual, version 2.1, April 2015.
[2] M-G350-PD11 Datasheet, 21 October 2012.

4.1   Rotation Convergence

Figure 4 illustrates 3 different iteration steps of our rotational convergence:

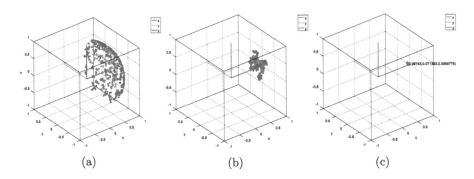

(a)   (b)   (c)

Fig. 4. 3-D rotational convergence to $(1, 0, 0, 0)$ (Color figure online)

In (a) we see the 1000 best results after filtering with sorting the initial seed phase consisting of 10000 seeds. In (b) we see iteration 3 and in (c) is iteration 10, our best result which belongs to quaternion $q_O^I = (0.999344, -0.00515105, -0.00317474, 0.0357037)$, and is close to the rotation reference estimate $q_{O,ref.}^I = (1, 0, 0, 0)$. The dots represent rotations of vector (1, 0, 0) according to the generated quaternion seeds. And the color transition from red to green represents bad and good fitness values respectively. Which means best obtained q_O^I will rotate vector (1, 0, 0) to new position (0.99743, 0.071393, 0.0059775) as in Fig. (c).

4.2   Translation Convergence

Figure 5 illustrates 3 different iteration steps of our translational convergence:

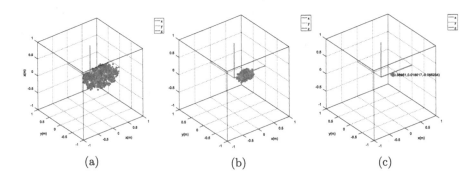

(a)   (b)   (c)

Fig. 5. 3-D translational convergence to $(0.40, 0.025, -0.07)$ m (Color figure online)

In (a) we see the 1000 best sorted results after filtering the initial seed phase consisting of 10000 seeds. In (b) we see iteration 3 and in (c) iteration 10, our best result which belongs to translation $P_O^I = (0.389506, 0.0160174, -0.0652339)$ m, and is closer to the translation reference estimate $T = (0.40, 0.025, -0.07)$ m. The color transition from red to green represents bad and good fitness values respectively.

4.3   Time Synchronization

For the obtained best results q_O^I and P_O^I, our best time match varied between 40 and 32 ms, which corresponds to five and four samples arriving at 125 Hz rate respectively. This has been justified by Figs. 6 and 7 representing the comparison between real and simulated values of the Gyroscope and Accelerometer.

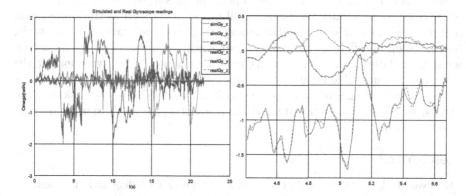

Fig. 6. Time synchronization comparison between simulated (solid) and real (dotted) accelerometer readings. Left full experiment plot, right is the magnified portion of the same plot.

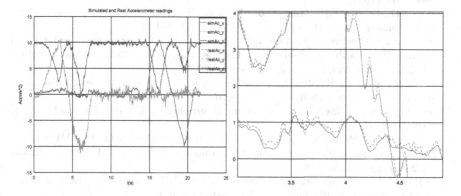

Fig. 7. Time synchronization comparison between simulated (solid) and real (dotted) gyroscope (right) readings. Left full experiment plot, right is the magnified portion of the same plot.

186 M. Pancholi et al.

Figures 6 and 7 indicate that both simulated and real accelerometer, gyroscope readings are significantly close to each other. Which justifies the resulted best orientation offset q_O^I and the translation offset P_O^I obtained in this experiment.

5 Conclusion

This paper described a novel approach to accurately determine the 3D rotational offset, 3D translational offset and a time synchronization in data between an optical target and an inertial measurement unit. It consists of creating simulated acceleration and gyroscope readings by applying 6-DoF offset to the optical target and compare them against the real ones from the IMU in an adaptive genetic algorithm. The experiments shown in the previous section suggest that the developed system delivers admirable results in all three tasks it has been designed for. Furthermore, it is not dependent on supplementary hardware or other constraints besides the factory calibration of the optical tracking system and its target as well as the inertial measurement unit calibration. Additionally, for operation in different environment, our method enables rapid re-calibration when the relative pose of the sensors must be changed. Thus, we consider the technique as applicable in the fields of augmented reality, robotics and automotive industry. We plan to continue our work in two directions - by making more extensive evaluations of our system and implementing a sensor fusion techniques, which relies on it.

References

1. Alves, J., Lobo, J., Dias, J.: Camera-inertial sensor modelling and alignment for visual navigation. Mach. Intell. Robotic Control **5**(3), 103–112 (2003)
2. Dam, E.B., Koch, M., Lillholm, M.: Quaternions, Interpolation and Animation. Københavns Universitet, Datalogisk Institut (1998)
3. Davis, L.: Handbook of Genetic Algorithms, 1st edn. Van Nostrand Reinhold, New York (1991)
4. Hol, J.D., Schön, T.B., Gustafsson, F.: Modeling and calibration of inertial and vision sensors. Int. J. Robotics Res. **29**(2–3), 231–244 (2010)
5. Kelly, J., Sukhatme, G.S.: Fast relative pose calibration for visual and inertial sensors. In: Khatib, O., Kumar, V., Pappas, G.J. (eds.) Experimental Robotics, vol. 54, pp. 515–524. Springer, Heidelberg (2009)
6. Lobo, J., Dias, J.: Relative pose calibration between visual and inertial sensors. Int. J. Robotics Res. **26**(6), 561–575 (2007)
7. McKinley, S., Levine, M.: Cubic spline interpolation. College Redwoods **45**(1), 1049–1060 (1998)
8. Mirzaei, F.M., Roumeliotis, S.I.: A kalman filter-based algorithm for IMU-camera calibration: observability analysis and performance evaluation. IEEE Trans. Robotics **24**(5), 1143–1156 (2008)
9. O'Haver, T.: A Pragmatic Introduction to Signal Processing. CreateSpace Independent Publishing Platform, North Charleston (1997)
10. Zheng, S., Chai, X., Su, S., Liu, X., Neta, K., Miller, W.: Relative pose calibration between inertial unit and visual unit in railway track inspection system. J. Balk. Tribological Assoc. **22**(2), 1253–1264 (2016)

Smart-Bike as One of the Ways to Ensure Sustainable Mobility in Smart Cities

Irina Makarova[1], Ksenia Shubenkova[1(✉)], Anton Pashkevich[2], and Aleksey Boyko[1]

[1] "Service of Transport Systems" Department, Kazan Federal University,
Syuyumbike prosp., 10a, 423812 Naberezhnye Chelny, Russian Federation
kamIVM@mail.ru, ksenia.shubenkova@gmail.com,
boykoaleksey94@gmail.com
[2] Chair of Logistics and Transport, Tallinn University of Technology,
Ehitajate tee, 5, Tallinn, Estonia
anton.pashkevich@gmail.com

Abstract. Ensuring sustainable urban mobility is based on the rational management of transportation system. This involves the infrastructure development and design of vehicles equipped with intelligent modules, which provide the control ability. The widespread use of environmentally friendly bicycles is constrained by a number of reasons. One of them is the absence of models designed for physically untrained people. This paper proposes the concept of the smart-bike control system, which was developed to help cyclist in the situations, when the values of his/her physical condition as well as parameters of environment are critical. Prototypes of the proposed system were tested in the laboratory environment.

Keywords: Sustainable mobility · Control system · Smart-bike · Sensors · Controllers

1 Introduction

The global trend of urbanization and population growth, which puts ever increasing pressure on the world's urban area, requires from the cities to develop a sustainable way of living. This sustainability is developed through environmental sustainable solutions combined with a full use of the possibilities, which are given by the digitalization of the society. This means enabling the technology to gather data, which can be used by the technology itself in order to adapt to the most sustainable and smart behaviour. Enabling the technology to communicate, to share the gathered data with people or other technologies, to borrow relevant data from elsewhere and to make the technology multifunctional - all of this provides solutions not only to one, but to multiple problems [1].

The Smart City concept can be defined as a model of the city development, which creates a surplus of resources through the use of information and communication technologies combined with sustainable and environmentally friendly multiple solutions. It emphasizes the need to improve the level of mobility and connectedness through collaboration and open source knowledge on all levels of the society [2].

© ICST Institute for Computer Sciences, Social Informatics and Telecommunications Engineering 2017
M. Magno et al. (Eds.): S-Cube 2016, LNICST 205, pp. 187–198, 2017.
DOI: 10.1007/978-3-319-61563-9_16

One of the main ways to create a Smart City is a Smart Transportation systems implementation, which is in line with the United Nations Sustainable Development Goals and the Transition to a Green Economy. As far as transport starts to be one of the main sources to produce air pollution, emissions of greenhouse gases, noise as well as one of the main reasons of the consumption of nonrestorable resources, household inconveniences caused, for example, by the neighborhood with a highway, etc. [3], the number of adherents of transition to a green economy is growing. They initiate the development of strategies and policy documents on sustainable development of the urban transportation systems.

Transition to a Smart Transport involves the development of appropriate infrastructure, which will ensure the rational management of transportation system, as well as the intellectualization of vehicles, which can provide a sustainable urban mobility.

2   Ensuring Sustainable Mobility in Smart Cities

2.1   Main Ways to Increase Sustainability of the City Transportation System

There are three main ways, using which cities can innovate to make transport more sustainable without increasing journey times:

- Better land use planning.
- Making existing transport modes more efficient.
- Moving towards sustainable transport.

Part of measures to ensure the transport sustainability is connected with planning for urban and suburban centers in accordance with the development, which is provided for a mixed fleet of vehicles and reasonable growth. Such principles of city development will help to reduce dependence on private vehicles and to ensure widespread use of public and non-motorized transport for short trips and for regular commuting into the city from the suburbs [4].

The UNEP report [5] states that, in order to achieve economic goals and objectives of sustainable transport development as well as integrated planning of this development and regulation system load, it is necessary to switch to fuels with lower carbon content and to implement a more extensive electrification of transport.

Safe public transport systems are considered often as an important tool to increase the safe of population mobility, especially, in urban areas suffering from growing traffic congestion. In many cities with high income, the policy to reduce the use of personal motor transport is particularly emphasized through investment in the development of public transport networks [6]. According to the Global Status Report on Road Safety 2015 [3], moving towards more sustainable modes of transport (such as cycling and public transport) has positive effects if associated road safety impacts have been well managed. These include increased physical activity, reduced emissions and noise levels, reduced congestion and more pleasant cities. Moreover, measures to promote safe public transport and non-motorized modes of transport are also in line with other global moves to fight obesity and to reduce noncommunicable diseases (such as heart disease, diabetes) [7].

2.2   Benefits of Using Bicycles as a Travel Mode and Examples of Their Implementation

Considering the fact, that the world community has set an objective to reduce the levels of greenhouse gases (first of all carbon dioxide) by 50% by 2050 [8], bicycles get an additional advantage, as this mode of transport does not produce CO_2 emissions. Furthermore, bicycling makes efficient use of roadway capacity and reduces congestion. The advantages of cycling include cheap infrastructure requirements and improvements of the public health. Bicycle pathways, lanes and parking require less space than their automobile counterparts. Cycling has direct health benefits: it is an aerobic exercise, which can minimize the risk of muscle and ligament injury, lower blood pressure and reduce the risk of heart disease [9]. Moreover, in urban areas, cycling can sometimes prove to be faster than other modes of transport and also allows cyclists to avoid traffic jams.

Thus, bicycling is a low-polluting and a low-cost transportation alternative and can be an important means to reach destinations, which are not serviced by transit [10]. But at the same time, cycling has a number of disadvantages, however, including a greater physical effort, the difficulty of carrying loads while cycling, being at the mercy of the weather, and, outside urban areas, travelling more slowly than motorized transport. Factors such as physical effort and speed also limit the distance, which a cyclist can travel [11].

Today, in some European cities – such as Amsterdam or Copenhagen – two-thirds of all road users are cyclists. In other words, it is perfectly feasible for a majority in a metropolis to ride a bike and not to travel by car. Not everybody can ride a bike every day, however, which is why the bike should not be seen as a competitor, but rather as complementary to public transport. Especially, on the way to and from work, there is a lot of potential: in London onle around 2.5% of all commutes to work are by bike, in Berlin it is 13%, in Munich – 15%, in Copenhagen and Amsterdam these numbers reach a whopping 36% and 37%, respectively.

Such a high percentage of trips to work or to education facilities by bicycles in Copenhagen is provided by the fact that the priority strategy of politicians is development of bicycles infrastructure as a way to create more friendly conditions to live in the city [12]. The so-called "carbon footprint" of Copenhagen is one of the smallest in the world (it is less than two tonnes per capita). But there is even more ambitious goal to become neutral on emissions has been set in its development strategy. To do this, there have been set very strict targets in order to follow energy efficiency standards, "green" construction and "green" energy. The city government approved the project of equipping bicycles with special sensors, which report on the level of pollution and traffic congestion in real time [13].

One of the most popular counter-argument about cycling are adverse climatic and natural conditions [14]. However, it is a matter of attitude and priority for cycle paths when clearing snow. It is confirmed by the example of Oulu, where there is a substantial proportion of people commute by bicycle, even when the temperature is below zero in deepest winter. This is ensured by 845 km of routes (4.3 m per inhabitant), 98% of which are maintained throughout winter because the main route maintenance prioritized over highways. Routes parallel to highways are separated with a green lane, which also serves as snow build-up space. There are underpasses in most busy crossings and it is possible to reach every place by bike using cycling routes [15].

Also, technology can be used not only to make better cars, but also better cycle paths, such as the proposed air-conditioned bike path in Qatar [16].

Introducing bicycle lanes is not enough to make a city attuned to cyclists' needs. Essential infrastructure in a city with the size and traffic volume of Moscow includes a strategy for secure parking lots and allows alternative ownership structures through a bike share system. Moscow decided to introduce various parking facilities appropriate for short-term and long-term parking and to introduce a bike sharing system similar to schemes in London, Barcelona and Paris [17]. To use such a system, person must register and receive a personalized card. In Barcelona, each one can rent a bike and leave it at any convenient point of the city, because there are bicycle parkings all over the major streets. An extensive network of bicycle paths and cycling facilities and services are also contributes to the development of this system [13].

Problem of the environmental pollution is a major issue in China with its notoriously poor air quality in large cities. Probably, this was the main reason of China's bicycle development [16]. In 2014 Lanzhou (Northwest China) was praised for integration Asia's second-largest bus rapid transit system with a bike share system (14,000 docks planned), bike parking, and greenways [18]. Bike share system is also implemented in such cities as Beijing, Zhuzhou, Shanghai, Wuhan and Hangzhou [19], where the popularity of this mode of transport is also provided by the widespread introduction of electric bicycles, which help physically untrained people to overcome steep climbs and long distances. That is why an increasing number of people choose non-motorized transport as a travel mode.

2.3   Ways to Increase the Attractiveness of Cycling

In conjunction with the foregoing, the population will prefer the cycling as a mode of transport in a case if there is a considerable advantage of its usage. The results of the population preferences research (Table 1) show that the number of people who choose bicycle as a mode of transport can be increased by the expansion of non-motorized model line-up and the integration of its infrastructure into the city road network system. What is more, cycling facilities and services should be developed. These steps, on the one hand, will help to enhance the attractiveness of bicycles for different groups of population and, on the other hand, will make roads safer and more secure particularly for non-motorized road users who are the most vulnerable.

In simplified form, ways to increase the attractiveness of non-motorized transport are shown on the Fig. 1.

Table 1. The results of the sampling survey of population.

Indicator	Students	Workers	Retiree	Other category	TOTAL
number of respondents	624	299	16	14	953
number of trips to work or education by public transport	313	109	-	-	422
number of trips to work or education by bicycles	50	7	-	-	57
number of trips to work or education by cars	163	133	-	-	296
number of trips to work or education by foot	98	50	-	-	148
number of bikes in the personal property	313	86	2	6	407
the number of drivers who are ready to transfer to bicycles, if there are:					
bikeways	127	56	0	0	183
bicycles parkings	129	46	0	0	175
bike hire system	75	28	0	0	103
the possibility to take the bike in buses or trams	76	21	0	0	97
E-bikes	78	22	0	0	100

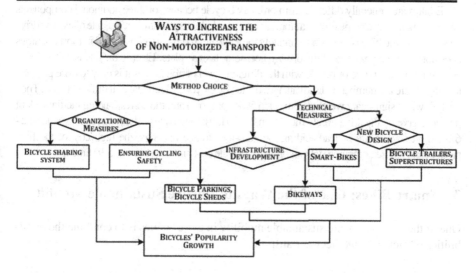

Fig. 1. Measures to implement for moving towards non-motorized modes of transport.

The case of Copenhagen proved that the attractiveness of cycling may be increased by the expansion of bicycles model line-up for different population groups and different use cases. In Copenhagen it is possible to rent not only conventional bikes, but also such models as [20]:

1. The Velomobile: it protects against wind, rain and drizzle; it is the best suited for long distances over 20 km and runs well on wide bicycle lanes outside the city; and also several users would cycle more in the rain if they had a similar cycle.
2. The Cargobike: it is good to transport children and to carry things and products; it is the best suited for short distances below 10 km.
3. The Recumbent: it is comfortable and good to ride on, especially, in headwind; it lends itself well to long distances over 20 km.

4. The Electric-assist Long John: it is good to carry cargo and children; it motivates to cycle more and drive less; it is fast, practical, fun and effortless to get around within the city.
5. The Electric Bicycle: it is fun and different to drive on; the electric slide is a good help, especially uphill and against wind.

Bicycle infrastructure planning should include the creation of bike parkings, bike sheds and bikeways as well as it should be taken into account the terrain and the structure of population, who want to use the bike to get around the city. Despite a fast growing literature on the bike lanes design [21–24], the problem of terrain identification and topographic conditions modeling is still actual. The most common method of bicycle wayfinding is the shortest path method.

As far as bicycle routing is not always possible to avoid hilly terrain, bike-lifts and electric drives creation can solve the problem of overcoming steep climbs. In contrast to the electric scooter or motorcycle, e-bike may be driven by pedals. At this time electric drive is off and accumulator is charging.

E-bikes are generally different from ordinary bicycle because of three additional components presence such as an electric motor, a storage battery and a battery controller. Despite of electric drive presence, electric bike is used approximately the same as an ordinary bicycle and in most countries does not require a presence of the driving license or license plate. Electric bicycle is suitable as a vehicle for a wide range of people with the different level of abilities, as it is easy to dose physical training. There is a number of disadvantages of electric bicycle, which makes it difficult to use. They are following: significant weight (from 20 to 50 kg or more) and the corresponding inertia; lack of power reserve on the drive (rarely more than 25–50 km); long battery charging (usually at least 2–6 h); short service life of lead-acid and lithium-ion storage batteries; the high cost of the final product and its use compared with an ordinary bicycle cost and use (from 2 to 10 times).

3   Smart-Bikes: One of the Ways to Ensure Sustainable Mobility

One of the ways to ensure sustainable mobility in Smart Cities is to combine the possibilities of bicycles and electric transport.

3.1   Idea of the Smart-Bike Control Realization

Electric bicycles are controlled by cycling computer (controller), which is supposed: to supply amperage from the battery to the electric motor in accordance with the user's settings; to show residual battery charge on the indicator; to determine the rotation/stop of pedals; to limit the maximum speed of the bicycle movement in order to save energy; to keep constant speed (cruise control); to charge the battery while braking.

At the same time, there is a variety of velosimulators, which are belong to the group of cardiovascular machines equipped to control the physical condition of a user. Also the main indicator to diagnose critical state is a pulse rate. As far as the parameters of the bicycle motion are influenced by both condition of the cyclist and the parameters of the environment, the rational management should be based on monitoring, analysis as well as taking into account all these factors.

Today there are two types of systems, which are used to analyze bicycle's characteristics and motion parameters. They are:

- Cycling computers – electronic devices to measure the speed and daily run of bicycle as well as such additional parameters as average speed, travel time, full speed, transmission (for multi-speed bikes), running time, temperature, atmosphere pressure, cadence (pedal rotation frequency), etc.
- Smart phones applications – applications, which duplicate functionality of cycling computer, except the ability to monitor the transmission and cadence, use built-in phone sensors such as GPS, accelerometer, barometer.

To implement the smart-bike control idea, it is necessary to design a system, which combines cycling computer, motorized wheel (it is the type of a driving wheel: complicated mechanism, which combines the wheel itself, electric motor, power gear and braking system) and velosimulator to control the physical condition of a user. Sensors readings are transmitted into the controller for the further analysis. In critical cases (when the physical cyclist's condition is bad) the system sends the request to turn on the electric drive and after receiving the confirmation from user electric drive control is transferred to the controller.

Thus, if to equip the bicycle with the universal module, which includes a pulse sensor, a controller and other components that are shown on the Fig. 2, and to manage it in accordance with the selected program installed on smartphone, it will help to increase the attractiveness of cycling among untrained population.

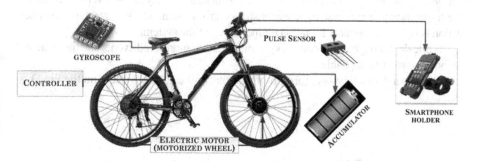

Fig. 2. The elements, which are included in the developed module.

3.2 Functional Requirements for the Control System

Existed sensors and controllers can be used to implement the concept of smart-bike. To determine the condition of the cyclist and to monitor travel times, the following devices are required:

- means of cyclist identification – to set his physical characteristics in the rest condition;
- pulse sensor – to determine heart rate;
- timer – to determine the travel time, setting training modes.

To measure the parameters of the bicycle will be required:

- gyroscope/accelerometer – to determine the position of the bicycle in the area;
- speedometer – to determine the travel speed;

– sensor of used chain sprockets;
– GPS sensor – to determine position and route setting.

Module, which determines the weather conditions on the route and transmits it to a smartphone, is required to establish parameters of the environment.

While designing bicycle control system it should be taken into account that the control system is completely autonomous, and the interference from the cyclist is impossible, so it may be unsafe for the rider. That is why the principle of feedbacks between control system and person should be implemented with the help of notifications. In this way, the possibility of accidents in electric drive, which could cause bicycle false alarm, will be excluded.

3.3   Algorithm of Smart-Bike Control System

Bicycle movement is provided by the cyclist, who sets the driving speed and the movement direction. It means that cyclist manages the process of cycling. But at the same time, cycling parameters depend on environmental conditions (including the terrain characteristics), natural conditions, time of the day and physical conditions of cyclist. In short, cycling parameters depend on everything, which affects the possibility of bicycle movement. If we consider the "bicycle" system, its functioning is provided by the interaction between such subsystems as "external environment" – "infrastructure" – "bicycle" – "cyclist". To ensure the traffic safety, it is necessary to establish a control system, which implements the interaction between subsystems for rational functioning of the system.

While designing bicycle control system, the list of monitored events and the system's responses was made (Table 2).

There is a data analysis algorithm of the smart-bike control system on the Fig. 3.

Table 2. List of the bicycle control system's events.

№	Event	Response
1	Cyclist's pulse > optimal heart rate (OTP)	Display of overcoming the training threshold, offer to turn on the electric drive
2	Road gradient > 15° (uphill)	Display of the warning of an uphill, offer to turn on the electric drive
3	Cyclist's pulse > OTP + 50	Display of excessive overcoming the training threshold, offer to stop for the rest or to continue motion completely on electric drive
4	Road gradient < –15° (downhill)	Display of the warning of a downhill, electric drive's switching-off, accumulator charging
5	Non-stop travelling during more than 1 h	Display of the need to have a rest, offer to stop for the rest or to turn on the electric drive
6	Non-stop travelling during more than 2 h	Display of excessive overcoming the training threshold, offer to stop for the rest or to continue motion completely on electric drive
7	Travel speed < 15 km/h during 15 s	Display of the offer to turn on the electric drive

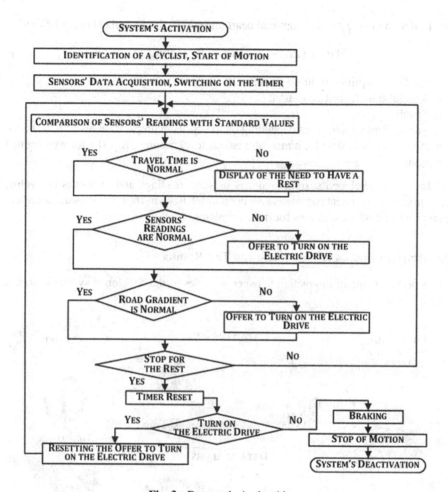

Fig. 3. Data analysis algorithm.

The Table 3 shows one of the system's operation scenarios. If cyclist's pulse value is higher than OTP and the movement speed is less than average speed that is usual for this person, the screen displays an offer to turn on the electric drive. When the pulse value and the speed become normal, the electric drive switches off.

Table 3. An example of the script «Turn on the Electric Drive».

Step	Event	Action
1	The value of the pulse exceeded OTP, movement speed is less than 15 km/h	User's condition data collecting (pulse, weight, height, location tracking, etc.) Comparison of these indicators with the "reference" values for a particular cyclist. Display of overcoming the training threshold. Offer to turn on the electric drive
2	Heart rate decrease	Electric drive's switching-off, resetting the display of overcoming the training threshold

To determine the cyclist's optimal heart rate (OTP) the formula (1) may be used:

$$OTP = (220 - A - PRC) \cdot K + PRC. \tag{1}$$

where OTP – optimal training pulse;
PRC – pulse in the rest condition;
A – cyclist's age;
K – coefficient which varies depending on the cyclist's preparation level: $K = 0.6$ for the freshman, $K = 0.65$ for a man of medium-level training, $K = 0.7$ for well-trained person.

Thus, the developed system analyzes sensors' readings and, if values of cyclist, bicycle and environment parameters are not normal, it warns the cyclist about the critical case as well as offers solutions for these problems.

3.4   Implementation of the System and Test Results

Conceptual scheme of interaction between modules of the developed system is shown on the Fig. 4.

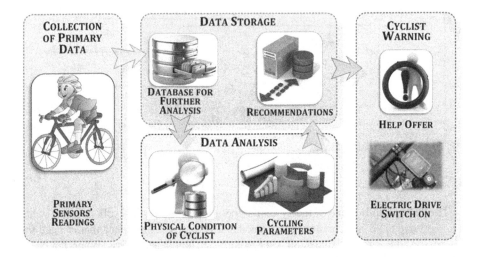

Fig. 4. Conceptual model of interactions between system's modules.

Primary data collection is realized using MPU6050 digital sensors and Pulse Sensor (plug-and-play heart-rate sensor for Arduino). These sensors being located on the steering wheel, on the frame and wheels as well as on cyclist are connected to the Arduino board via the I2C protocol. The motor-wheel MXUS XF39-30H is controlled by Arduino board. Connection to the smartphone is realized via the Bluetooth wireless connection. Sensors' readings are transmitted to the smartphone and then they come into the Microsoft SQL Server database for storage and processing. An example of the control realization scheme is shown on the Fig. 5.

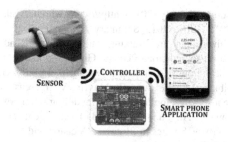

Fig. 5. Control realization scheme.

The application for smartphones, which was developed with the help of Android Studio in Java, allows to manage the sensor system according to the above-described algorithm and taking into account the state of the external environment as well as the cyclist itself.

The prototype of the developed system was tested in laboratory conditions. The results of tests confirmed that even physically weak category of people can use a bike equipped with the developed system as a mode of transport. Moreover, the widespread introduction of bicycles with such system allows to improve the road safety by avoiding accidents, which are related to fatigue or to a sharp deterioration of cyclists' physical appearance.

4   Conclusion

Despite the obvious advantages of using bicycles for short distances, there are still a lot of obstacles to the widespread use of the bicycles as an alternative travel mode. Some of these problems can be solved by use of smart-bikes with adaptive electric drive, which turns on when it's necessary. Since the intellectual smart-bike control system uses sensors' readings of the cyclist's physical condition and of the environmental parameters for decision-making, it will help even physically untrained people to overcome steep climbs and long distances without overload. The development of bicycles infrastructure and its integration into the public transport system will contribute to use of bicycle and public transport.

Moving towards non-motorized modes of transport is one of the key elements to ensure the sustainable urban mobility. Moreover, the experience of developed countries shows that this clean and efficient kind of transportation contributes also to the development of economy. Besides that, the health and longevity are also benefits from cycling. As it is seen in Denmark, the cycling benefits are seven times greater than the cost of accidents, in money value the total health impact is worth 230 million Euro.

References

1. GREEN CAPACITY. http://greencapacity.ru/ru/information/smart-cities
2. Smart cities Preliminary Report (2014). http://www.iso.org/iso/smart_cities_report-jtc1.pdf

3. Global status report on road safety (2015). http://www.who.int/violence_injury_prevention/road_safety_status/2015/GSRRS2015_Summary_EN_final.pdf
4. Share the Road: Investment in Walking and Cycling Road Infrastructure. http://www.unep.org/Transport/sharetheroad/PDF/str_GlobalReport2010.pdf
5. Global "green" new deal. Policy Brief. http://www.unep.org/pdf/GGND_Final_Report.pdf
6. Makarova, I., Khabibullin, R., Belyaev, E., Mavrin, V.: Increase of city transport system management efficiency with application of modeling methods and data intellectual analysis. In: Sładkowski, A., Pamuła, W. (eds.) Intelligent Transportation Systems – Problems and Perspectives. Studies in Systems, Decision and Control, vol. 32, pp. 37–80. Springer, Warsaw (2015)
7. Global Report on Human Settlements. http://unhabitat.org/books/planning-and-design-for-sustainable-urban-mobility-global-report-on-human-settlements-2013/
8. Share the Road Programme. http://www.unep.org/Transport/sharetheroad/
9. Tsenkova, S., Mahalek, D.: The impact of planning policies on bicycle-transit integration in Calgary. Urban Plann. Transp. Res. Open Access J. **2**, 126–146 (2014)
10. Handy, S., Xing, Y.: Factors correlated with bicycle commuting: a study in six small US cities. Int. J. Sustain. Transp. **5**, 91–110 (2011)
11. Heinen, E., Wee, B., Maat, K.: Commuting by bicycle: an overview of the literature. Transp. Rev. **30**, 59–96 (2010)
12. Bredal, F.: The case of Copenhagen. In: Changing Urban Traffic and the Role of Bicycles: Russian and International Experiences, pp. 24 – 28. Friedrich-Ebert-Stiftung, Moscow (2014)
13. Smart City. http://city-smart.ru/info/125.html
14. Ernits, E., Pruunsild, R., Antov, D.: Links between road accidents and winter road conditions. Transport **4**(4), 2681–2703 (2015)
15. Tahkola, P.: The case of Oulu. In: Changing Urban Traffic and the Role of Bicycles: Russian and International Experiences, pp. 2943. Friedrich-Ebert-Stiftung, Moscow (2014)
16. Appenzeller, M.: Cycling – past, present and future. In: Changing Urban Traffic and the Role of Bicycles: Russian and International Experiences, pp. 11–18. Friedrich-Ebert-Stiftung, Moscow (2014)
17. Mityaev, A.: The case of Moscow. In: Changing Urban Traffic and the Role of Bicycles: Russian and International Experiences, pp. 72–79. Friedrich-Ebert-Stiftung, Moscow (2014)
18. 4 Cities Developing The World's Best Sustainable Transport Systems. http://www.fastcoexist.com/3025399/4-cities-developing-the-worlds-best-sustainable-transport-systems
19. Zhang, L., Zhang, J., Duan, Z., Bryde, D.: Sustainable bike-sharing systems: characteristics and commonalities across cases in urban China. J. Cleaner Prod. **97**, 124–133 (2015)
20. Bicycle innovation lab. http://www.bicycleinnovationlab.dk/activities/data-popular-bikes?show=lgg
21. Parkin, J., Rotheram, J.: Design speeds and acceleration characteristics of bicycle traffic for use in planning, design and appraisal. Transp. Policy **17**, 335–341 (2010)
22. Larsen, J., Patterson, Z., El-Geneidy, A.: Build it. But where? The use of geographic information systems in identifying locations for new cycling infrastructure. Int. J. Sustain. Transp. **7**, 299–317 (2013)
23. Forsyth, A., Krizek, K.: Urban design: is there a distinctive view from the bicycle? J. Urban Des. **16**, 531–549 (2011)
24. Rybarczyk, G.: Simulating bicycle wayfinding mechanisms in an urban environment. Urban, Plann. Transp. Res. Open Access J. **2**, 89–104 (2014)

Author Index

Printed in the United States
By Bookmasters

Printed in the United States
By Bookmasters